Y'ALL (NOT) GON' MAKE ME LOSE MY MIND

NOTES FROM A HIP-HOP UNICORN & SUICIDE SURVIVOR

EMILIA A. OTTOO

FOREWORD BY
PHAROAHE MONCH

CONTENTS

Select Praise	vii
Foreword by Pharoahe Monch	xvii
Definitions, Myths & Realities	xix
Introduction	xxi
1. I Put My Lifetime in Between the Paper's Lines	1
2. Incarcerated Book Nerds, Karate Monks, and Hue(man) Nature	8
3. Girls Go to College to Get More Knowledge, They Said	13
4. I Was Running Through (Hypercreativity) with My Woes	20
5. Six Million Ways to Die, Choose One	30
6. Hardcore and Miseducated Invasions of Privacy	40
7. Just Got Paid. It's Friday Night (at the Psychiatric Ward)	56
8. I Know Why the Caged Birds in the Trap Sing McKnight	64
9. We on a Ward Tour, Prison Song & Prison Letters	79
10. DMX, All Caps When You Say the Man's Name	102
11. Act Like You Know the Sequence Is Kollage	106
12. If You've Cried on Your Birthday, Make Some Noise!	117
13. Will the Real Afeni Shakur Please Stand Up?	130
14. Valentin, A Hip-Hopera & Self-Care Story	144
15. Rebel Soul Burnout & Meeting thee Kathleen Cleaver	154
16. Ladies Who Lunch (with Immortal Technique)	166
17. Tough Girl: A Mini-Career in Tackle Football, Pt. 1	178
18. Tough Girl: A Mini-Career in Tackle Football, Pt. 2	196
19. The Real World Is Faker than Wrestling, Pt. 1	211
20. The Real World Is Faker than Wrestling, Pt. 2	224
21. Dead Prez, Politics & the Model United Nations	244
22. Wall Street, Nipsey Hussle & Hip-Hop Business History	258
23. The KRS-One Guide to Being Irreplaceable	272

Please take care. I love you. Thanks for reading.	301
Resources, Organizations & Support	305
About the Author	313

Wahida Clark Distribution
75 Washington St
PO Box 383
Fairburn GA 30213
1-866-910-6920
www.wclarkdistribution.com
www.wclarkpublishing.com

Copyright 2023 © by Emilia A. Ottoo emiliaisemmalee@gmail.com
Bronx, NY, 10454
(646) 704-1374

All rights reserved. This book, or parts thereof, may not be reproduced in any form without permission.

Library of Congress Cataloging-In-Publication Data:
Emilia A. Ottoo
Y'ALL (NOT) GON' MAKE ME LOSE MY MIND: Notes from a Hip-Hop Unicorn & Suicide Survivor
ISBN: 978-1-957954-50-9 Hardcover
ISBN: 978-1-957954-51-6 ebook
LCCN: 2023922030

1. Mental Health- 2. BIOGRAPHY & AUTOBIOGRAPHY 3. SELF-HELP / Motivational & Inspirational- 4. SOCIAL SCIENCE / Ethnic Studies / African American Studies

Cover Art & Interior layout by NuancArtLLc.com
Printed in USA

SELECT PRAISE

"... exciting to witness the evolution of EMMA LEE—an amazing Hip-Hop artist transforming into a force for wellness! This book gets real about mental health as she gets it right, telling her story, sharing insights, and representing brilliantly."

- Toni Blackman
U.S. Hip-Hop Ambassador
Creator of Lyrical Meditation Cypher Podcast

"... tugs at your heartstrings, caresses your soul, and inspires you to believe that there's a way to overcome and transmute your trials in life into a true masterpiece. I found myself at home with her references and curious to learn how EMMA LEE M.C. interpreted and experienced her journey into that beautifully complex world. I recommend this book to anybody feeling frustrated and defeated by the pressures life may bring. I also deem this a 'Must-Read' for those passionate about music and the arts."

SELECT PRAISE

- Napoleon Da Legend
Bilingual Hip-Hop & Afrobeat Artist and Community Activist

"Of course, EMMA LEE wrote a book! I mean, what *hasn't* she done?! I've had the pleasure of working alongside this juggernaut of talent so much that I'm seldom surprised but frequently in awe of all the things she has brought to fruition, this book being one of those manifestations in the best way . . . This will become a point of reference for many in the years to come."

- Fred Ones
Visual Artist, Studio Engineer, Producer & Community Advocate, The Art of Lyrics, Peasant Podium, Guerrilla Grooves Radio

". . . a high-level M.C., but she's also an amazing writer. If Dyson and Cornell coparented a daughter of Dr. Cress Welsing at The Wu-Mansion annex in The Harlem School of the Arts, Panther Division, 'Bong,' you get this. Great read, cop that!"

- Curtis Sherrod
First-Generation Hip-Hopper and Community Advocate, Executive Director, Hip-Hop Culture Center

". . . powerful and inspiring . . . My friend is also a Hip-Hop music aficionado, and her love of the genre is woven into the fabric of her life story. Her passion for music is a testament to her creative spirit, appreciation of art, thirst for knowledge, and self-expression. But what truly sets her apart is her determination to pursue her dream of becoming a professional wrestler . . . requires not only physical strength but also mental fortitude, discipline, and perseverance. As she trains to reach her goal, she serves as inspiration for anyone ever told that their dreams are too big, too crazy, or too impossible . . ."

SELECT PRAISE

- Valentina Grimaldi
Marine Ventures (NYC)
Financial Technology and Investment Philanthropy

"I wasn't aware of the trials and tribulations of EMMA's struggles. I only saw a happy, energetic woman who would shoot and edit videos for our weekly radio show . . . I also saw a creative M.C. who would rap in an almost spoken-word manner. This book takes you through a journey of ups and downs, down and outs, and rising highs. I love the way she titled the chapters as songs or verse titles. It really shows her connection with music to her personal life . . ."

- DJ Riz
Rap Is Outta Control, **Shade 45, SiriusXM Radio**

"Beautifully written! Profoundly deep and existential. Yet, a prose-poetry that is accessible and relatable. EMMA LEE holds the Philosopher's Stone. Her inward exploration and metaphysical practices are heroine. Her Hip-Hop sensibilities and proficiency make EMMA LEE M.C. a true Unicorn and Hip-Hop Genius."

- Martha Diaz
Founder, Chief Curator & Operations, Hip-Hop Education Center Chair, Archives, Curatorial, & Educational Affairs, Universal Hip-Hop Museum

". . . glimpse the illustrious consciousness of EMMA LEE M.C. The multihyphenated artist weaves through the mind-body-soul tapestry with musical references while showing a relatable vulnerability on her life journey. If M.C. means 'move the crowd,' then EMMA LEE is moving us . . . This body of work reminds us of the subtlety and significance of the breaths we take . . . It is a must-read about survival, validating feelings,

SELECT PRAISE

emotions, and experiences; the complexities of growing up; and it affirms why we are and belong here."

- **Kashema Hutchinson, PhD, Urban Education**
Fresh, Bold, And So Def, Hip-Hop Education Center, Director of Arts Education, Caribbean Cultural Center African Diaspora Institute

"You don't know what paths people's lives take; it's an honor and privilege to be a small part of that cog. Martial arts and Hip-Hop are very near and dear to me, so to have a next-generation still doing the work and pushing the envelope of using the platform of these cultures, what they're about, and what we represent to it means a lot. The journey this young lady's on is a very important one."

- **José Manuel Figueroa**
Chen Taijiquan World Champion and Kung Fu Hall of Famer, Author, Filmmaker, Choreographer, Instructor, Holistic Consultant

". . . I describe her as 'the female version of Pharoahe Monch.' This analogy perks ears up and signals that lyrically, I'm speaking on a dynamic, megaminded creator who offers cryptic and delicious food for thought . . . She's a generous person in service to the greater good of the collective . . . People we experience as strong, kind, and intelligent individuals often overcome intensely difficult circumstances which forced them to unearth gifts in extraordinary ways. I seek to learn from these types graciously . . . to have one open up in detail intimately about what they went through in life helps me understand and connect to my journey . . ."

- **Señor Gigio**
Emcee, Musician, Cartoonist & Tarot Reader

SELECT PRAISE

"... simply blown away! Her work's vulnerability, strength, intellectual rigor, emotional depth, and clever lyricism are completely engrossing. EMMA LEE's clarity of voice and purpose always inspires me and keeps me grounded in the beautiful struggle of life. She reminds us to claim our story, our imperfections, our greatest, our trauma, our recovery—all of it—because it helps us survive and thrive. I'm genuinely grateful for this work. I know so many of us can relate. This book is so necessary and could save someone's life. In a way, it's already saved mine!"

- Dafina Roberts
Award-Winning Writer, Director, Producer & Arts Educator

"... makes me feel like I'm being taken on a deeply personal and profound journey by someone who cares greatly for me. It gives an intimate and vivid look into life and struggles with the purpose of equipping the reader with tools to better themselves. The writing has the same rhythm as the Hip-Hop songs it mentions, making the author's relationship to music palpable to the reader. Truly worth reading."

- Kyle Haynes
Rap Is Outta Control, **Shade 45, SiriusXM Radio**

"... a poetic force of life breaking down myths while distributing Hip-Hop medicine. She writes with the spirit of the ancient griots in this imaginative, brave, and vulnerable piece of her story."

- Nejma Nefertiti
Hip-Hop Artist, Social Justice Educator, Sound Designer & Natural Perfumist

SELECT PRAISE

"... a supertalented artist who puts in the right amount of work and effort necessary to reach the top. Her life experience, which she graciously shares in the book, can help many, and one can learn to do much better and succeed in life and career. I find it so well done that it sounds like true guidance for people of all ages to do the right thing and skip falls. Keep reading, and you will discover more than expected. Thank you, EMMA LEE!"

- Valentin Peytchinov
Award-Winning Bass & Metropolitan Opera Principal Artist,
Legendary Vocal Technique Expert, Singer & Producer

"... a natural-born lyricist, EMMA LEE guides the reader through pivotal times in her life when conflict and hope come together to create opportunity and growth. Seasoned with dashes of quotables from rap legends and underground heavyweights, she tells a tale that is sometimes heart wrenching, other times comedic, but always conveyed with the linguistic swagger of an elite M.C. EMMA LEE's journey is an inspiration for any artist, Hip-Hop and otherwise, searching for the delicate balance between art and the pursuit of happiness in a world where 'life is like a jungle sometimes.'"

- Sebastien "Seb" Elkouby
Award-Winning Hip-Hop Educator, Writer & Producer,
Founder of the Longest-Running UC/CSU-approved CTE Hip-Hop Course in the U.S.

"Who is rich? I think of myself as a rich person. What is rich? Are the communities who make people monetarily rich, rich themselves? Do you have to be wealthy to create wealth that gives back?" "Positivity, love, self-awareness, self-belief, vulnerability, respect, empathy, and compassion abound in Emilia's inspiring debut book of survival, postsurvival, accomplishments, and personal growth. She talks candidly and with alacrity ... To contemplate living

SELECT PRAISE

intentionally, start here with Emilia. She's the community builder that humanity needs."

- Giles Sibbald
Cofounder of MÜ Magazine and South London Arts Lab, Creator of Hey Sunday and I Wanna Jump Like Dee Dee Podcast

"Sometimes an event comes along that pivots your perception. Sometimes . . . is now! EMMA LEE is . . . that 'unicorn' of magic. She's that sunshine glimmering off the bodega-front glass that makes you accidentally sight the soul mate you've searched for all your life. She's who makes you miss the bus that crashes blocks later that you could have been riding in. She's that childlike magic, brutally yet innocently honest, that enamors your spirit with unapologetic bravery . . . and this is such a book . . . right on time for the healing we all need, though we barely admit to needing it . . ."

- DJ R-Trane
The Time Travel Mixshow
Disco Originalz

". . . a seminal work about the intimate journey of self-growth and introspection. *Y'all (Not) Gon' Make Me Lose My Mind* has been born to be that match struck in the midst of the 'inkiest' of darkness. I feel privileged to have read EMMA LEE's work and (I dare say) ministry. This is a necessary endeavor."

- Princess
Legendary R&B/Pop Singer, UK Top Ten & Gold Recording Artist,
Co-Owner, OnDa Ground Music Label

". . . a 'lyrical assassin' rapper and author, EMMA LEE 'spits'

SELECT PRAISE

venom that destroys myths and misconceptions. Having been afforded a peek into the psyche of a 'suicide survivor,' I am heartened by her approach to 'life after death.' EMMA's work is an important message about a journey to kill or remove what does not serve her. The antidote to the sense of loneliness she must have felt, 'Quiet Storm' . . . denotes that a hurricane will be unleashed as she moves forward. This is already a celebration of living, and I eagerly await more . . ."

- Donovan Heslop
CEO & President, OnDa Ground Music Label
The International Reggae Train, LLC

*To the dreamers, doers, architects, and teachers
. . . and Professor Oseye—who said the best writers take notes on life.*

FOREWORD BY PHAROAHE MONCH

The struggle with depression and suicidal thoughts is not a singular event but an extended war fought on multiple fronts. It's an internal conflict where the mind becomes both the battleground and the adversary. The desire for relief clashes with the innate survival instinct that tortures you through every waking moment. In this struggle, time becomes a paradox. Each moment feels like an eternity, an endless loop of pain, while the prospect of a future appears as an unreachable horizon. The nuances of joy, once vivid and vibrant, fade into a grayscale existence, and the simple act of holding on to hope becomes a grueling task.

Yet, amid the darkness, there exists a flicker of hope. A fragile glow that persists against the prevailing shadows. It is the glimmer of resilience, the innate human capacity to endure, and the potential for healing. This struggle is a testament to the incredible strength that resides within individuals who confront the abyss and choose to persist.

EMMA LEE endured incredible pain, both mental, emotional, and physical but through it, she chose to move, to act, and to embrace the potential for transformation. In each deliberate step, in every intentional action, lies a quiet revolution—a testament to the resilience of the human spirit and the possibility of rediscovering joy, purpose, and vitality amid the shadows. She lived through every moment of it, welcoming the opportunity to get better and stronger.

Through this, every motion forward became a courageous act of defiance. Her story is a testament to the hope that even in the face of overwhelming darkness, there exists a reservoir of strength that can be tapped into through the simple act of putting one foot in front of the other. As EMMA LEE says so profoundly about her experience with Hip-Hop, "it's the testimony of young veterans who were supposed to die, but didn't." Through her music and this "Y'all (Not) Gon' Make Me Lose My Mind" book, she has *definitely* given us her testimony! There is no doubt in my mind that she is part of a larger narrative, and that her presence is a source of light within the Hip-Hop community and culture, and far beyond.

Reading this book strikes a chord personally, reminding me of when I was spiraling downward from hardcore cocktails of prescribed medications. It explores deep into the multiple layers of trauma that humans can internalize. Yet at our lowest, somehow, we can find within ourselves the fortitude to discover hope, if even in just a pinhole of light.

- Pharoahe Monch

DEFINITIONS, MYTHS & REALITIES

The following is an excerpt from "What Survivors of Suicide Want You to Know" by the Suicide Prevention and Early Intervention Network of Maryland's Department of Health. Please see the back of this book for more resources, support organizations, and help.

What does it mean to be a survivor of suicide?
The phrase "survivor of suicide" can have several meanings. Someone who lost a loved one to suicide is referred to as a survivor of suicide loss. Someone who has survived a suicide attempt is referred to as an attempt survivor.

Many myths about suicide still exist.

Myth: Someone who is going through or has experienced a suicidal crisis cannot help others.

DEFINITIONS, MYTHS & REALITIES

Reality: Helping others can be part of healing from crisis. It is important not to make assumptions about what a survivor of suicide can or cannot do. Instead, approach survivors of suicide by listening, asking questions, and providing empathy and support.

Myth: A person who attempts or dies by suicide is selfish.

Reality: When someone attempts or dies by suicide, they often have experienced a disruption in their social connections. To assume someone who attempts or dies by suicide is selfish assumes that the person did not consider how their decision would impact those around them—which is often untrue. People who attempt or die by suicide usually *do* think about how the decision will impact those around them, but their thinking is generally incorrect. People thinking about suicide often feel like a burden to those around them and (incorrectly) think their loved ones would be better off with them no longer around.

Myth: A person who attempts or dies by suicide is weak.

Reality: Remember the saying, "Don't judge someone before you walk a mile in their shoes"? The problem is, when we try putting ourselves in someone else's shoes, we usually bring our brain too; meaning, we view their situation from how we would think or respond to it, *not* how that person might think or respond to it. It's important to remember that everyone experiences things differently, thinks about things differently, and responds to things differently.

INTRODUCTION

CHAPTER 1
I PUT MY LIFETIME IN BETWEEN THE PAPER'S LINES

AIGHT SO, *BOOM.*

I had no idea rapping along to the original "Quiet Storm" was saving my life. (The classic 1999 cut from *The Infamous* Hip-Hop duo of Mobb Deep, not the Smokey Robinson masterpiece of 1975, which helped create an entire subgenre of R&B-soul radio programming and the modern "slow jams" algorithm.) Of course, numerous examples of music literally saving a life exist, but I didn't think this would count.

Many know music can help create meditative states or consciousness in the body. Rhythms that can keep you alert while studying, traveling, or operating machinery; compositions that can inspire new ways to live; songwriting that can induce better decision-making; voices that can enable spiritual breakthroughs; ambient frequencies which can break up diseases; and energy that can balance or replenish almost any mood. I didn't think deeply about how much I liked "Quiet Storm." I just thought it was a great song. My engagement with the track was as mindful as it was mindless. Still, even though I knew every lyric, I was often engaged beyond them.

It was a covert and gradual affair. I noticed a feeling of "home" when I'd put it on, though I didn't know why. The music took me places further than my mind. The lyrics cleverly and repeatedly unfastened themselves without force. It brought me inside its choices and instruments. I was walking through it in a raincoat, sitting by a fire in its cave, gazing at the fight scenes of its wildly drawn anime, caught comfortably in the pupils of its predator animal. There was a spirit of a thing there that I couldn't explain. A persistence in darkness that tapped at my nature and reminded me of something secure yet still wild. The testimony of young veterans who were supposed to die but didn't. A sermon for those who had to become warriors quickly.

The moody, anthemic, relentlessly confessional "Quiet Storm" by Prodigy and Havoc of Queensbridge, New York City, became a go-to for my vocal practice and "performance-ready" artist training. Initially, I chose it because I had all the lyrics memorized and, thus, could use it to enhance other exercises without the need to read off something. I'd jump rope, do jumping jacks, hold planks, run, or do cardiovascular movements alongside it. Other fully memorized or lyric-heavy songs requiring strategic breathwork joined this directive, including the Wu-Tang Clan's "Triumph," Queen Latifah and Monie Love's "Ladies First," Big Pun and Fat Joe's "Twinz (Deep Cover '98)," Lauryn Hill's "Everything Is Everything," and Anita Baker's "Fairy Tales."

Legendary writer Arthur Miller once said, "I guess we're all, every artist, has a tendency to throw himself into the world to see if he floats." There's something profoundly thoughtful about the recklessness of throwing yourself into something in life. This is something I've done almost stubbornly since I was a baby. I love seeing what I'm made of. Maybe because I truly believe I'm something greater than anyone has ever seen in me. This profound recklessness to dive in feels to me like humanity that will not be conquered. The evidence of a soul living, bucking the truth of being smaller than a grain of sand in the physical universe. Maximizing the gift of life, answering its call with action, and making something out of something. Creating what's already possible.

Nobody told me to practice like this, and nobody had to. These songs transformed into physical challenges which required me to work with my body as it was. To learn it, cooperate with it, and master its command. To not just release tension to make movement possible but to open my heart, to believe in what I was doing for myself. No one taught me this at home, school, or otherwise.

In college, I always kept two sets of notes, one for what was said and the other for what I noticed or questioned. I've likewise always kept a private space for exploration in music and performance. The likes of high-intensity physicality to "Quiet Storm" put me in tune with something fundamental I needed to feel. Emotional connections and aspirational images met the vulnerability of simply relearning how to breathe. Meanwhile, riding the secure tone of Prodigy's vocal delivery was like reciting a soldier's prayer. It was a therapy discovered unintentionally between counselors who are also counseled.

Each time I was in the act of performance training, monitoring my respiratory system, coordinating my movement, reminding my body parts to maintain good form, and doing my best to focus away from the temporary agony—I'd also put myself in the mastery, playfulness, mystery, and imagination of the accompanying lyrics and sounds. I imagined how the artists might've felt as they recorded these songs. What it felt like to write such words, to swiftly illustrate details of life with acute wit and flow. To be doing what they love. To be present in the freedom of a gift. To go from being a relative unknown just creating in a room to a headlining, global, public figure. To come through a culture dismissed as a passing trend that became a billion-dollar industry, and unlike anything in human history, significantly shifted the world in less than fifty years. To be part of a meaningful blueprint, an original within a unique energy duplicated to death, sometimes even beyond recognition.

Inhales and exhales would dance across thin lines inside my "Quiet Storm" aerobic body, daring me to hang on. Under the physical stress of performing, each breath suddenly had an assigned or improvised purpose. They carried voice, sustained silence, or gave the body fuel, which meant any waste or misuse would be felt immediately on the next breath. As discomfort and fatigue grew, and my brain would start fight-or-flight negotiations, I'd will my heart rate to beat toward a higher power. I'd also use my third mind to pray, as legendary jazz-pianist Herbie Hancock's twenty-seventh album said, *Feets, Don't Fail Me Now*.

I'm more than familiar with the iconic "Quiet Storm" remix featuring Lil' Kim too, for the record. I usually can't resist performing along with her monstrously secure energy, especially on this track, which may be one of her tightest verses and most extraordinary vocal deliveries of all time. The mix of her unabashed grit, decisiveness, richly colored vocal tones, sexual freedom, audaciously divine feminine, and visual decadence make rapping along to any classic Lil' Kim song an energy-raising, transformative, and, in some cases, therapeutic experience. But where her outstanding presentation on this remix moved me with its stylishly declarative "I Am" energy and outward performance, the original "Quiet Storm" moved me from the inside. A delivery of thoughts more concerned with the processes of being than the act of stating or presenting. An inward exploration that gave "I Am" an armored and attractive soul.

Prodigy and Havoc seemed to employ a different care on the original. The usually acceptable bravado of street lore seemed stripped of its need to perform for a sensationalized or identity-hungry audience. Instead, subtleties, soft thoughts, and small exchanges were given the limelight. Success was significant because it represented personal power, access to expansion, untouchable spiritual promotion, and the ability to uniquely survive, ascend, and choose to have something more to offer. Motivations felt less overtly "Money, Power, Respect" and more love, redemption, and fulfillment. Growth signifying details like the "banging of jewelry on glass tables" or childhood memories of an influential loved one were immersive yet whipped by in seconds, prompting more listening. I listened . . . and indeed became addicted to this diction. These were not rhymes. These were prescriptions.

This book is about intentional living, suicide prevention and awareness, and my journey with Hip-Hop, always with me through multiple fields and industries. I am a suicide attempt survivor. I'll do my best to describe a series of events surrounding my death after life and "Life After Death." I've called myself a "unicorn" because I've (finally) embraced being different, and there seems to be magic everywhere I go. They say children always find magic because they look for it, and all withstanding, I've found some in nearly every part of my life. A heightened level of passion in all my relationships, drive in all my goals, revelation in all my loneliness, resonance in all my adventures. I like to believe this is also because I'd have it no other way. Though I wasn't always accepting or listening to them, every experience has also been met with messages, symbols, downloads, and reflections brought through nonphysical, highly coincidental, or mystical means. I've found synchronicity often tells me what time it is.

Simply listening and accepting these many times gave me the courage and clarity to live through a difficult day, night, or moment. They helped me respect my inner voice, open my mind, grow tired of repeating lessons, learn from others' mistakes, and discern the wonder which still exists in people, places, and things. Though many know me as a rapper, poet, vocalist, or someone who's generally positively spoken and outwardly encouraging, there was a period in my life when I was almost entirely mute, as well as those in which I didn't smile. I constantly swam in my inner conflicts and disappointments, pondering, as in the Mary J. Blige *My Life* album, whether I'd genuinely ever "Be Happy." I'm relieved to be more so on the other side, where it does get better, where there are many meaningful things to say, smile about, and enjoy observing, doing, and being . . . where silence is about peace, not punishment or precaution.

I wrote this book because I believe light is more powerful than darkness. I believe the heart could use another advocate, intelligence could use more promotion and bravery, and love could use more visibility. I believe natural sensitivity can be a superpower. I believe you can grow beyond your circumstance. Possibly, my life has been preserved through death and trials so others can be inspired back into themselves or preserved for the better. Often, people who can't see the value or beauty in themselves can't see what is in others, making vision very important.

I believe in the power of uniqueness, my own visions, and the visions of greatness in others. I believe in human warmth and how stories connect us. I believe few are truly living but could be. I believe the COVID-19 pandemic skewed and drained a lot of energy that can be reclaimed, transformed, or clarified at will. I believe the biggest lies are about who we are, where we are, and what we can do. I believe many of us are ready for better. I believe I must tell truths.

This is the kind of book I once needed but couldn't find, so the feeling is amplified that I simply can't or don't want to hold these thoughts exclusively inside me anymore. I believe the called are qualified. I believe in imagination and creating into existence. I believe in the good work and good thinking of those who came before me. I believe better living comes from better thinking and better feeling. I believe there's better to experience here and now, which makes unlearning necessary for most. I believe in a power within us more than any power over us.

It seems everything positioned to kill, minimize, or enslave me to the point of no return hasn't, and this is, first and foremost, for my understanding. I believe this writing is a match for my readiness to be happier, more alive, more fulfilled, and more bada**. I believe we're being shown something with every example, interaction, and experience, first and foremost, about ourselves. I know I'm one of infinite examples of possibility, as are you.

Throughout this book are examples of humanity, creativity, and ideas that have inspired me to feel something, keep going, embrace my uniqueness, develop my self-care, and see much more life to live. I graciously introduced some meaningful people who directly shaped my evolution. Many people, places, and things are not named because this is *not* a linear story of my life, and perhaps some are better in a different book or project. There are details of traumatic events in numerous sections surrounding my suicide attempt, medical emergencies, the terrorist attacks of September 11, 2001, imprisonment, substance abuse, and sexual violence. If you're susceptible to triggers, please be aware. Again, please also see the back of this book for more resources, support organizations, and help.

I reference cultural icons, other "unicorns," and survivors throughout whose uncommon existences make me want to, as legendary musician Jimi Hendrix said, "wave my freak flag higher." True to his inspiration and being somewhat of an oddball for most of my life, I've been encouraged to learn that some of the most outstanding examples of truly living come from unpopular places, unpredictable sources, and the unlikeliest packages.

CHAPTER 2
INCARCERATED BOOK NERDS, KARATE MONKS, AND HUE(MAN) NATURE

FROM A CALIFORNIA PRISON cell in the 1970s, Black nationalist revolutionary icon George L. Jackson said, "It's not revolutionary to disconnect things." He'd been in prison for eleven years, mostly in solitary confinement, on a one-year-to-life sentence (now illegal) for a $70 robbery as a minor. On his journey into adulthood and becoming an acclaimed author, organizer, cofounder of the Black Guerrilla Family prison gang, and leading theoretician of the Prison Rights movement, he brought greater awareness of social politics, prison labor, inhumane treatment, and basic self-determination to the world. He did this, most notably, by reading books.

In fact, according to "From Freedom Summer to Black August" by Dan Berger of *Dissent* magazine, George and others read many books as part of a California state prison program that made numerous titles available. Unfortunately, as they read, the seeds of the world's biggest prison boom were also being planted throughout the United States. George's writings from this period reveal intense studies which clearly opened his mind. He was exposed to different ideas of living, making new connections, and becoming more in tune with his own intelligence and ability to observe, think critically, and discern.

Registering these psychological changes in George and other inmates, authorities made certain this program was systematically shut down. Books became less widely available, and some were even banned or provoked consequences (to this day). This class of incarcerated individuals was notoriously dubbed "hyperliterate" inmates. According to the National Academies Press, the incarcerated population of the United States increased sixty percent from there, doubled in the following decade, and by 1990, grew four times its 1972 size across all facility levels.

A little over twenty years later stood a stark cultural parallel in Hip-Hop. From one of his last recorded media interviews with Rob Marriott in 1996, bestselling global music icon Tupac Shakur described a rejuvenated mind-set since being released from prison and gaining chart-topping success with the legendary collective of Death Row Records.

He was a superstar at the time who may not have needed to do much else beyond making chart-topping music, yet he had expanded his consciousness about nearly everything. Doing better business in the entertainment industry, venturing into new industries, giving more artists equitable opportunities, investing in more community wellness, organizing better leadership in the Hip-Hop community, and even American politics were all discussed with the same passion as his most signature rap lyrics, if not more.

It's not the money that I'm bragging about, when people see me with the jewels it's not that, it's [manifestation] to show that the last time you seen me I was in cuffs, shot up, in a wheelchair with my head wrapped up. And you see me less than a year later . . . I got this whole s*** shook up. The day I stepped out, that's power. I didn't get this power from guns because there's no guns in jail. I got that power from books, and from thinking, and by strategizing. That's what I want little n***** to see.

The June 1975 issue of martial arts-, boxing-, and wrestling-focused *Black Belt* magazine featured an article titled "From Monastery to Tournament Floor" by Jon E. Topham. In it, a young Filipino yoga monk named Dada Jii Shishir described what shaped his persuasion to join a karate tournament he came to watch in Canada at nineteen years of age. It was his first time out of the monastery in over five years. Though he entered the tournament as a startling unknown, weighing just over one hundred pounds, he reached the final rounds of both the lightweight and heavyweight divisions. By the end, he was regarded as a legend, achieving this feat despite never being in a tournament nor training in karate in over four years. He graciously spoke with interviewers:

What is your official title?

"I am an acharya, which is teacher by example. It is like a priest or minister in this country."

Why would you come to Canada or the United States if your duty in life is to serve and help the suffering and starving?

"Well, the way I see it, there are many people here that are suffering and starving mentally for some way to gain peace and contentment. This is why I am here."

What made you become a monk and dedicate yourself to the Brotherhood?

"When I started in the monkhood, I don't think I really wanted to become a monk. I didn't even know what is a monkhood. I just got fed up and frustrated by all the things in society, like money, cars, dress. You have to have money all the time and be looking good all the time, being with the ladies all the time. I got into some really deep thinking, and I got to know myself a little more. You know, why am I doing something, why am I eating, why am I doing karate. I was a black belt already at this time. But it seemed to just make me too proud and very emotional. I guess I just couldn't control my emotions. It was

also too violent for me. It got to a point where I reacted with violence."

What finally allowed you to leave the monastery?

"Well, every three months or so there are these examinations. The exams are different because the higher monk will just look at you and maybe ask you a question. I knew everything, and I said I was going to pass this time because I had already failed six times. He would never call me. He would call others but for six times he would not call me, and I was crying and saying he was unfair. Finally, I got more mature, and he called me. The exam was more intuition. He just looks at you and knows if you're ready to go. He just asked me one question. He asked me, what is man's nature? This is a very fundamental thing that every monk should know."

What is man's nature?

"Man's nature is to realize his potential."

Lupe Fiasco opened his masterful 2015 Hip-Hop fusion album *Tetsuo & Youth* with a nine-minute, no-hook magnum opus titled "Mural." In it, he brilliantly proposed, "life is not a dictionary; it's a thesaurus." He'd go on to make lyrical synonyms out of an abundance of provocative and sensual images. Legendary hoofer Bill Robinson "tapping in Morse code" for generations of barrier-breaking Black entertainers who'd follow him, apparitions using apps, suggestive parallels of the art of Stevie Wonder and Salvador Dalí. It's one of the most relentlessly vivid paintings of "pictures in word form" I've ever heard. More than impressed at the lyrical accomplishment and bold choice to start the album this way, I admired the imagination, vision, and literacy that put everything together. I too believe in the power of synonyms, associations, and relationships. Making connections with an open mind fuels imagination, which is often necessary to eclipse suppression or limitation of any kind.

I remember reading the word "hyperliterate" regarding

George L. Jackson and immediately relating it to all the psychological battling I did in formal education. I was often angry at the audacity to seemingly try to control, corrupt, or demean rightfully growing minds. How unlike the United Negro College Fund adage, good minds often *do* "go to waste" due to poor educational vision, execution, administration, or curriculum, even at the wealthiest institutions.

CHAPTER 3
GIRLS GO TO COLLEGE TO GET MORE KNOWLEDGE, THEY SAID

I WAS ALWAYS A "LOVE to learn, hate school" person. So, I can relate to the frustrations of Dada Jii Shishir in *Black Belt* magazine regarding his readiness to leave the monkhood as much as he was ready to join it. The monastery was important in affirming his direction and steering him away from the temptation to use his karate power violently. He'd come from significant achievement at a young age and gained mastery in this craft he loved. Yet, with all the discipline and focus this took, he still found himself unhappy, uninspired, unfulfilled, and even unhinged.

It took the combination of physical, mental, energetic, and spiritual training to equip Shishir with the knowledge that not only made him balanced and matchless but also fulfilled him and made him feel good about himself. I took from this a concept of dynamically bespoke education: creating a multidimensional knowledge base that suits your strengths, visions, and desires.

Thanks to intellectual breadcrumbs left by the likes of the Wu-Tang Clan, my sincere love of kung fu movies, and two semesters of Chen-style Taiji with award-winning martial arts master José Manuel Figueroa, I too was intrigued by the likes of the Shaolin Temple as a learning institution. Joining a monastery for at least a year and eventually becoming a Shaolin nun was something I briefly considered. (Women can't become Shaolin monks in certain countries but can usually receive kung fu training.) Regarding education, I was looking for a change of pace, scenery, and approach to life which also had my mental and physical health in mind. This was part of my endless search for a knowledge base related to my skill set, who I really am, how I want to live, and what I want to do.

I remember hearing about prolific women of the Black Panther Party, who, while running most of their community and national programming in the 1960s and 1970s, would form their own schools and often restructure traditional learning approaches. Sometimes, they'd do away with the grade-level system in favor of more intuitive, communal, and ability-based methods. I always thought this was incredibly bold and out-of-the-box thinking. I never heard of anyone challenging the grade-level system used by Western education since "Jimmy Crack Corn." But there's a lot of sense in such thinking.

Education is no small thing, whether from solitude, public school, private for-profit settings, ruthless competition, or wise, loving elders. The connections or disconnections of the mind create powerful molds. What people teach themselves or are being taught is how they're being conditioned to think. This will shape their lives and ability not just to exist or follow but create reality.

In the third grade, my parents were approached about skipping me ahead or sending me to a "gifted" school. They declined both. Had I gone, I wouldn't have met my artist community like I did. Also, major news outlets, national institutions, and educational nonprofits have reported controversies about gifted programs, especially for Black children, so I'm not mad at their decision. However, there wasn't much for me academically from then on. I wasn't told of this decision until much later, but the effects showed themselves almost immediately. I was routinely bored and felt I was being given "busy work," which didn't have me or my "gift" in mind at all.

Left to my own devices, I had the most stimulating adventures, conversations, and independent studies, which continued to be the case. In contrast, stock, pipeline, or "brand-name" education seemed inconsistent, limited, and impersonal despite the social passes it offered. As a result, I became suspicious about how the world treated intelligence regardless of gift.

The singing chant of a children's handclapping and jump rope game I played on many playgrounds provocatively suggested that "girls go to college to get more knowledge." By nine years of age, I decided the *real* knowledge was being hidden, and I needed to find it for myself. I just knew this knowledge had to be somewhere; I just knew it. Somewhere were special books, special facilities, special lessons, or special teachers eager to share with someone like me.

I know some soldiers in here. Where they at, where they at?
  —*Destiny's Child, "Soldier"*

I didn't trust the college hunch per se, but from being on college campuses where my parents worked, I noticed they *felt* different and had more extensive libraries. It stood to reason that maybe "real" brain-power training was going down in the hallowed halls of university.

Counterintuitive to some "underprivileged" narratives, there was a lot of insistence from the so-called urban community to go to college. By my midteens, however, I felt I'd found gold in entrepreneurship, music, writing, training, coaching, performing, understanding concepts, being a cultural bridge, and having people skills which would surpass the classroom. Now in high school, I went from a straight-A honors student to a straight-F student. I dropped out, dropped out again (this time from trade school), got a GED, took a semester of community college, and transferred to a four-year university, eventually graduating with honors, academic awards, a hard-fought major and two minor degrees.

I was already unimpressed with the prospect of having a degree by then. Common sense, vision, and practical wisdom seemed understated, and the high costs of education made no sense to me. However, I understood it meant a lot to people socially, was an easy signifier of competence, and a method of mobility. My father worked full-time as a college professor and was in education most of his life. It was why he could leave our birthplace of Uganda and move me and my mother to the United States. Imagine telling an immigrant educator you don't value traditional education . . . How much audacity you got? "A lot." *21 Savage voice* We had a handful of vigorous "debates" about this. I eventually decided, as my inner child had years before, maybe I'd find what I was looking for in college. It also seemed smart to take advantage of not having to pay tuition costs at the university which employed my father.

"Don't Get It Twisted," though . . . there were still costs. Putting an unorthodox degree combination together moved me out of the usual gimmies, so I paid for some classes. It was also still a juggle every semester with the insanity of books, supplies, course requirements, travel, and food fees aside from general bills. I was wide-eyed at students who were taking up to $100,000 in bank loans to cover the college tab. Financial consultant, college graduate, and author of the *For the Hustler* book series Trevor Cassaberry would counter that "a degree without a clear return on investment is a liability." Depending on your field and job market it's advantageous, but this isn't always the case.

Working full-time while going to school full-time also remains in the top five hardest things I've ever done, even with taking a couple of breaks just to work and "stack." But while I had this chance and some financial support, I chose to "play the game." *Triple H theme voice* In fact, I remember looking at my loaded transcript one year with all its numerical codes and proposed controls and thinking, *this is just one big video game, SMH!*

Stress from the juggle, classes, commuting, traveling across campuses, overnight research, essays, test prep, deadlines, and presentation missions indeed replaced that of *Crash Bandicoot, God of War, House of the Dead, Mario Kart, Def Jam: Vendetta, Madden, Sonic, Mortal Kombat, Splinter Cell,* and *Grand Theft Auto* —but it was fundamentally the same. It was a game of points, credits, lives, and profits. My father, even with a PhD, astounding credentials, and a positive reputation, was also enduring professional challenges which affected me. Though he was still well respected by most, he was going through "the game" too, particularly as one of few Black faculty members. I was routinely uncomfortable for us both. I swallowed the overall bittersweet scenario and let go of a romantic idea of college. I'd stay open to an experience I hoped for, but I reconciled simply needing to rack up the points required to level up and get out with my remaining life.

I'm sure never having the "typical" student experience also made a difference. I was doing non-school shows, rehearsals, socializing with the streets (my mentor Jamal Joseph calls this "The University of Lenox Avenue"), chopping it up with colorful characters, helping run several youth programs, and had my own apartment to maintain an hour off-campus. I was more disappointed in society's false advertising of the college experience, even just regarding the curriculum. Someone like me should've been having a ball intellectually, but I wasn't.

Save for a few exceptional professors and classes I went out of my way to be in, it was more "busy work" just like in the fourth grade, only at the college level. I'd also wanted to attend an HBCU (historically Black college or university), but it wasn't feasible. Ratio: I couldn't commit to the likes of Black student union meetings at my very international, private, PWI (predominantly White institution) campus nor most activities outside my major and minors. As a result, I barely got to socialize with other Black students, and a feeling of alienation became normal.

Being in the Financial District meant proximity to world-class venues, top-tier guests, and the cultural neighborhoods of New York City. It also meant everything was subject to the city's skyscraping, concrete jungle, name-branded backdrop. High prices, heavy police presence, and constant crowds, yet no grand homecomings, yard shows, or campus football games. There was a lot of vibrant activity, cool events, and locational privilege, but I desired a warmth and collective conscience I often didn't feel.

I loved New York and being a New Yorker, but it was the same big city life and subway ride, just now with different stops and a different schedule. Sometimes, I felt like I was in the thirty-sixth grade. I also noticed a lot of challenges to my spirit, identity, and background, even in my diverse, arts-centered courses, which I joined specifically to grow as an artist and bring me joy. I was grateful for the opportunity to be there and meet sincerely good people of more outstanding talents and abilities. But in resisting assimilation to it all, I almost lost my mind.

Though I was still an excellent student and achieved notable things on paper, the experience began to drag. Midway through my degree, I aged out of an excellent health coverage program for youth and young adults, which Mount Sinai Hospital had been running through a facility on the Upper East Side. It provided free physicals, testing, OB-GYN visits, and more for years. I'd found an amazing American-Black woman therapist and Puerto Rican-Italian psychiatrist there who hit it off with me very well, much needed after I'd given up on therapy years back from several negative experiences. But suddenly, the only people I could see were break-ready receptionists asking, "Well, who is your insurance?"

A rug had been pulled from under me. I was graciously given a chance to speak with Dr. Suzanne Ross, the grandparent of one of my youth program members, who was also a clinical psychologist and key organizer in the movement to free political prisoner Mumia Abu-Jamal. I remember sitting in her living room numerous times, emotional over what felt like a battle for my soul. I'd had a vision for my life before this; I felt I had a lot right in my mind already. So why did I have to go through this cookie-cutter experience and battle every day?

I could feel my energy draining and an illusory sense of time-a-ticking. Why couldn't I just go with my gut? I didn't want to waste the financial and networking opportunities present, not to mention my father's hard work to get me there. But at what cost to *me*? I certainly almost quit many times. Toward the end of my degree chase, my mantra was "finish strong." By the end, it became . . . "just finish."

CHAPTER 4
I WAS RUNNING THROUGH (HYPERCREATIVITY) WITH MY WOES

WHERE GEORGE L. JACKSON was called a "hyperliterate" inmate, I'd probably be called a "hypercreative" one. In my mind, there's rarely a time when creativity has no place. A major part of survival is resourcefulness. Business thrives on ideas; nature is filled with more colors than we can name. The human body can transform itself with its own weight; there are over thirty ways to cook a potato. The insanely ornate temples of Ancient Egypt are still standing. Endless examples imply creativity is a bedrock of our existence.

Though it's a very normalized mindset, I've always found the *disapproving* energy of art to be odd. I understand worries about security in a creative career and numerous nouns called "art" which are credibly questionable. However, many "throw the whole art away," completely dismissing its history, power, utility, and opportunity in the practical world. Likely, art will always be subjectively and selectively "too (something)" for someone. This doesn't erase its ongoingly significant place in human evolution, necessitating creative minds at every level of society. But to each their own. The phrase "if I'm too much, go be with less" comes to mind.

Since I didn't have to pay for most of my classes, I filled my college transcript with dance, art, arts management, and marketing courses wherever possible. I'd never been exposed to this level of formal art instruction and needed creative balance. My final degree title read "bachelor of arts in political science with a double minor in dance and arts and entertainment management." (Say *that* five times fast!) Majoring in political science was intellectually up my alley, though quite a hefty workload. I wouldn't have made it through its dense, complex, legal, and historical readings without being able to sweat it out in a dance class, site visit a theater, (badly) draw some still life, or attend a lecture about media production.

Some view my degree combination as odd or wonder why I didn't just "stick to one thing." In one perspective, I've never really been a monotasker and my fundamental living environment has changed several times. With the combination of immigrating from Uganda to the "Black Mecca" of a bustling, post-"crack era," pregentrification-Harlem in 1990, to my family dynamics and our economics, resources, and exposure, to moving around once my parents divorced, joining a touring performance group, the journey of becoming a U.S. citizen, and more—foundational gears were constantly switching.

A panoramic view of life, intense stimuli, and multiple things to do was just how it always was. I never had the luxury to focus on one thing for an extended beat of time. Multitasking throughout the day and multitasking codes of identity were part of my survival conditioning. I've thus always been awed by people who pursue dreams in a linear fashion from childhood to adulthood. Or those who base their entire lives and futures on one educational focus. I believe had I grown up differently, this would be normal for me too.

Singular focus or monotasking is still a necessary skill I've had to learn. It serves you in every area of life and recenters and calibrates your mind when your lifestyle has you constantly on a swivel. Some do this by signing up for classes or doing something that takes them away from their usual environment, requiring siloed attention. Yet, for example, I've also seen people texting repeatedly during their one-hour boxing lesson with gloves on and all. Creating singular focus conditions for yourself is essential, especially to avoid burnout.

An occupational health collective named Workplace Wellness Systems notes on their website, "Several studies have shown high multitaskers experience greater problems focusing on important and complicated tasks, memory impairment of new subject matter, difficulty learning new material, and increased stress levels." Sometimes, we don't have the logistics to do otherwise. But when we do, where we can, it helps significantly to monotask. Practicing this with intention, even when unnecessary, has helped me sharpen and create beneficial habits without force. Unnecessary monotasking for me looks like specialized journaling, learning how to cook my favorite foods, and often exercising without music because I've gotten deeply into communicating with my body and programming my own thoughts.

My wake-up routine best exemplifies necessary monotasking, which has needed more focus than I thought. I'm not one to roll over from sleep onto social media. Still, I'd often jump straight into work, Google a runaway stream of consciousness, or make myself available to numerous energies. In the process, I'd deplete my precious wake-up brain and set my day off on an imbalanced, "chase" driven energy. I've learned I can't just give myself more time, either. I had to create flexible rules, give the routine rituals, segment it, know what each segment was for, and accept why this was best for me. The resulting peace of mind and feeling of being collected before I interact with the world creates invaluable returns. Having a wake-up routine has dramatically improved my life, body, and mental health. Singular focus still comes most easily when I'm focusing on something creative, be it physical or intangible.

In managing hypercreativity, I often use intuition and understand one focus doesn't eliminate focus from all other things for good. I do my best to create priority and placement for each craft according to their demand, resonance, and timing. I'm a detail- and results-oriented person. I've learned balance by trial and error and in recognize the relationship of all things to all things. Somewhere between my energy, mood, and discipline is the allowance, space, and proper respect for each of my creative experiences.

I don't limit myself mentally. Even if I keep something compartmentalized, I let myself be curious. I follow the search, have seventeen tabs open, make bookmarks, organize folders, and eventually close the tabs and set things aside. I do a lot of visualizing of people, places, and things . . . even what I haven't yet done, said, or learned how to do. In my physical space, I make room for things that don't physically exist yet. When I have intense feelings about someone, I may explore why with the diligence of a news report. I have vivid dreams almost every night and often document and analyze them. I look up definitions even if I already know what a word means. I observe people (and other animals) who are "in the pocket" with their instruments in life. I enjoy exploring, and I've figured out a way to be functionally curious. I'm drawn to connect with how different things feel, taste, smell, look, sound and can be experienced.

At times, it's felt like a crime to be deeply engaged in multiple passions like this. Wherever the drawing power was natural or even slight, I've naturally engaged with quality and intention. Sometimes though, it's seemed like a crime *especially* if I had clear intentions and unique qualities about my engagements. Artful being, nonlinear thinking, and dynamic curiosity are regularly treated as niche, threatening, or unnecessary instead of natural, complementary, and valuable ways of self-actualizing in the world. This under-spoken conditioning has social implications. For instance, in my early teens, I noticed less and less imagination and autonomy in people. While doing my best not to internalize limitations, I also sensed my nature and vision were attempting to be tamed. Allow me to back this up with math and science . . .

Cited by curator and world-renowned art advisor Maria Brito in *How Creativity Rules the World*, a creativity and innovation study for problem-solving at NASA conducted in 1968 by Dr. George Land and his wife Dr. Beth Jarman inspired them to apply its test to 1,600 children enrolled in a Head Start program. Ninety-eight percent of the age five children scored at the highest level of creativity. They were tested again at age ten. Only thirty percent scored this high, and at age fifteen, only twelve percent. The same test given to 280,000 adults averaging age thirty yielded only two percent with the score of "highly creative." I repeat, that's *two percent from ninety-eight*, y'all! The general systems and social environments in place are simply not designed to support creative intelligence. Thus, I consider it a blessing, accomplishment, and asset to be part of a coveted two percent (gang gang!) and still be "hypercreative" in adulthood.

I don't know what to tell those looking to tame vision or creativity **Jordan shrug** about how we're wired, our nature, and what it can still become. Scientifically, there's distinct wiring in all of us for the initial purpose of maturing and preventing sensory overload. According to neuroscience and philosophy educator John T. Bruer and his book *The Myth of the First Three Years*, when we're born, something like 15,000 synaptic connections form for every hundred billion neurons in our brains. By age sixteen, half of this network is gone. The bulk of these connections are apparently eliminated to arrive at what forms our unique decision-making, strengths, and personalities. This is something scientists continue to study. Barring their inconclusions and any injury, disease, or barriers to development in the brain, it seems nature has given us a deliberately miraculous serving of exactly who we are, whether or not it's compromised, and whether or not we're using it.

The uniqueness of brain makeup allowing for a "strengths-based life" (say *that* five times fast) was explored by social scientists from the 1980s through the early 2000s by the likes of Dr. Donald O. Clifton. He's been cited by the American Psychological Association as the "Father of Strengths Psychology," the "Grandfather of Positive Psychology," and worked extensively in analytics with polling, research, and intelligence consulting giant Gallup, Inc. After over twenty years of research, he compiled a program of "34 dominant themes" in people such as the "Arranger," the "Maximizer," "Ideation," "Input," the "Futuristic," the "Context" person who always looks back because that's where answers lie, or the "Harmony" person who aways looks for areas of agreement. The themes and corresponding case studies cover thousands of personality combinations which identify different strengths in proven personal and professional success. Coauthored by Marcus Buckingham in *Now, Discover Your Strengths*, these types of perspectives deserve a revisit. The myths of monolithic success have already been broken.

As far as my distinct personality in evolution, living in the faith and leadership of my strengths has given me a completely different life. I decided long ago *Whitney Houston voice* as a small child, that "déjà vu (I've Been Here Before)" *Teena Marie voice* and *this time* I wanted to be part of significant change. What stood out to me was human suffering, power in words and expression, and the joy of wonder. I knew having life didn't mean one was living and I'd use what I'm made of primarily because it feels good, right, and true to do so. Someone flipped a passion switch to "on" when I was born and froze it, passion is my norm, so feeling anything less has been a signifier of off-ness or changing stages in my life. I've also reasoned, why would we be interested and good at multiple things if we weren't meant to explore, use them, and enjoy ourselves? Right?

. . . *right?*

Before anyone "taught me how to hate myself" as Malcolm X so eloquently proposed in 1962, I'd naturally decided everything about me was no crime, it was great! It was me. People, places, and things existed for it all and every day of my life would include the enjoyment of this. This decision was an early and soulful one, predating the concept of authenticity and any drive for redemption, revenge, or approval. Even when this drive stopped growing, it simply persisted like an echoing conscience. A tiny computer fan whirling in my core; a small crackling fire I can hear when quiet. The evidence of my strengths is more than being meaningfully engaged in multiple interests. It's continuously satisfying, significant, successful, personal, and in some cases, world-class experiences with each interest. It's like someone's holding up a big "YES! KEEP GOING!" sign every time I choose to really live, especially through these strengths.

So, do I dare continue in them? . . . Do you?

This wide range of experiences aren't the prettiest fairy tales either, by the way! Sweet accomplishments have been alongside sour failures, bitter low points, dramatic lessons, saddening and humiliating ordeals. For example, I've been a featured showcase artist at Hip-Hop's legendary End of The Weak collective as well as third-place winner in their world-famous, five-round "MC Challenge" competition, but not without being moved from sixth performer to twenty-sixth (last up) at their popular open mic years earlier *and* crashing and burning in front of the five people remaining in the audience. I've auditioned for the prolifically renowned Alvin Ailey American Dance Theater and at seedy local strip clubs. I know what it means to wear a gown and host the formal event launch of my own transnational nonprofit organization in a United Nations building *and* what it means to wear a nametag and deal with lewd, entitled, and disrespectful customers at five in the morning, load heavy commercial garbage into dumpsters at night in the rain, and cry in the bathroom at work.

Tough contrasts are not just potential character-building moments but skill-building opportunities for those who can get past their cliché and apply wisdom. While singing my first solo in church I got the dismaying encouragement heckle of a stern but soft-spoken "take your time, baby" which, while ironically a sign to get it together or wrap-it-up *expeditiously* (chile!) for me was not a deterrent, it meant there was more to learn. While singing backgrounds with the Impact Repertory Theatre choir at a sold-out show at the Apollo Theater, I watched thee Patti LaBelle, Nona Hendryx, and Sarah Dash murdering solos and harmonies right in front of me. I marveled at their command of themselves and the adoring audience hanging on every note. It was a LaBelle anniversary concert, and this audience would've done *anything* for them on-demand! Having the ability to move people just from a connection to your nature, what you believe in, and what you create seemed wild and possible. I found encouragement in how "bad" I was in relation to how great they were because the example of mastery was literally at my feet.

When we attempt to live by passion, nature, or our strengths, negatively sourced energies and the inner saboteur can ask, "who do you think you are?" In doing their best to rock us internally they emphasize the real battle or affirmation is in ourselves. For many years, I believed in cancerous suggestions to "shrink down, adjust to fit here, too much, ideas too big, give us a piece, not enough . . . " when I didn't have to. As a survivor of multiple traumas, I also unknowingly had post-traumatic stress disorder and coping mechanisms which shaped my interactions and went mostly unchecked. I cycled through poorly reconciling what the limited world had for me instead of what I wanted to create in the world with my unlimited self. What it meant to be "overqualified" or not ready for things I really wanted and being too accommodating about what I'd already outgrown. I often stumbled in finding what was right for my life.

Thankfully, I've also had several experience-highs which not only felt good and right immediately but sustained. My first time jumping in a rap cipher in the fifth grade was a life-defining, unforgettable, ripple-effect moment. It made Hip-Hop personal to me, began my love affair with "moving the crowd," being a connection-driven lyricist, and being unafraid to be the only "anything" in a room. Due to my high level of activity and continued creative exploration, it's likely before my suicide attempt, I'd had more experience-highs from childhood to young adulthood than the average person. Yet, life between these highs felt increasingly low, demanding, and complex. I still had my strong conscience and multiple passions, but I seemed to live a daily inner battle and outer war. My real motivation for vigorously exploring my talents, curiosities, and hypercreative abilities was that I was looking for reasons to stay alive.

ENERGY, WELLNESS & MENTAL HEALTH

CHAPTER 5
SIX MILLION WAYS TO DIE, CHOOSE ONE

ON THE DAY of my suicide attempt I did what many people need to do (or choose to) regardless of their mental health status, I went to work. I was a waitress and service bartender at Mars 2112, a space-themed restaurant that eclipsed its "tourist trap" attraction and became a pop sensation at the far tip of Times Square. Through a series of lucrative, body-aching, and foot-skin peeling double shifts, this job made it possible to afford my first apartment and moving expenses to start my independent living era. I'd also temporarily quit school to focus on it after a hellish go of doing both. Again, respectfully, working a physically demanding full-time job while successfully in school full-time remains in the top hardest things I've ever done.

As taxing as it was and as much as I hated it sometimes, I've always been excellent at service and hospitality. At tuning in with people's wants, needs, and energies in real time. So, though I was "one of the quiet ones" I had no problem becoming one of the top revenue earners and thus placed in more "important" sections of the huge, high-volume restaurant.

It was the most tip money I'd ever racked up, upwards of $500 per shift, even after splitting percentages with support staff. Seeing and feeling the most cash I'd ever had undoubtedly motivated me for a long while. It was also the most people and commotion I'd ever had to focus around, not counting a show, and no doubt the hardest I'd ever worked outside the arts, sports, or quitting smoking. To me, though, it *was* an art, a stage; and meaningful victory was involved.

In this job, I found a similar science and flow to all things in life, and true to form, I was learning while doing. Even this, a position which, on paper, was below minimum wage without benefits, where I was contractually obligated to wear a costume and play a committed role in somebody's random, wild idea brought to fiscal life. A supported hunch, a full-on creative experience, a corporate fantasy . . . Even this, which many would find demeaning, unforgiving, or too stressful to deal with, was a deep reflection of the world and possibility.

I'd done so many things at this job, from multitasking chaotic dining disasters to being part of the frequent "dance breaks" done for the customers (including alien mascots, soul music, feather boas, and tambourines), to serving several celebrities and their families. For a while, I slept, woke, showered, dressed, and traveled strictly to be "Space Captain Emily" at this underground restaurant "on Mars."

Years before this, around age fourteen, my goal to legally gain "independent minor" status was stalled due to not yet being a U.S. citizen. Its title would've allowed me to enter into my own agreements and contracts, be my own legal guardian, choose my own work, services, education, and leisure in New York state. This was music to my ears. While I appreciated what my hardworking immigrant parents made possible for me, I discerned they were (rightfully) busy chasing and positioning their own decisions about themselves in this wholly different American reality. I was essentially on my own and wanted to operate freely as such.

My visions for a unique, strengths-driven life were already clarified by this age. I resolved independence would enable me to think clearly and effectively and choose my own destiny. I'd already perceived existing systems (like public and private schools, religious directives, and government programs) were offering me less than what I could create for myself. I was deathly determined to be independent and create a life no construct could deter. I saw no other way of truly living or achieving my desired goals than to be responsible for myself.

Even in meeting and cocreating with good people of merit as I remained active into my teenage years, I repeatedly noticed a quality of control, possession, or prejudice to dodge, especially as a young Black woman. Whether or not I internalized it, I just didn't want to deal with it. It was something I'd have to actively phase out of my desired life, wherever possible. I needed to be all in about what I saw for myself to overcome all this, even without paperwork or material prestige to claim a status. The stretch of time between this realization and working for the Mars 2112 restaurant, which was my first job out of bartending school, was no straight line.

There were many uncelebrated years in between—much like the time it took for legendary performer Tina Turner to leave Ike Turner for good, gain independent stability, and eventually go double-diamond as a solo recording artist and stadium Queen of Rock 'n Roll via the *Private Dancer* album. These were years of rote survival, obstacle coursing, treading water, figuring it out, weightlifting, and staying alive without acclaim. T. J. Martin, codirector of the 2021 HBO documentary *Tina* called it "being in the wind" or "wilderness." This is a fluid condition of life's many experiences.

Like the acronym PUSH, which stands for "persist until something happens," I was certainly there pushing, keeping myself busy, steering through the human traffic, convincing myself of my own hunches, of what I felt I had in me. I debated against projected limitations, simple doubts, trauma anxiety, and severe depression, which would cripple me if I let it. I was feeling my way to a horizon I knew had to exist . . . any significant change for the better. It was more of a gritty *8 Mile* or *Hustle*

& Flow than a glossy *Belly* or *Paid in Full* montage of success, but finally, some firm steps had been made, and I was a workingwoman with a plan. This Mars 2112 restaurant moment of my life would prove a most memorable level of focus, raised level of inner dignity, and work experience I'd never forget while in the background, I climbed.

Ratio: I didn't know what burnout was, nor that I was headed to it early.

The physical and psychological demands of the job also played a part in running my vital energy into the ground. To make matters worse, I'd mismanaged some of my moving expense money by rushing to overpay an ill-suited company. This hiccup added to the dissolution of my financial cushion under unforeseen costs. I still needed to work just as hard to keep up with my new bills. The apartment I'd wanted since age fourteen was mine, however, my deathly determination now seemed to be a slow death march with a finish line that kept moving back.

Caught up in the hustle (cue "Everyday Struggle" by The Notorious B.I.G.), I had yet to think of a new route and didn't have the energy or desire to restart school. Things quickly felt limited, though I figured getting financially stable was important, and a plan would come to me. Still a teenager, I was tired . . . to my bones. Growing up how I did and where I did, I'd had to grow up fast. I'd been thinking like an adult and processing mature things since childhood. I'd been numbing painful situations and the absence of a family connection since childhood. My senses of stability, innocence, privacy, and protection had already been violated, interrupted, or accelerated for the convenience of the world beyond my good. Now here I was, fighting to get to the *starting* line. I felt like a stunted pawn on a chess board and was deeply frustrated because I knew I was really a queen piece, with the additional ability to be a maker, to create my own game. But the constant give-and-go with little increase was beginning to catch up. In hindsight, I went to work this fateful day not just because I needed the cash. I was hoping something, *anything* there this last shift would inspire me to put off the suicide at least one more day.

The "business of death" always seems to be booming and well marketed. But while some plan to live and some plan to die, the cliché still fits . . . most fail to plan either way. Freestyle, improvisation, and intuitive spontaneity have always been huge parts of my creative and spiritual foundation. Numerous scientific studies have proven the power of these for productivity, balance, and even happiness. Yet and still, *"I'm a Method Man, baby, accept it, utmost respect it and . . ."* I'm also a loyal child of order, methods, and having a plan. In this case, with suicide as the objective, I wouldn't stray from either of my natures. Once I affirmed the decision to do it, I carefully moved it in my mind like a bomb needing rewiring. I took it from thought to consideration and then into a planning phase. It was a serious decision, not a pretend one, which I would do alone. I created a separate space from my emotional mind to logically think about its elements and the action steps involved.

I decided jumping from a roof (in my hood) was tricky and not my approach. I also didn't want a bloody scene that someone would have to clean up or in case my father would have to identify my body. I considered the person(s) who would find me. Because I wasn't too into Western medicine, hated the idea of taking pills, and was no stranger to binge drinking, I decided pills mixed with hard alcohol would have a profound internal effect on my body. I didn't have these things handy, so I figured I'd go to work and use the extra cash on these "materials."

I'd picked up an afternoon shift on a Tuesday, not necessarily a moneymaking shift, which proved very slow. A few of us were cut early for labor-cost balance. Unlike me, I volunteered to be one of them after making only $22 on a couple of tables in a few hours, which felt like days. This alone was defeating, and I'd had enough. I was just done. Simply done.

Many details of this day are still hazy. I believe I reached out to someone in earnest, one of my close friends at the time, Jasstina Featherstone, with whom I'd bonded over a shared love of video games, laughter, and entrepreneurship. We also shared being only children of divorced parents with our spiritual curiosity, playful sensual natures, and dark mental health experiences. I called or texted her and said something about feeling suicidal. We had a code that predicated not to call authorities or certain people. I was to text her something every hour or so to let her know I was still alive or how I was feeling.

I'd done so, reassuringly, though I went from whole phrases down to single words and emoji-like figures. Smartphones weren't in full swing yet, so I had no GIFs, stickers, or high-resolution emoji options to express the likes of indifference, worry, face palms, a monkey bar, seamstress, a needle and spool, or its "hanging by a thread" equivalent, which was how I really felt. She did what she could to comfort me, but I also believe I wasn't letting her know how serious I was or how truly hopeless I felt. Nothing had managed to inspire me to an excitement for life that day. As I grew numb and detached, the day itself grew fuzzier and everyone more monotonal. Everything began to blend and fade into a very simplistic landscape. The wild, detailed, vibrant jungle of my human life and sensually calculating mind became slowly muted, like a time-lapse or gradient of a Basquiat painting turning into a Rothko.

In one of my favorite romantic comedy movies of the 1990s, *The First Wives Club* (spoiler alert)—it's expressed the main character who commits suicide was a bright, good-hearted, affluent woman voted "Most Likely to Succeed" in high school. That "when she decided to do something, she just went ahead and did it." This always struck me, firstly, because of how bold a character trait this is. Secondly, the fact that this kind of person found themselves, as the movie portrayed, successfully living in a beautiful penthouse overlooking Central Park while also deeply depressed, in the outs of a painful and publicly embarrassing divorce, lonely, distraught, and without her dearest community. The phrase "check on your strong friends" comes to mind. I've always been fascinated (for lack of better words) at how strong people can surrender or divert their strength and often do overtime, or on "any given (Sun)day." How this strength itself is human and can be worn down, thus needing revitalization.

In the "Not Another Monday" episode of the Emmy award-winning television classic *The Golden Girls*, the main character Sophia's elder friend Martha is tired of her lonely lifestyle, afraid to die alone, and burdened by the numerous health complications of her advanced age. After attending her best friend's funeral and swimming through its grief and depression, she formally asks Sophia to be there and hold her hand when she commits suicide. In the days leading up, Martha uses her life savings to get her hair and makeup done, buy new clothes, eat her favorite foods at a high-end restaurant, toast with top-shelf cocktails, and purchase a diamond ring on lay-away (ha!). She attributes this to a "new attitude called eat, drink, and be merry," inspired by her fatal decision to "change her life" by ending it.

I wondered if I'd been in a different financial position, might the days which led to my decision have been different, perhaps more like Martha's? Would I have simply taken better care of myself or done something special for me, and would it have mattered? Does one really want to sit alone indoors and die with a fresh fit ready to be worn and "hair did, nails did, everything did!" ***Swizz Beatz voice*** Debatably not (shrugging). Would the feeling have lasted? Might my attitude have been different? Would I have gone to work that day? Would I even have that job? While I see so many things money and social class could've corrected or Band-Aided, my mind was still fixed in a sad, mentally limited place of silent struggling.

Also playing a part was my genuinely happy relationship

Y'ALL (NOT) GON' MAKE ME LOSE MY MIND

with my first boyfriend of over two years suddenly disconnected . . . over . . . and freshly tearing my heart apart. He'd broken up with me soon after I moved into my new place, leaving to not only to start a new life in a new country but to be with a new woman distinctly different from me—the totality of these colliding and contrasting circumstances I couldn't fully process at the time. In addition, the weight of overworking at a tip-based job to keep up with the new apartment (which was still pretty barren and beginning to visually affect me) was getting heavier. I felt chronically unappreciated and intellectually under-stimulated by my surroundings. I'd had the most cash I ever had and *still* ended up broke. "How, Sway?"

I missed performing but was worn out physically and mentally. I felt a plateau in my creative goals and activities. There was so much heavy lifting to do by myself, and still manage to smile every day. I knew many people and had relationships in many circles, but by choice or sum, I was routinely lonely. My closest friends were close, but also not that close, and I'd outgrown several others. My immediate family had fallen apart since my parents' long and bitter divorce, which began when I was about eight. I wasn't in warm, regular communication with the rest of my family who were on different continents. My passionate visions seemed to mock me for not believing in myself enough. My desires for pleasure seemed ceaseless and fleeting. My unresolved trauma was still working through my physical body and mental conditioning.

Aside from running away or taking myself on an elaborate vacation, more money would likely have only meant a bigger budget for my production of self-inflicted casualty. I was low in my mind about something bigger and deeper. I was a young, active, attractive, college-adjacent girl with talent. By MTV standards, this was supposed to be "the best time of my life." Instead, I questioned happiness itself constantly. What was it, really? Would I ever be truly happy here? Were pain, hard work, and disappointment all I'd ever know in a real way? Was I out of the strength which turns pain into power? Tired of these franchise questions and empty answers, I proceeded to checkmate.

One might say you can (try to) take the girl out of the game, but you can't take the game out of the girl. My plan to die was the clearest I'd felt about anything at the time and ironically demonstrated my skilled quality for production and execution in a lively way. In the vein of our beloved *First Wives Club* fictional character Cynthia Swann Griffin, I was still all business about this bereavement. The auditor of my expiry, the project manager of my mortality, the executive producer and show runner of my series finale. I was the CEO, COO, and CBO of this last curtain call. In continued illustration of the ability in myself I couldn't see as worthy, the power of my dynamically creative and prosperous mind (which could've been used successfully almost anywhere else) had turned strictly to bowing out.

Unlike Ms. Griffin, I wasn't sitting on millions, so I had moves to make to support the creation of this surreal episode for my ultimate move. I bid the restaurant adieu ahead of schedule and pooled the $22 with the remaining cash I had on me. I headed across 50th Street and Broadway dashing by men in suits, men begging for spare change, women in lights, hot dog vendors, and the colorful, circuslike neighborhood of "the Great White Way." I walked into a Duane Reade to look for medical pills or a supplement combination that would do the job. As I went downstairs to the pharmacy aisles, I was a bit overwhelmed by the rows of medications, though still determined about my decision.

Remembering I also had hard alcohol to purchase, I narrowed down my search, began label reading, and evaluating. Unsatisfied by the choices I had left, my disappointment turned to frustration. I began to get irate, also fairly but irrationally, at the fact no one had asked if I needed help. I thought to myself, *I'm suicidal on a budget. S***! Why is everything so expensive??!*

Another part of my brain began intellectually combing through the political economics of "big pharma," the trickle down to corporate chains and neighborhood variety drugstores. Elders, youth, or active professionals who, in polarity to me, were determined to stay alive and happened to "need" any of these pills for any number of discomforts or imbalances, who may have also found themselves coming up short monetarily or standing in an aisle just like I was, feeling helpless, overwhelmed, and frustrated about how to help themselves. The whole thing disgusted me. As the poets Jay-Z, Scarface, and Beanie Sigel once said, "This Can't Be Life."

This wasn't living, and I was glad I was going.

I calmed myself down, rationalizing I had no idea what I'd say if someone came up asking, "Could I help you?" or "Do you need help?" The jig might've been up right there. I wasn't sure. Was I secure enough to give a stable, nonweird, emotionless answer? Did I know how to pose my need scientifically to get medical information without raising suspicion? I couldn't say. This was my freestyle element, as well, making a scene in a Times Square big-box store incurred the high possibility of being escorted out by hypermilitarized police or questioned into an institutional corner. Again, not my style or approach. *Not* what I wanted in my story's end and would undoubtedly stall my existing plan. The prices were ridiculous, but I held my disdain for society, purchased some generic pills, and exited.

When I got back uptown to Washington Heights, I purchased the alcohol, bid adieu to the living soap opera of the hood, and headed home quietly. The world had gotten enough from me. My sadness for leaving certain things was overridden by the mantra "no more pain." Also, the prospect of new adventures for my beautiful soul, which was so capable and deserving of better. I guess this was it. The sun was going down, and as much as I could help it, I was going out on my own terms.

CHAPTER 6
HARDCORE AND MISEDUCATED INVASIONS OF PRIVACY

THE NIGHT CAME. I showered, put on some plain clothes, sat on the floor, and exhaled. I sat cross-legged on some sheets between my futon and a colorfully hand-painted wooden bench made by my third-grade class, whose childlike giggles I could hear in echoes. Now positioned as the home furniture of an alleged adult, it was my "coffee table," office, and adventure center, narrowly holding my laptop, extra speakers, notebooks, current reads, and a featured end space for miscellaneous. The miscellaneous feature of the night would be my suicide aids. I exhaled again, resting my head on the edge of the futon, taking in the city's silence. The things I'd managed to fill the apartment with and my inner clutter while somberly enjoying the freshness of my clean skin in clean clothes. Feeling the directive to "get on with the program," I turned to my nearest and dearest friend, music.

What makes a "committing suicide playlist" one may ask? I guess it depends on the person and situation, of course. My memory is fuzzy on this too, but sticking out in my mind has always been "Maggot Brain" by the legendary band and personal favorite, Funkadelic. My operative and counterintuitive aim was to *feel* something in my numbness. Even if that was my own projected insanity or out-of-bounds imagination. A sense, to give me the energy to carry this out. For all I knew, I was completely sane, albeit living in an insane world. The amount of drain I felt would've made it easy to drift and cry myself to sleep again. But I didn't want to reface this world or this-me another day. I had to "consciously" *do* the act of suicide. After all, that was the decision. I had to show God I was being for real. I meant it. "Got My Mind Made Up." **Method Man, Donnie McClurkin, or Instant Funk voice***

"Maggot Brain" seemed perfect for the ambiance of the moment. I wanted to ascend to a more incredible experience so badly. I wanted to *feel* better, to be in touch with something more profound than artificiality. I was not of this. I was not like them. I was from something, somewhere else. I had to be. Maybe I just wanted to return? I also felt like I was drowning, in general. The slowest drown, the slowest death, happening day to day. Now, I was about to drown myself, alter my consciousness, and willingly leave my body in a swift, energized action. The ten-minute classic and cover art of George Clinton and his galactic soul band seemed to cover all the bases. I let the music soothe and transcend me for a bit, then set a big bottle of Bacardi 151 rum on the bench next to a tall glass and a big bottle of generic acetaminophen pills. Then I cried.

I wiped my tears, started pouring, and with an iron throat, began drinking rum like water. Never being a "pill person," I knew I needed to approach them with strategy. After a few rounds of overproof drinking, my idealized "iron neck" gave way to the soft, impressionable tissues, muscles, and organs lining my swallow tunnel, making both the rum and pills have a hard way down. My body became aware of what was happening, and resistance began to set in.

A self-preservation siren went off inside me, and emotions suddenly took on metaphysical traits, turning spikey and sharp, fighting me back. My crying intensified and took over my whole body, increasing tension everywhere and making simple swallows difficult. Finally, I slowed down and started taking pills one at a time.

There were at least 100 pills in the bottle. Determined to take most, one at a time clearly wouldn't work for my tolerance level. I calmed myself as best as I could, drank some more, and began grouping pills in bunches. Not only was this even more dangerous, but it was also scary, and combined with the overproof rum, it was beginning to physically hurt my throat.

As if my voice box had its own brain and eyes, my singing, rapping, poetry, and public speaking life thus flashed before it, indignantly petitioning. I apologized to myself for what was happening, for what would no longer be happening, but this had to be done. I had to override. I hadn't thought about the effects on individual parts of me standing out like this, but we were a package, and as far as I was concerned, we all had to go. I forced down at least three or four more handfuls with sorrowful tears. My throat burned badly, and I began to question if the pills were strong enough. But there was no turning back now. This was really happening, and it needed to work.

What had become of me? Bright, gifted, soulful me. Now, here, doing this. I'd decided I couldn't take the burning in my neck anymore. Nothing else would pass my throat. I chugged what I could of the rest of the rum and crawled to my feet, stumbling through the apartment as my playlist continued. My *beautiful* apartment, my dream come true. I'd begun adorning it more and more in the past year as I realized the plain white walls were probably "driving me crazy." In an initially unplanned and perfect unfolding of my design, each wall and every section took on a distinct energy, role, and presentation.

In my drunken yet aware and painful bliss, I admired how I'd reorganized and decorated so far. My moody and colorful lightbulbs—different in each space yet camouflaged and only triggered by certain light switches. Visual art, posters, revolutionary memorabilia, dance mirrors, and black chalkboard paint filled with proverbs, goals, and affirmations. Hanging rows of jewels and cultural icons collaged along walkways. A lamp resembling a professional stage lantern, a working mic stand, and laminates from all my production gigs. Tower speakers, physical music, histories of culture and entertainment. An extensive collection of fabrics and Japanese fortune cookie message slips. Books, cards, candles, intriguing article clippings, human interest pieces. Wax African prints from Uganda quilted together with custom paperclips into a gallery-worthy clear-vinyl-lined shower curtain. Cream and black gun range silhouette papers from a very memorable date night with the first boyfriend. Black electrical tape geometrically lining a few floor tiles to keep up with my old football and weight training exercises . . . The floor, which I always did my best to keep clean . . . The open space I prioritized so I could move, practice, and rehearse freely.

My heart had exploded decoratively in every direction of this apartment. The threat of the shrinking, plain white walls was now obsolete. I'd even strategically covered closet frames which made for a flush entrance way and secret doors. As a result, I and anyone entering would always walk into not just a home but a living, breathing idea . . . an experience. I'd utterly transformed the feeling of the hollowed prewar one-bedroom-turned-studio. The surviving white walls peeked out from my adorn in sips, serving as punctuation and lining my spiritual design.

As evidenced by my generally private nature, lack of seating, and formal furniture, I never planned for this to be a well visited apartment. All my design work was really for my sanity and creative outlet. The more it became known as a *spot*, I thought people would think I was "bat**** crazy" upon seeing what I'd done. That while well-coordinated, it was a raging mental vomit, overwhelming, unconventional, and just too much. It was also a bit vulnerable, having much of my inner consciousness out on display, in some cases for complete strangers.

But it all gave *me* so much life, incomparable to what any opinion could give me, especially in times when I was most alone, physically, and psychologically. So, when I had company, I'd tuck my most personal valuables away, mind my precious floors, and proudly open my door. To my surprise, at every gathering or party, people were damn near mesmerized by what they saw. It seemed to endear them and give off an uplifted vibe, like, "a real live human being lives here." It sparked many conversations and ciphers. The lighting was a perfect complement for events, and the open space and walkways made it feel adventurous. I often saw people standing by themselves in areas looking closely at something to their own intrigue. Some would ask to come over just to be in the space, sober or otherwise, to decompress, zone out, or recharge. I was even asked to do the interior design for someone's future apartment, which was mind-boggling in my unworthy mind-set.

In hindsight, my last moments of consciousness were an expression of my love of this perfectly imperfect expression—this unconscious act of what was my right consciousness being itself. A creation, always creating. The gatherings and voices of the past were swept away in an echoing fade, but as I looked around, the fact an oasis had been created set in with gratitude. This place, which could've been any regular set of rooms, was a homage to my uniqueness, a reminder of inspiration existing in all of time, and had brought a lot of good together. Yes, I could still agree. The raw me and the raw essence of true living were pretty damn special. So much had gone wrong, yet there was a lot to appreciate.

I just couldn't reface this matrix another day. I could no longer fake being okay with all of it. Something in me was happy to let it all go. In some ways, albeit self-violence, I felt I was choosing peace.

I stumbled, moving in and out of a few blackouts. Soon, I was laid out on the floor of my main room, halfway off my twin air bed, officially toxified like never before. I prayed it was goodbye and not just another blackout. As my eyelids grew heavier and my throat continued to sting, I thought, *this final pain is a small price to pay for getting out*. I drifted face down, feeling the heave of my chest and my breath slow before blacking out a final time. I felt a rupture and a slight slip of my consciousness. I rolled over, already feeling sharp pains in my gut, but a small smile came on my face. I put my head in my hands, cried, and felt my goodbye.

The depth of night fell as the event progressed, and I had an out-of-body experience while unconscious. I'd felt the separation from my body. It felt obvious, but I went into a deep, dreamlike, interdimensional state as I lay there. I was used to having vivid dreams or nightmares almost every night since I was a child. Yet, this was different.

I'd arrived at a bright place, the only thing existing for miles. It was suspended amidst a dark, starry, hazy universe. It was a small amphitheater with circular rows of stone and gold going up and up into columns. On these were a congregation of dignified beings. I say beings because they weren't all humans. Some were like jellyfish floating in the air with translucent or holographic flesh. Some were shapes of light. They "stood" and "sat," conversing, gathering, studying, reporting, joking—they arranged themselves orderly around the coliseum-like space. Though I couldn't make out faces or recognize voices, I felt the presence of my ancestry, which was endearing. I was also weightless, and this alone was a relief.

I heard something say, "Aah, so you've arrived." Then the space went quiet. With some trepidation, I said energetically, "Yes, I'm here!" I was eager to hear anything about what would happen next. I looked around wide-eyed and intrigued. They were not as enthusiastic. They continued.

"You're here, but you're not supposed to be here. You have to go back."

"Say what?!"

"You're not supposed to be here, and we're sending you back."

All the other beings nodded, "mhmm-ed," shifted, gestured, adjusted their fabrics, and toggled their elevation, color, or light emittance in agreement. Now, this was bonkers, for real.

I began resisting, denying, and pleading against this. After all, taking myself out was as challenging as some of the living I'd done. It couldn't have been for nothing. Sending me back to what, the same scenario? I just couldn't. How could they not know that? Also, here were these beings apparently aware and watching me the whole time but only now telling me something definite? I went on a confused inner rampage.

Respectfully, "f*** is on your mind, kid?" ***Raekwon voice*** I mean, what gives? What the dilly with dat doe, dun? ***Mobb Deep voice*** I mean, what you meannn? What *is* the meaning of this? Nahhhh . . . This ain't it, chief! That's not gonna work for me, brother! ***Hulk Hogan voice*** I mean, "What's Really Good?" ***Diplomats and DMX voice***

I was vexed, to say the least. Stuck, screw-faced, and pacing on a nonexistent floor.

They continued.

"We understand you're tired. We've seen how much you've been doing. But you can't leave now. There's still more for you to do. So, we're sending you back because there's more work for you to do."

"More work???!"

Sheesh, this was the last thing I wanted to hear.

I felt an odd mix of enlightened, esteemed, and very disappointed. I didn't know what else to say. I also sensed there was no argument to win here, although I couldn't see what all this meant. I had no idea how I would pick things up and keep moving as is.

Accepting the possible reality of these beings accurately speaking of my destiny, a destiny which I was too tired to "single-handedly" *do* anymore, I saw no better alternative than conceding to this higher power collective. I agreed to be sent back, but not much else was said. I was also too far gone to ask a million more questions or even take their answers. I felt something communicate the likes of, "Don't worry." I communicated back, "How can I not?"

Anxiety overcame me as I felt the weight returning to my human being. A part of me wanted to stay there, roam this place, and engage with the ascended directly. I became paradoxically calm as I let Spirit move me in its exponentially enormous waves, seemingly back to where I belonged, for now.

I passed swiftly through dimensions like Dorothy in *The Wizard of Oz* (or *The Wiz*), back through the interstates. It felt like it'd only been a short time at the coliseum, a few minutes, if that. But I had no idea of the perceived time or how long I was there. I greeted a quiet blackout once again.

I knew I was alive because I could feel pain. My eyes were sealed shut, though eventually, I could tell it was daytime. I'd slipped back into consciousness but wasn't fully back in my body until I felt a shooting pain from my core. Simultaneously, I noticed I had a brain, albeit wrapped in a headache because it began thinking about this pain and its location. Finally, my mind registered my entire body was still laid out, down on the floor of my apartment, and it was heavy, sore, and hurt. I was alive. I started to cry, sob really, as it became clear the suicide hadn't worked, and here I was, right where I left me. Also, now, I was injured internally, and to what extent, I didn't know. I stayed down and cried until I couldn't anymore, which wasn't long because my body was running on fumes.

I tried to get up, but it was horribly difficult. I also felt the remnants of my severely irritated throat and knew I needed to get some water. I slowly crawled to make this happen. Groveling also to my resentful but forgiving body, which I humbly asked to cooperate with me. It wouldn't stand up yet, so I slowly crawled back to the main space. I was still at a loss of what to do and wrought with numerous pains. I curled onto my air mattress and sobbed back to sleep as more hours went by, and night fell again.

I was awakened by two things: the vibration of my phone for the first time, which jolted my eyes open, and the intense cold moving through the apartment. I was shivering noticeably but could barely move. As I tried, the attempt brought me to tears again though something in me really wanted to pick up the phone and, no doubt, close the windows. I rolled off the mattress onto the floor, letting the momentum put me back into a crawling position. I stayed on all fours until I had the strength to move and knew which way I would go. Then I began the crawl.

The apartment was dark except for a hallway light. Yellow, light brown, and burnt orange glows poured into the main space from its reflection, as well as the streetlights and building shadows. I painstakingly made my way to each window, the bitter wind pushing me back so hard I had to turn my face and keep my eyes closed, putting my weight on each lid to push the panes up or down. Exhausted from this simple task, I moved to the wooden bench which held the phone. When I got to it, long after the buzzing of the call, I saw it had been Raymond S. Johnson. Mentor, cofounder, and artistic director of my Oscar- and Grammy-nominated performing arts group, Impact Repertory Theatre.

I tested my voice and collected myself to call him back. When he picked up, he answered with so much energy I was almost startled. There was also an abundance of sounds and noises behind him. He was the first human voice I'd heard coherently since regaining consciousness.

"Ray?"

"Em! Aye! What you doing, what's going on, where you at?!"

I didn't know how to answer.

"Umm, I'm just at home in the Heights. What's good with you?"

"I'm here with Vibe (Impact's senior collective); we're at the office. Eating, having a creative session, and kicking it. Why don't you come chill with us?"

"I don't think I can, Ray."

"Awww, come on, Em! It's pretty cold out, I know. That snow was something terrible last night!"

So *that's* why it was so cold. I limped to the window and, with clearer eyes indeed, saw snow scattered about. I sat on the ledge and listened as I looked out.

"Well, listen, what if we come pick you up? We want you here with us!"

I felt tears coming back to my face with warmth. Those words hit me like a sweet gong.

"Umm, I don't know, Ray. I'm pretty out of it. I don't know if I can be around a bunch of people right now, even if it is Vibe."

"Well then, you can just sit with me all night. It's settled. Let me see what we can do, and I'll call you back."

I exhaled. "OK."

I hung up and started wrapping my mind around leaving the apartment. The best I could do was grab a scarf, identify some shoes I would put on, drink more water, and sit back down. My body was a chore to move. I needed to play this gracefully to avoid questions about what had happened.

I looked at the phone again. The date read Thursday. *It was Thursday night?!* This meant I'd been unconscious for at least twenty-four hours and then another half-day before Ray called. Perplexed, I did my best to stay in the feeling of having a grip. I started warming up to the idea of seeing folks from my performance family. Maybe it was just what I needed.

After a long, anxious wait, the phone went off again.

"Em!"

"Ray, is everything OK?"

"Yes and no."

He described the snow being worse than they thought and having car troubles. Though I'd warmed myself up to the idea, my swift disappointment took over, and I regarded it as a sign. I thought about how much it took for me just to close my windows and answer the phone. On second thought, maybe it was best I didn't go out.

"Oh, that's OK. Maybe it's best I stay in anyway."

"We could call you a cab and make sure you get to and from safely?"

"That's very kind of y'all, but no, Ray, it's OK. Thank you so much."

"OK. Well, just know we love you. Have a good night."

"Love y'all too. Have a good night."

I hung up, sniffling and crying. I made my way back to the mattress, collapsed, and fell back asleep until morning.

The phone buzzed wildly once again, urgently yoking me out of sleep. I rolled off the mattress, feeling the bright morning on my eyelids. I crawled to the phone, faster this time, yet still feeling pain. It was Ray again.

"Ray, what's good?"

"Em! Listen, Em. We were worried about you last night..."

"Oh, I'm OK, I'm good, really. I don't want y'all to worry."

"No, you don't understand. See, we thought you needed help, and we thought about getting you some help. But we didn't realize exactly what we set into motion..."

"What are you talking about, Ray?"

"They're coming to take you away, Em."

"SAY WHAT??!"

I prayed and begged this wasn't real. I had to be dreaming again. Please, let it be a bad dream. *Please.*

"We're really sorry. We didn't know that's what they would do, but it was too late."

"When are they coming?"

"Right now, Em. You have to leave right now. Just come here.

We're at rehearsal. I almost don't care where you go, but you must leave your apartment right now."

"OMG. OK. OK, thanks. I will."

I hung up and tried to stop from becoming frantic. This was crazy! But he'd never lied to me before. Although I'd never been in this situation, I sensed the "right now" directive was spot-on. I didn't know who "they" were or where "away" was exactly, but I knew I didn't want to be "taken" there by "them."

Adrenaline surged as I snapped to attention and grabbed the scarf, a hat, zip-up hoodie, keys, and wallet, and did my best to put on some Onitsuka Tiger sneakers quickly. Not exactly what you'd want to go dodging authority through New York City snow in, but it was the quickest decision and lightest for my post-regaining-consciousness feet. I looked around the apartment unbeknownst at what was ahead of me and was thankful, all withstanding. I couldn't believe I was now on the run for my life. This was really crazy.

I threw the scarf around my neck, got out the door, locked it, and shuffled down the stairs. When I got through the double doors of the front entrance, the cold met me and induced me to bundle up with fervor. It was too late to go back for a proper coat. I looked out over the courtyard of the three-building complex, noticing a police car outside the main gate and some officers milling about the yard. I'd left just in time. I was never more thankful for prewar architecture than this.

Due to the vast, circular courtyard, the height of stairs to each building entrance, and the lack of clear numbering on each building, they'd been stalled in their search. I told myself to remain EXTREMELY calm, slowed my shuffle down to a normal gait, and swiftly came down the external stairs of my building as though I was on my way to throw out garbage. I literally slipped right past the officers who were coming to get me.

I kept it moving (and praying) as I made my way to the main gate, past the officers' car, and down the block. I headed for the nearby 1-train subway station. I picked up my pace and briskly moved to the elevators at the 191st Street station entrance. Once the elevator doors closed to go underground, I knew I'd gotten away. I traveled through Washington Heights, West Harlem, and the Upper West Side to the 3-train, into the heart of Central Harlem between 135th and 145th Street. I walked to the well-known community center named Minisink Townhouse on 142nd Street and Lenox Avenue into an ongoing Impact rehearsal.

I arrived, briefly greeted, and sat at a table off the side of the main space practice.

Phew! I caught my breath.

Everything was surreal. What did this all mean again? And now, could I never go back home? How long would I have to keep running? I started to get depressed again. As well, the pain in my body returned.

Ray came to me, apologizing again, telling me how glad he was that I was okay. I told him I didn't have the energy to do anything but sit there and maybe sleep. He said not to worry, just enjoy the warmth, and stay safe until we figure out what to do next. Anxiously, I was thankful.

I felt so disheveled sitting there, having (literally) run out of the house without washing my face or brushing my teeth after being laid out on the floor for days, too drained to do anything but sleep. The psychological discomfort, bodily pain, and anxiety of trying to "act normal" in such a loud, open community environment started to be too much. I thought about things intensely as the rehearsal went on at a distance in front of me . . . All the answers I didn't have, all the answers no one could really have. I went back to Ray.

"Ray? I'm gonna leave. I can't stay here."

"Where you gonna go?"

"I think I'm gonna check myself into a hospital and get some help."

"Mmm. OK. Are you gonna be OK? Do you know where you're going?"

"I know of a place, St. Vincent's Hospital. They came to do

counseling at my high school after 9/11 happened. They seemed caring. I think I'll go there. Take the 3-train straight down to 14th Street."

"OK. I'm proud of you, and I love you. Are you sure you can make it on your own?"

"Yes. I'm good, thanks. I have just enough energy to get there. I love you."

We hugged. I rebundled, quietly bid rehearsal adieu, and left for the train.

By the time I got to the hospital, whatever was happening inside my body had progressively worsened. I don't remember exactly how it happened, but I found myself on the other side of the emergency admittance, on a hospital bed, now in so much pain I couldn't sit normally or stay completely quiet.

A security guard, an American-Black man, was standing near my bed. He looked at me and asked if I was okay.

"What you doing here, Queen?"

I told him I wasn't sure, that I was looking to get myself some mental health help but was in a lot of pain and unsure of what was happening.

"Sorry to hear that, sister. You don't belong here, but I feel you. I hope you get the help you need for this pain."

In the rest of his address, he told me to "be careful with these people" and that he was praying for me. He carefully came to my bedside, stealthily held my hand, and squeezed it, telling me to stay strong. Though usually not up for being touched by people I don't know, I was thankful, it was a big help in the moment. If the look in his distressed eyes was any indication, I wasn't looking so good and really needed medical attention. He stayed within eyesight when he could, and when someone came to relieve his duty, he let me know he was leaving. I really appreciated it. I couldn't hold back tears because I was in so much pain. True to many hospitals, especially for the uninsured, I was just sitting there for what felt like hours. The pain was so intense it shocked me back to sleep.

I was woken by a doctor frantically making sure I was conscious. As I returned to lucidness, I noticed a clipboard with yellow and white forms in her hands. She waved them in my face and said something like, "We want to help you," urging me to sign. I emphasized I'd come to get help yet questioned the forms. She stressed again that they couldn't help me until I signed the papers, giving them the legal right to provide care. I doubted this and asked if something could be done to at least stop my pain. She resisted and again pushed back about the forms.

It was all a bit hazy, and I regretted not coming with someone, as the pain wouldn't allow me to think straight. I had no cell phone service in this area of the hospital, and with my security friend gone, the thought of "making a break for it" on my own seemed trickier. I didn't understand why they were withholding the "help" we all agreed on, and, sadly, I became desperate. I skimmed the legal language and signed the papers which said something about a 72-hour period and my right to petition in court. She thanked me and said, "OK. I'll be back after we look at what's going on in your stomach."

I've heard, seen, and read in numerous places how Black women are less likely to be believed when they speak of pain or their discomfort to authorities, doctors, nurses, or medical personnel. This is part of the reason Black maternal mortality rates (death from childbirth or pregnancy-related causes) in the United States are three times higher than other races, according to the Centers for Disease Control. Sadly, in this situation, I empathized from firsthand experience, and this would prove itself with a vengeance in a matter of days. It was now Friday or Saturday, which meant at least three days since the suicide attempt and ingesting hazardous doses—three days of intense stress, depression, physical shock, anxiety, self-harm, and corrosive substances sitting in my body.

They examined me, yet whatever was going to appear on whatever they were examining apparently wasn't there yet. In addition, my words about the excruciating pain I was in weren't enough. I told everyone I could about it and was all but pacified at every turn. I suspected the suicide attempt made it seem as though I was incoherent or irrational. However, I remember being mostly collected. I was just tired, drained, and in a lot of pain.

They drew my blood, said they would keep me there for a couple of days and check the blood, then wheeled me to another part of the hospital I'd never seen before. I clutched my core tightly every second and kept asking for ice or ice water, the only thing they consented to offer me for relief. My stomach felt like it was eating itself. I still couldn't stand up for more than a few seconds without leaning on something or slinking to the floor.

I also still wasn't sure what was happening.

That is . . . until we arrived at a door that had to be unlocked from the inside *and* buzzed open. As we rolled in, I felt an immediate wave of not-it-ness. The people who wheeled me there, including sign-these-forms-Barbie, talked to the administrators, handed over files, and walked out. I wouldn't see them again for some time.

What I'd signed in the emergency room was my at-will admittance into St. Vincent Hospital's psychiatric ward.

CHAPTER 7
JUST GOT PAID. IT'S FRIDAY NIGHT (AT THE PSYCHIATRIC WARD)

CONVENTIONAL HOOD WISDOM SAYS, "never get locked up anywhere on a Friday." This was no different. While it might've been a halfway good idea to send me to an "appropriate mental care facility" immediately after getting the "appropriate medical attention," I still felt in this situation, I'd been:

- A. Had
- B. Took
- C. Tricked
- D. Bamboozled
- E. Led Astray
- F. Run Amuck

All of the above, chile! And I wasn't sure what to do about it.

The ward staff now had all the belongings I came with in a place I couldn't access. They also wouldn't allow me to say or do anything within feet of them, which took me aback. I soon realized my attempts to speak with anyone sanely, calmly, and rationally were futile. Because I was there, I was not to be trusted. I was now a mental patient and considered much less than sane. In fact, I was now also delusional, cunning, conniving, full of stories, and a hazard to be monitored and controlled.

The doors to go anywhere were all double-locked and remote-controlled. The windows were all barred, except for one high up a wall with cracks and circular indents, presumably from someone unsuccessfully bashing their head against it. You ate everything with special spoons. Anything remotely close to being able to be a weapon was treated as "contraband." The floor staff were called nurses but were more like corrections officers with a bit of pharmaceutical knowledge. The air was filled with a sanitary, gloomy, gritty energy. Loudspeaker announcements called for meals, lockdowns, recreation, or medicine-taking time. It was a psychological-hospital-dystopia. This wasn't the "help" or "care" I had in mind, not by a long shot! What would happen now? What had I gotten myself into?

I was told I was committed to a single room for the weekend (which made me wonder if they give people roommates in psychiatric wards?) and put on "suicide watch," which carried the infamous "24-and-1." Contrary to the stifling "23-and-1" concept in prison facilities, which gives inmates only one hour of recreation time outside their cells a day, 24-and-1 in the psych ward meant a hospital staff person would be assigned to me, stay in my room, watch me sleep, go with me to the bathroom, follow me everywhere, for twenty-four hours. I discerned the premise being I was now the state's property and not to die on their watch.

Since my 24-and-1 assignee was a Black woman, I was hoping she'd be inclined to listen to me about needing help for the continued pain. Unfortunately, this wasn't the case. She was also immigrant-Black, likely from the islands, so Caribbean-West Indian-Black, and seemed very annoyed to have to watch over me in the first place. Be it learned posture or just personality, she had zero empathy for my situation. At the most, she was concerned about me doing anything that might jeopardize her job.

She mostly rolled her eyes and insisted on staying close. Kudos to the effectiveness of the 24-and-1 training program, as she wouldn't even let me wipe myself in private. I mostly lay in bed, slept when I could, and cried as I felt my body worsening. I had no appetite and continued asking for ice to ease my stomach. Sometimes I'd get it, and sometimes they'd refuse. They continued to take my blood, and by Sunday, I felt there wasn't any more to give. They made me walk to get my blood taken despite how much pain this caused me. I'd make it by using every wall for support on the way. I felt drained of what fight I had left.

The sustained agony, lack of food, and loss of blood also hardened me like nothing had before. I stopped trying to convince people of what they didn't want to believe and stopped talking altogether, just letting the staff do their jobs. After watching me do nothing but cry, sleep, and eat ice for days, my suicide watch assignee compassionately asked me if I was okay and let me wipe myself in private. I appreciated it but stayed mute.

The weekend grimly passed by like a war passing a small town. As early Monday morning crept in, a commotion grew toward my room. A team of doctors, including the one who'd urged me to sign the forms in the emergency room, rushed in. Startled, my 24-and-1 and I asked what was going on. While helping me into a wheelchair, the doctor explained they were taking me to the medical part of the hospital right away.

"We looked at your bloodwork and the examinations from days ago, and you're headed into liver failure. You might need surgery right away. We don't know. But we must get you upstairs *immediately*."

"Oh my goodness!" exclaimed my 24-and-1, wide-eyed with hand over mouth. She'd been watching me die internally for three days.

My jaw all but dropped open, and I was bitterly satisfied. I knew it. I'd known it. I *knew* something was off. I knew something wasn't right inside *my* body. I rationalized having been kept from Friday to Monday with no knowledge of this and the fact I could've died over the weekend . . . being stuck in a ward while being drained of what life I had left. It seemed the pressure was quietly on them now to avoid my death . . . or a negligence lawsuit.

As they frantically wheeled me out, I raised my faint voice and a faint finger to exclaim, "I told y'all! You wouldn't listen; nobody listened! I told y'all I was in pain!!!"

Legendary gospel singer Mahalia Jackson described being closer to God in her popular 1952 single "In the Upper Room." I soon found the upstairs of this medical and intensive care hospital to be a completely different energy from the downstairs dungeon of the psychiatric ward. I was put in a private room, so bright, clean, and encouraging, as opposed to the dingy walls of the barred ward. I had a large window showing a *Metropolis*-like view of the city on-high. The sky seemed bluer; the sun seemed to shine brighter. They even had a hospital pet program with service dogs, and a beautiful golden retriever came around to cheer me up! I cried at his warmth and free love, so relieved and happy to be momentarily out of hell.

I couldn't escape it all as they sent 24-and-1 staff along to stay with me in this part of the hospital too. More Black women, this time African-Black, each one equally broody and just as pissed to see me. One took it upon herself to verbally shame me for wanting to die when so many people "back home" wished they were living my privileged life. I didn't have it in me for rebuttal. Part of her was right, though part of her had no idea what she spoke of.

While there, I remembered a passage I wrote in an old journal about suicide. What brings anyone to such a point? How deep and touchy this subject is, the chords it strikes in people. How normalized it is to view suicide as nothing but a selfish, unnatural, anti-spiritual act. Why? Why is it so dehumanized when the vulnerability and emotional awareness involved are peak human? People being angry and indignant at those who choose this is understandable, but why? Knowing this is not an unusual act among us, why aren't we looking at the root causes and ingredients of this? Even if one disagrees, why is it such a reach to understand the desire not to want to live a certain way? I let the "SHAME!" lady *Game of Thrones **voice*** have her opinion and righteousness. I pondered over the dream I'd had that fateful night.

What now? When I heal, as I heal . . . What now?

They took more blood, hooked me to an IV, and a doctor came to explain what was happening with my liver. Though he was very nice, he wasn't at all optimistic about my state, describing the damage as so significant a transplant was likely. However, he said first they'd try a specific presurgical liquid medication for a few days and see how my body responded. He also said that my father and emergency contact, Ray, had been informed.

My phone and other items were momentarily returned. I would soon communicate with friends and ask them, among other things, to bring me food. To my surprise, my first and now ex-boyfriend came to see me, which would've been sweet, and it still sort of was, but he was (understandably) angry. He paced, stared, yelled at me for "doing this" (which was only the second time he'd raised his voice at me in three years), then left. It was an emotional blow as I still loved him very much. I felt helpless to do anything worth anything. I wasn't expecting him to share emotions or show up at all, and I felt terrible he felt this anger. I went to sleep that night with some tears and a great degree of numbness.

The following morning, my father came. As I woke, I saw him staring out the window, arms folded, looking uncharacteristically helpless and stoically heartbroken. I looked at him quietly and, for the first time, thought, *he really loves me*. It was all a lot to process.

Though I wasn't much of a TV person, the huge perk of television in the private room led to more cathartic inspiration. A mini-marathon of the makeover reality show *What Not to Wear* came on the TLC channel every afternoon during my stay. I'd briefly seen the show before and, desperate for some positive distraction, voted it most worthy of my jaded eyes. *At least I'll see some nice colors and patterns*, I thought nonchalantly. Perhaps, people with intriguing knowledge who were doing something meaningful in life with drive. It would be a far cry from the dungeons of the ward, either way, where one small TV for over twenty mentally imbalanced people meant I was usually playing cards or chess, if in the rec room at all.

Even with the numbing and negative qualities we understand about excessive "screen time," my creative, athletic, intellectual, and sensual muses first seen on television have remained significant. Witnessing shows from the 1950s–1990s provided different perspectives on self-determination, beauty, culture, morals, ethics, race, class, and gender politics. In addition, I always appreciated the neatly conclusive nature of sitcoms and informative programming. Usually, in less than an hour, all conflicts cleared, and all objectives were resolved.

The premise of *What Not to Wear* was hosts Stacy London and Clinton Kelly typically ambushing a frumpy, seemingly miserable, aimless, or disastrously overzealous person of potential with a $5,000 budget for new clothes. The key was giving them a whole new outlook and knowledge based on style, perception, and dressing their bodies. Finally, they'd give them a new haircut or hairdo, address skincare or makeup, and specifically encourage their desired advancements in life, love, work, self-concept, and fulfillment. Featured subjects were different shapes, sizes, colors, genders, ages, and professions.

The makeovers were described as "life-changing," and they were. I got deeply into this show unexpectedly, amazed at how a change in wardrobe, hair, attention to detail, and self-expression completely changed people's lives. How stubbornly the guests held onto their old selves even if they knew it wasn't working well for them. How negatively and short-sighted they saw themselves before the makeover and how a whole new world was suddenly open to them.

Even if I didn't love all the looks, I was thoroughly impressed at the consistent result of the unique transformation. Insecurity becoming confidence, close-mindedness becoming more creative, doubt becoming curiosity about more things one could do in this same world now full of opportunity. If strangers could help a person change their entire axis and point of attraction through the clothes they wore and elimination of self-sabotaging habits, I reasoned I could help myself too. It was entirely possible to change my life and create a living I was excited to experience daily.

The head doctor returned to my room a few afternoons later, emotionally beside himself. I carefully sat up, perplexed by the look on his face, praying for good news. *Tell me something good.* ***Rufus and Chaka Khan voice*** By this time, I'd completed one round of the disgusting liquid meds, more needles, and harrowing IV attachments. While extremely thankful for a few visits from mostly clueless friends, I'd hurdled over conversations about how I got there. I'd overestimated my stomach and failed at eating most of the food they graciously brought me (including Red Lobster cheddar biscuits I'd specifically requested). I knew my days of "just chilling" with them were over. I'd let the pain have its way in my system, returning to silent cries for hours, facing away from my 24-and-1's who still wouldn't let me wipe my a** in private. It needed to be up from here. So, what now? The doctor cleared his throat.

"You've made a 98 percent recovery in three days. I've never seen anything like it. You don't need a liver transplant; you don't need any surgery at all. You're gonna be fine. Just lay off the alcohol, anything with acetaminophen, and don't ever do this again, OK?"

"Wow . . . OK. Thank you *very* much, Doc."

He told me he'd start the discharge process and left the room. Wow!

98 percent, a number I wouldn't forget. Without parade, pomp, or circumstance, I reckoned this had been a miracle. Either I was Superwoman (or Wolverina), or a very powerful force really wanted me here. Or both! I felt the echoes of my dream on the night of the suicide. *"More work for me to do,"* they'd said.

I was supremely excited to have my life, health, and strength back in miraculous fashion. Also, the lessons from *What Not to Wear* and all those who came into my room gave me so much new fuel. I was ready to see about all this . . . about my new life.

The hospital was too, in a very different way. I soon found out why the doctor hadn't specified "you can go home" or to whom or where I was being discharged. After three days "In the Upper Room," it was back to the barred dungeons for me. I was being sent back to the psychiatric ward for an undisclosed amount of time, and I could do nothing about it.

CHAPTER 8
I KNOW WHY THE CAGED BIRDS IN THE TRAP SING MCKNIGHT

SINCE I WAS NINETEEN, it was decided I'd be kept in the adult ward. I quickly noticed I was the youngest person there. The floor was filled with full-grown individuals—most double, triple, and beyond my age of all types of nationalities. Some had been there for years. Others were there overnight on arrests, in and out of court, or transferred from other hospital programs.

The grip which prescription medication had on most of the patients was astounding. Even if I had a great, eye-opening conversation with someone, once medication time came and went, that person was no longer that person. In fact, the entire floor would be sedated to sleep for hours after pill-popping time, like clockwork. A few would walk the floor in a daze before they crashed into bed. They looked like literal zombies, something I'd never seen, which was scary for me. I came to regard this time of day, every day, as the "zombie hours." At this time, you could hear a pin drop throughout the ward, except for the shuffling of the administration office and the moans and wails of those still awake, fighting or merging with chemical substances.

While standing in line at the pill distribution window, I quickly noticed people being given three and four hard-core-sounding things while I was given one simple antidepressant. I wondered if this was a sign I honestly didn't belong here or if it was only a matter of time before they started adding more pills to my cup. You were to take your medications right there and prove you swallowed them before you got off the line. Security guards also stood by the nurse administering the pills. All this kept me tense and distrustful of the program.

Younger people were admitted to our floor at one point, including two regular, hood, American-Black kids from Brooklyn. I was momentarily relieved, feeling more represented by their youth and cultural knowledge and thinking maybe we'd vibe in such a vibeless place. We did vibe, but the relief was short-lived, as I learned they'd been brought from the children's ward to the adult ward as "punishment." We huddled briefly, but nothing lasted as they were "disciplined" and taken back. I certainly wasn't encouraged about what I faced then, and this practice repeated. I witnessed a big commotion with one who received an injection from a giant needle filled with a fluid that rendered them lifeless, even days after. After that, they never caused a commotion again but continued to ask (as I also wondered) what was in that needle?

The next youngest person from me was in his mid-twenties. A very sweet soul who didn't watch TV, was mostly quiet, owned a radio, read newspapers, did yoga every morning, and whom all the staff always greeted with a smile. He had his own private room but was never on a 24-and-1. I engaged him in conversation and learned he'd been in the ward for five years. He didn't have much to say and was apparently very comfortable there. He was fair and clear-skinned, tall, lean, toned, very polite, and soft, both in speech and carriage of his body. He seemed quite institutionalized. His room didn't even look like other rooms. It looked custom and very lived in. It gave off a perception he'd made himself comfortable in this scenario over time. In the window of my arrival, he was awaiting transfer to another facility, which would house him with the prospect of full release soon after.

Another facility, a *prospect* of release. The uncertainty of words kept me uneasy. He and the staff were very excited, and, indeed, this transfer was momentously great news. Yet, this also seemed horrifying to me. I couldn't imagine being locked in a psychiatric ward for five years since being a teenager. His remarkably well-adjusted attitude impressed me, and I greatly respected his peace. In fact, his inner harmony was exemplary. He was a serene picture of health, a walking advertisement for the power of yoga and no TV. He was sincerely kind and never had an emotional outburst while I was there. Yet, for all I didn't know about why he was there, his example mostly moved me not to become so well-adjusted.

I decided this scenario was not going to be mine. This was not my home; no ward would ever be. As others chose to dress in the clothes they came with or had family bring them, I chose to remain in hospital gowns, socks, and slippers—anything to emphasize in my brain that I was *not* home. I was in a hospital, a ward at that. I was in an alternate reality that was not mine. Home was where I was going. Then and *only* then would my "reality" clothes be put back on. As far as I was concerned, I was in a lucid dream. Each day, I was learning how to navigate the terrain and get closer to the definitive moment when I would wake myself up.

I spent hours imagining walking out of the main door. The metal unlocking, being buzzed out, hearing the weighted clicks for the final time. I also held a fascination with keys as I realized how meaningful the keys to my apartment were to me. I loved the feeling of them in my hands and what they symbolized. I'd fought hard to have those keys, to use them to enter and leave *my home* when *I* wanted. Here, there were very few places to go, and there was no door you ever controlled. You'd never hold keys as they'd be considered contraband, and you'd never enter and leave anywhere when you wanted. I spent hours gleefully imagining the jingling sound and weight of keys in my hands.

Fascination also came in the form of words, or rather, lack

thereof. My simultaneous acceptance and resistance to my position there rendered me mostly expressionless. My creative mind was dangerously scraping the far left "E" when a lady came around with a rolling shelf of old books and magazines. There, I first read copies of the famed *New Yorker* magazine, full of spicy, long-form pieces, cultural commentary, and clever cartoon sections. It made me laugh, think, and stimulated me in ways I hadn't felt in a long time. It moved me far from the physical experience of where I was and enabled my mind to travel across planes through intelligence, humor, wit, and imagination.

It moved me to begin writing again, which I hadn't considered through this ordeal. I was reminded of a 1995 interview with Tupac Shakur from Clinton Correctional Facility, where he essentially said, "Everyone thinks a rapper will come out of jail with multiple albums of material, but really, it's the most uninspiring place to be. It's *not the spot*." Creativity thrives differently when the autonomous mind is constantly suppressed amidst tension, and I certainly understood this better. I'd had not one poem or rap bar in me, not even a haiku. Also, I'd gotten used to certain words, phrases, simplicities, and limited imagination being around the same institutionalized people and processes daily.

The New Yorker thrust an explosion of vocabulary, ideas, questions, voices, and concepts back into my brain. It entertained me and recentered the value of substantial stimulation. I returned to my desperately barren notebook and turned the page from the one lonely lyric I'd managed to write in over a month. (It read, *"How long's the planet gonna tolerate the way we treat it?"* A line that would open the second verse of *"What We Do Now Matters Forever"* by Impact Repertory Theatre. I'd complete and record the verse the day following my release.) On a fresh page, I began writing all the words in *The New Yorker* which stimulated me, from every single page, from every copy I'd get. Then a synonym to every word, an antonym to every word, a rhyming word to every word, and multisyllable rhymes to every word. I never wrote an entire poem or rap while there, but this practice happily continued until my release and did more for me than I could fathom.

Several other living characters would cross paths with me and create memories in my heart. They'd keep me company, encourage me, and keep me entertained in this grim state of "State Property."

An elderly American-White lady in her 70s who'd taken a lot of LSD in the '60s had wild stories of Woodstock and losing all her money in the '90s. Apparently, before being committed to the ward, she was a prosperous interior designer, and so (when she was lucid) we had great conversations about fabrics, culture, being a businesswoman, and staging homes. It was clearly and understandably hard on her daughter, who sometimes came to visit. Nevertheless, I found it encouraging that, in her mind, she was still running her own business and would instruct her daughter about keeping things in order until she got home. Even if this was a mental defect by medical standards, it was a far cry from the stagnation many others had willingly fallen into. So what if the business in her mind was only in her mind? Once a boss, always a boss!

An elder mixed-Pacific Islander brother told me he was successfully faking his mental illness to remain in the ward because, essentially, "You can't beat the guaranteed bed and three meals a day." I'd heard this type of thing said but never met someone who was living it. He was really pulling it off too. In fact, he was one of the regulars in the hallway during "zombie hours."

An elderly American-White man was locked up for hard drug possession charges. He spoke openly about his disgust for authority and using the ward for a few nights' sleep. He'd petition in court, leave, cash his next Social Security check, scam his way into other checks, get more drugs, and hit Atlantic City until the next go-round. He was nonchalant and unintimidated about the entire institutional setup, which was inspiring in its own way.

An older American-Black woman with very big auntie-energy sort of adopted me during her stay. It was a blessing because when my 24-and-1 period was over, they moved me into a room with three other women, which wasn't always peaceful. The idea of four-bed boarding in a psychiatric ward never sat right with me. Also, being the only child of a small family, I'd never shared a single room with multiple people other than my parents as a standard.

One of our roommates routinely woke up at night to eat fruit and crunchy snacks loudly and profoundly. I was usually level-headed and quiet, but this drove me bananas (ha!) mainly because she seemed to do it on purpose. Though regular sharp pencils weren't even available per contraband protocol, I hit a boiling point and threatened to find one and stab her in the neck in her sleep if she persisted. This violent outburst caused big auntie-energy to keep me under her wing from then on. She told me I was a sweet girl who needed to get out of there and letting people ruin my release wasn't worth it. The old prison adages of "This isn't you," "Don't let them . . ." and "Serve the time or let the time serve you." She was right, of course, and a mother figure I greatly appreciated.

When good and ready, she could have a nasty attitude herself. She even got the "discipline" needle once, fighting her way through the process in a manner I hadn't seen anyone fight it. But usually, she was a joy, and to be in her good graces was to be among the best and most respected of the ward habitat. She was full of soul, cool to be with, and easily carried a beautifully voluptuous body and divine feminine energy, which was admirable and rarely found there. She seemed to believe she was beautiful, something many of us seemed to have lost. She took care of herself, doing her hair and fixing her face, and was selectively generous with gifts her family would often bring. She'd share them and her wisdom with me, though she too was "out like a light" *Drake voice* every day for "zombie hours."

Once, her family brought her a large collection of scented body washes and lotions. She offered me a set, which felt like a feel-good Christmas. I was usually very picky about what I put on my sensitive skin, but after months of dry hospital air, low-grade one-for-all generic hygiene products, sterile institutional scents, and the agony of the entire floor sharing one single shower—the packaging, colors, and fragrances were a luxury for bath time. Plus, coming from her, it was like being crowned a princess. I was never so proud to smell like peaches. I truly felt relaxed, among royalty, and like I was at a family cookout whenever I sat with her and an equally charismatic man named Willie Will.

"Willie Will, the man who drives a Coup-de-Ville," spoke almost exclusively in rhymes. He was an American-Black Southerner-turned-Brooklynite whose jokes, anecdotes, and freestyles kept me in stitches for the greater part of his stay. We had a grandfather-granddaughter or uncle-niece relationship, which was sincere and heartfelt. We took a liking to each other almost immediately, and he'd tell vivid stories of his street adventures. When the fancy, scented body products came, he'd call out "queens of the ward!" in a British accent as we walked through, bowed, and used the scents to justify we were the sweetest things in the world. It was routinely comforting to play cards or dominos with them as they exchanged tales and grown folks' business. I'd often pull up a chair as they rhythmically connected dots. It always amazes me how Black people seem to have many of the same experiences, even though we've grown up in different places.

I worried about him as he seemed to have a lot of trouble with the institution. Numerous conflicts, "zombie hours," and unsuccessful court appearances also began robbing him of the vibrance I so adored. However, we had an encouraging hallway talk before he left the facility, where he said he felt we'd "done time together." He'd been in correctional facilities and commented on the ward being run like a prison, not a mental health institution, so it was not my imagination where it felt like it. Always giving me his sunshine regardless, he also entertained my big sister Stephanie Amoh and Raymond S. Johnson from Impact when they visited me. It was one of my only visits down there, so I really appreciated Willie making them laugh, it being an unsettling place to be even temporarily.

Stephanie and Ray also came to sneak in hair products I'd requested and arranged to keep. (The rat tail comb, wide-tooth brush, and oils, creams, gels, or sprays were considered contraband.) I'd made a passionate and convincing argument to the Jamaican-Black head nurse about the injustice of cheap, hospital-grade shampoo, conditioner, and needle-tooth combs allegedly supposed to "work" on natural Black hair. After appealing about the failing state of my mane under the circumstances and how this affected my mood, security, and identity, she eventually agreed to keep the combs, etc., locked in her office. I was to remain quiet about it and, upon advanced request, be placed alone in a monitored room to do my hair. On the brink of severe damage by then, I buckled down and learned to protectively style my kinks using these smuggled-in tools and strategic reflections off sunlight (no mirrors allowed) to hook up some "Iverson braids." This gave me confidence, self-determination, a feeling of control, and personal order and contributed to my natural haircare journey, which continued after release.

A young, quite handsome, warm-beige-skinned, very muscular, and well-mannered Caribbean-West Indian hospital orderly spotted me some time into my stay. He was subtle, but I noticed him noticing me right away. Due to the physical environment and exclusive hospital food diet, my skin and body changed beyond my comfort. I was also still rebelliously dressing only in hospital gowns. Though he didn't seem to mind any of it, I was uncomfortable being analyzed by such an attractive man. I reasoned there were "bigger fish to fry," and resenting everything hospital-related anyway, I decided not to care.

I was minding my biz-nassss ***Ludacris voice*** just "Me & My B****" ***Biggie voice*** (my notebook, that is) when among the buzz of the recreation room, he bravely made his way to me one afternoon. He small talked a "how you doing?" (surreal question in a ward) and asked if I'd like to play chess. At first, I was uneased by the sight of the uniform before me. Then I noticed his voice was slightly different than I was used to hearing from staff. It had a kind tone and peaceful address. The way his large and physically fit frame pronounced itself, humbly amplifying his uniform, made me think he was cast as one of the hospital intimidators. Perhaps part of the "discipline" needle staff and, thus, not to be trusted. I looked him in the eyes, reading for danger, aesthetically approving of how his well-groomed locks complemented his enjoyable face, careful aura, and noble approach. I obliged. Though he was stationed on a different floor, regular sweeps by all the employees allowed him to stop for more chess meetings with me after that. Still skeptical, we played on, and I grew to like him.

We reconnected after my release, and he promptly disclosed his full attraction and desire to be with me. Due to the blurry soundscape of my new readjustment stage, I was astonished. I was still getting used to being in a freer environment, once again surrounded by the millions of people in the city of New York. The rumbling, noise, lights, architecture, nonstop traffic, and omnidirectional energy sharply contrasted with the routine life with twenty-five or so patients on a single sectional hospital floor.

Though I experienced a hard withdrawal of sexual expression and "touch therapy" during my stint, which also prompted curiosity, growth, and new ground coverage in my fantasies and idle thoughts—still, dating or partnered intimacy hadn't been on my mind as a serious consideration. I felt out of place more than anything and was also still ruminating about the spiritual message I'd been given on the night I attempted to die. While it would be easy to say a small part of me felt like "damaged goods," it more accurately felt like I was pure and placed back into a place of generally damaged goods.

Pure as in reset, as in my slate wiped blank while retaining the soul of who I was, even though my sensitivity was more pronounced, and I could still feel old wounds. The hospital diet had flushed out my body. The lack of TV, media, and my attention to the essence of words and strategy had flushed out my mind. The separation and basic human interactions had flushed out my perspective, senses, empathy, and sense of self. I'd be hyperaware of the non-malicious or willingly pervasive quality of "good which had been damaged" in people and partners who desired to associate, see, touch, or be with me from then on. There was a whole new spin on the phrases "damage repair" and "damage control."

When I responded to my handsome former caretaker's proposal by asking "how he knew I wasn't crazy," he admitted to observing me for weeks prior to the day he first approached me, looking through my files, reading my reports and diagnosis. He noted numerous staff meetings in which head doctors cited me as an "unusual case," flagging several things about me which were atypical for staff to register and compare. I'd been scoped and scouted! Finally, he said, "Girl, I know you not crazy!" That made me think, *damn, so* they *knew the whole time too?* Outrageous...

I was perplexed about this for a long time. Them knowing I wasn't "Out My Mind" ***Erykah Badu voice*** but still detaining me meant what? Perhaps all suicidal people aren't insane. Perhaps all psychologically unorthodox people aren't crazy. Perhaps unprovoked, all mentally unbalanced people are not a threat to themselves or society. Perhaps the word "crazy" itself is grossly abused and manipulated for social packaging . . . to invalidate, pity, instill fear or intrigue . . . to build up or tear down.

One of my favorite iconic pro wrestlers whose career was in climax in the 1990s was the uniquely, athletically, and creatively talented "Luna Vachon." Distinguished among a small group of women in pro wrestling history to utilize "crazy" as a personality, she drove the concept to world-class, Broadway-worthy proportions. While blurring the lines of her actual condition of bipolar disorder and contrasting her natural beauty, she spoke in a hauntingly monstrous voice, shaved half her head, adorned her face with painted veins and skulls, and carried a terrifying body language. After a series of harsh disappointments, difficulties, and traumas within and outside the wrestling business, she was found deceased due to an apparent overdose in 2010. Multiple stories, such as "The Many Faces of Luna Vachon" episode of the Vice series *Dark Side of the Ring*, highlight her competent abilities while noting the questionable habitats around her.

Many sources regard the term "lunatics" to originate from observing mental health patients during full moons. Luna—re: the moon, luna-tics, was heavily believed in and carried from the fourteenth century into modern Western cultural development. Research magazines like the *Scientific American* have widely covered the validity of lunacy, habitat, and moon theories for years:

Greek philosopher Aristotle and Roman historian Pliny the Elder suggested that the brain was the "moistest" organ in the body and, thereby, most susceptible to the pernicious influences of the moon, which triggers the tides. Belief in the "lunar lunacy effect," or "Transylvania effect," as it is sometimes called, persisted in Europe through the Middle Ages, when humans were widely reputed to transmogrify into werewolves or vampires during a full moon.

Even today, many people think the mystical powers of the full moon induce erratic behaviors, psychiatric hospital admissions, suicides, homicides, emergency room calls, traffic accidents, fights at professional hockey games, dog bites, and all manner of strange events. One survey revealed 45 percent of college students believe moonstruck humans are prone to unusual behaviors. Other surveys suggest mental health professionals may be still more likely than laypeople to hold this conviction. In 2007, several police departments in the U.K. added officers on full-moon nights in an effort to cope with presumed higher crime rates.

On the fringe of imbalance or otherwise "normal" people being affected by habitat and (scaling this idea) the cycles of nature, which also sway gravity, light, crops, animals, and the ocean's tides, has been a moldable concept for centuries.

My prolonged detainment at St. Vincent's also echoed of me being a ward of the state and them wanting to "protect their investment." While it may have made them hesitant to release me, I was clearly competent and able. Again, why? I reasoned the words of one of the most insightful comedians of all time, Dave Chappelle, on *Inside the Actors Studio*, discussing the likes of Richard Pryor, Martin Lawrence, and Kanye West. At critical points of their prolific and trailblazing careers, they were all reputed (or unfairly discredited) as some version of mentally unstable in public mainstream popularity. This was particularly after they were well situated in their upward mobility, considered thought leaders, monetarily rich, and significantly famous for their unique contributions. Chappelle noted:

The worst thing to call somebody is crazy. It's dismissive. "I don't understand this person, so they're crazy." That's bulls***. These people are not crazy. They're strong people. Maybe their environment is a little sick.

My big, strong hospital aide seemed unfazed about my suicide attempt and attendance in the psychiatric ward and was seemingly sincere about wanting to see me. He was also very gentle, caring, and protective about things from there, perhaps genuinely feeling he could protect me effectively. Perhaps interacting with him was an imperfectly perfect transition for my return to the general population. I appreciated his honesty, was relieved not to be treated like a victim or danger, and sincerely enjoyed his masculine company. Nevertheless, I remained perplexed and a little uneasy. Even though my stint was over, hearing the information of my widely regarded sanity made the whole ordeal feel different.

Weeks prior, I did not know of when my release from the hospital would come, and I continued to seek every opportunity to work my way through the system. Apparently, the liver-failure fiasco had me miss the 72-hour window to petition for myself in court, so it was almost entirely up to doctors whether I was cleared to go. They'd ask me every day, sometimes multiple times a day, to repeat the story of my suicide. This took a toll mentally, which seems counterintuitive, but I understood much like a police report, they were also looking for a consistent story. It appeared their primary (and legal) concern was a demonstration of not being a hazard to myself or anyone else. I worked these understandings to my best. I wanted to get out and go home more than anything.

As the day neared, I was given outdoor recreation time essentially due to "good behavior." I had no idea the ward even had an outdoor space, so I was very excited. Apparently, this was where the children's ward patients would play. After months of wearing the hospital gowns as my rebel uniform, I immediately got dressed. I was going outside! No one else was with me except the monitors and security guards, which felt weird. Still, they brought me to a rooftop with a completely matted rubber floor, tall railings, a netted ceiling, some toys, gym equipment, sunshine, and all the open air I could breathe. I stood at the entrance, overwhelmed by the fresh air and view, salivating at partial freedom. Before I did anything, I asked how much time I had, and they responded, "Now, 26 minutes." So, I proceeded to "Wild Out" *The Lox voice* on this rooftop.

Running, sprinting, playing, doing pushups, jumping jacks, spinning in the sun, staring out at the adjacent buildings and birds flying far away . . . Going from zero to a hundred up there,

I got lightheaded and almost passed out! They laughed, offered me water, and told me to take it easy. I sipped, panting, and took some breaths but I didn't want to waste a second of those precious 26 minutes. I was also a step closer to being outside—outside for good. It was great to feel the sun again and feel my physical strength returning. Soon after, my release was up, and the discharge process began. It was almost three months of never knowing when I'd see home again.

My big brother Luther Isler from Impact came to get me on release day. He'd also graciously communicated with my father to help me keep the apartment while I was detained. I was so thankful to be going home, to *my* home, as I'd visualized so many times. I thanked the Jamaican-Black head nurse for helping me save my hair and promised never to be back. Then, we walked out from the buzzed locks, weighted clicks, and elevators for a final time, just as I'd imagined. On the street, the air was different in my lungs and crisper on my skin. It was also a new season, spring—how fitting. The swiftness of people walking with a purpose in every direction was almost dizzying. I wasn't used to the normal gait of concrete street natives and immediately felt my muscles being challenged. I had to get my New York legs back!

I was overwhelmed when we got in the subway underground to head uptown. Every sound seemed extremely loud; the train seemed to move extremely fast. I closed my eyes, covered my ears, and buried my face in his collarbone for most of the ride. The people, the train itself, the screeching of the tracks, the subway stops whipping by on the express . . . It was a lot.

I got home, thanked Luther goodbye, settled in, and ordered food from my usual Chinese takeout. I felt almost delirious eating so much salt, grease, texture, and flavor in one sitting, compared to the *extra* swagless 2-D hospital meals I'd gotten used to. I immediately realized my stomach had also shrunk from the stay, failing to get through half a meal where I could previously polish off twice that without issue.

I walked around the apartment, looked out the windows, and watched the block, which, of course, was living on as if nothing new had happened during my absence. I opened and closed every door, examined every wall, and took in all my things. Finally, I showered, changed clothes for the first time in months, and curled up to rest from the short but exhaustive trip. The nightmarish lucid dream was over, and a new life was just beginning.

"More work for you to do," they'd said.

CHAPTER 9
WE ON A WARD TOUR, PRISON SONG & PRISON LETTERS

I WAS ABOUT fourteen when the Impact Repertory Theatre rental van drove up to the Green Haven Correctional Facility in upstate New York. Our show schedule was packed in those days, and gigs would roll continuously. As a result, we often wouldn't know the details until the week of rehearsal or the day we traveled. Prior to this show, we'd signed preregistration forms as a security protocol which was out of the ordinary but still just something to roll with.

I was relatively new to the program and relished performing at every chance I got, especially for the various audiences we faced. I was moving up in the ranks, finally on the dance line and being considered for more parts in the show. This meant a lot to me. Being among a stacked roster of talent, I was usually behind in the chorus. So, I didn't think much about the forms we'd signed nor tried to guess what would happen. I was generally clueless that we'd be traveling to a maximum-security prison to perform a one-hour show.

It was clear and sunny when the cars pulled up and parked. Our crew was smaller than usual, but as always, we'd stretch the repertoire in whatever way was needed to make it work. I hopped out of the cramped van and immediately took a stretch from the ride. While unassuming and blank of expectations, my carefree stretch was interrupted by my increasing stare at the incredibly tall and menacing wall in front of us. It seemed to grow taller and move closer with every motion of my eyeballs, silently introducing its pronounced watchtowers and generally unnatural, simplified architecture. I looked around its corresponding prison town. Amidst peacefully swaying and manicured nature was suddenly—*plop!* A big, old, brow-beating prison. We were a world away from many things. There was no way of knowing how much life was behind this lifeless façade.

I remember this day fondly because alongside (and maybe even ahead of) Impact performing at the 2008 Academy Awards as a "Best Original Song" nominee, it's one of my favorite show memories of all time. It was also the inspiration for a mental health decision that sparked another unforgettable journey over the next sixteen years.

As far as the show itself, I had little idea what I was walking into, even as we walked into the facility. We proceeded with armed officers on an elongated, dark mode, campus crawl of sorts through at least five detailed security checks before arriving at a surprisingly "normal" looking auditorium and stage area.

At first, the experience seemed tense and alert, but for lack of better words, it was also adventurous, thrilling, and almost fun. The prison reports it originally opened in 1949, but its architecture felt older. Like we were slowly traveling "Through the Looking Glass" to another world where light and dark played differently and time was measured altogether otherwise. The campus crawl soon became daunting, concerning, and depressing.

We crossed paths with several incarcerated men lined in hallways who were told to stand back and let us pass. This meant "All Eyez" *definitely* on us *2Pac voice* and to mixed reviews. Most didn't have the behavioral "privilege" to see us perform or even knew what was happening. We were literally "Passin' (them) By" *The Pharcyde voice* and sadly, I could feel this energetically. I can only imagine what a sight we were walking through their reality unannounced and heavily escorted.

A few looked with loving eyes as if we were their children or family. As if they were immediately reminded of their own inner child and an affirmed world outside of this one. A few looked disdainfully, insulted to have to step aside for us, vocalizing their feelings to match. A few stared as if we were aliens, intruders, or golden tickets. A few looked as if we were their food, grinning greedily, trying to scare us, and saying lewd things which would undoubtedly be censored by primetime TV. By the fourth or fifth checkpoint, with all types of signatures, frisks, metal detectors, handstamps, and black-light checks completed yet still walking to our destination, we'd seen a great deal of the facility and its repressive ethos. Clearly, we weren't in a spoof, joke, or TV special, and it was no longer adventurous or fun.

We huddled in the wings of the stage, anxiously going over formations, solos, the run of the show, and things to remember not to do per the institution's instructions. The stage was huge, and though sounds would carry, our smaller performance team meant being conscious of filling out the stage effectively to reach every area of the audience with what little we had. Still, usual stage mechanics were the last thing on our minds.

We were more anxious than usual because, firstly, it was a one-hour show, much longer than our usual sets. This meant we'd be out there, number after number, with little rest, facing the unknown bottom line of an audience we had no clue how would feel about us. Secondly, this wasn't a themed event; no audience members were going home or to something enjoyable after. It was specifically for them, but how were they feeling that day? Perhaps they'd treat us as those in the hallways had—or worse. Thirdly, there was nowhere to go. One way in and one way out—and the way out was a twenty-minute escort. So, what were we facing exactly? Did they even *want* us there? What would happen if they didn't like the show?

We'd soon have our answers.

Founder and artistic director Jamal Joseph Sr. (who'd been incarcerated for nine years due to his revolutionary activities with the legendary Black Panther Party, "Back in the Day" *Ahmad voice*) came with us as a point of contact with the facility and to host the show. He came out and spoke while we collected ourselves for a final time. In the wings, we prayed, told some jokes to lighten the mood, and made our way to hit our first marks. We opened as usual with one of our most popular monologues, "Frankenstein," about society's role in the making of troubled Black and Brown youth. We flanked behind the spoken word soloist in two groups of still poses before physically coming together for the concluding dramatic moment. An inner "call to action" was expressed with the closing lines, "Frankenstein made a monster; what will you make me?" As the mic moved from the soloist's lips and our heads raised for the final poses of the scene, you could hear a pin drop, butts shifting in wooden seats, guards' fingers on country metal guns, and the proverbial "church mouse pissing on cotton." My guy, it was quiet!

Thankfully, the opening music hit, heading straight into a bright, up-tempo, inspirational R&B Hip-Hop track that showcased singing, dancing, rapping, and energetic choruses. Peeking out from the dance line, I saw many eyes glued to the stage. Then as the track faded to its closing notes and dancers grooved through their last counts, we put our index fingers in the air to hit our final positions with gusto, and again, tumbleweeds . . . crickets!

I could hear and feel our collective hearts beating out of the building. As my first trickle of sweat came down, I took my first real look at our audience. The room was packed—every seat holding a grown man staring at us like outer dimensional life forces. The rumor (or truth) was everyone in attendance had at least one life sentence to their name. (How does one declare or serve multiple life sentences in a single lifetime, you may ask?

We wondered too.) The seconds between hitting our final marks and panting in the surrounding silence felt like forever. Time ticked by agonizingly as we waited for a response or our next cue, like the birth of a baby behind closed doors. Then finally . . . something happened.

Something *amazing* happened. The entire auditorium erupted . . . in applause! I took a real look again and saw nothing but smiles. Then the applause *grew*. They started standing, yelling excitedly, and expressing glee, which I couldn't compare to anything then or anything since. Hardwired by our training, we stood frozen and eyeballed each other while holding our positions. Nervously enthused, we listened for group veterans who were low-key debating whether to take an early bow or remain still. To my knowledge, this had never happened to this degree so early in a show before.

We held for the cue to the next piece, but the applause continued. It continued for so long and got so loud that not only did our arms begin to shake, but the correctional officers charged their shotguns at each corner of the room, yelling for the men to sit and calm down—or else! I know I wasn't the only one thinking, *Lord! Don't let them start shooting in here!*

But while achingly holding our index fingers in the air, we started smiling too. I'd never experienced an audience reaction like this in real life. Jamal came back out, taking advantage of the spontaneity of the moment, telling us to melt down our positions and stand at ease. He warmly addressed the audience as they finally retook their seats, buzzing with chatter about what they just saw. He took a beat and came at them with cheerful enthusiasm.

"So . . . y'all liked that?!"

They erupted *again*. I'd never seen anything like it. It was the most engaged I'd ever seen an entire audience, especially for something we just did! We stood there, as baffled at them as they were at us. Jamal humbly requested they mind the instruction to stay calm so they could enjoy the whole show and we could stay the entire hour or more without problems. We segued into our spoken rundown of the acronym and credo of Impact:

We are youth activists who view the creative arts and leadership training as a way to develop ourselves and change the world in a positive way. We believe that we must be the message that we bring through hard work, focus, discipline, unity, and the principles of S.O.S. Safe space, outstanding effort, and service to our family, friends, and community.

Inspiration
Motivation
Preparation
Activism
Commitment
Teamwork.

Jamal wrapped this with a Malcolm X quote we were all very familiar with, asking, "If you don't stand for something, you will what?" and us answering, "Fall for anything!"

They lit up the room with applause once more, this time from their seats, captivated even deeper. They mouthed, "Wow," spoke across rows and aisles, and aggressively shushed each other so we could continue (ha!). Jamal asked if we should keep going, and almost in unison, they roared, "YES!" So, we did.

The show kept rolling, and with every single number, they exploded in a standing ovation. I mean *every* . . . *single* . . . *number!* Even better was seeing the genuine appreciation in their faces, eyes, and body language from the first seat to the last. I stood next to Jamal in the wings at one point of the set, catching my breath as we remarked how well it was going. Then he lowered a boom on me.

"Em, I want you to go out and tell your 9/11 story."

"Say what?!"

"I want you to go out and tell your 9/11 story, the one you told the other week in the rehearsal circle. It's a powerful story, Em. Come on, please? Just trust me now. All you gotta do is tell it to them how you told it to us. Then we'll come in and do "Raise It Up" or something. Simple, no worries!"

He said it so casually while I was reeling inside. It was hard enough telling the story the first time to people I knew!

We both knew I was going to do it. I implicitly trusted Jamal Joseph from my time around him in the company. When I first joined, I nicknamed him "million-dollar mouth" in my mind due to an aura I swore I could see and the fascinating way he pulled words of conviction together at any point in time. The things he'd say made so much sense and had so much power, direction, and forthright emotion in them that I swear I could hear "cha-chings." I respected my father greatly, but he wasn't an outwardly expressive man, or had the inclinations of a performing artist. So along with staff and veteran members of the company, this was the first time I'd been around so many Black men, particularly, who consistently had something powerful to say about themselves, the world, and me in relation as a norm.

He'd explained one of his spoken word inspirations was the illustrious H. Rap Brown, former chairman of the prolific Student Nonviolent Coordinating Committee (SNCC) during the heights of the 1960s and 1970s Black Power movement. Along with notable members of the Black Panther Party, he'd give rousingly passionate, humorous, stylish, and intelligent speeches, which profoundly moved Jamal in his youth. Decades later, I was fortunate to have quality time with Jamal, experiencing his inside voice, private jokes, and quieter words. I also shadowed him on a few projects, visited his home, his lovely family, and his office at Columbia University, where he was a professor of screenwriting and chair of the film department.

He once told me as a little boy or young man, he wanted to become a healer, like an indigenous medicine man. This fascinated him, and he'd begun studying various methods. Upon further life experience, he reasoned he could either heal people one at a time this way or hundreds of times more at once by being a filmmaker and artist. Despite his esteemed OG status, ongoing accomplishments, legacy as walking history, and authoritative tunnel vision, I continued to look at him as the little boy who wanted to heal people. I was personally honored he continually saw something in me. He also occasionally advised me on spiritual matters, the ways of the professional world, and how to get in better tune with myself metaphysically. There are constructive things I still do to this day because of those talks. So, at the time, we both knew I would do whatever he asked.

Indeed, I'd been directly at the location of what became known as Ground Zero on the fateful day of September 11, 2001. I was attending my first week as a freshman at the High School for Economics and Finance, a block away from one corner of the renowned Twin Towers. Around our third period, the first plane hit and shook our building's foundation. We were evacuated from the building floor by floor. We didn't know what was happening because the lower floors of the building had no windows, and communication lines in the area were immediately skewed. Nevertheless, we smelled smoke, faintly heard emergency vehicles in the area, and hurriedly descended narrow staircases. Once we stepped outside the building, we were on our own as students and human beings. The rest was fortunate but grim history.

I'd made it out by immediately moving south through Battery Park, then sheltering under the Battery Tunnel. I stayed there with a hundred or so terrified adults and a few brave classmates until the first Staten Island Ferries were brought to dock to take us off Manhattan. I remembered my thoughts in every moment of this day, looking up in overwhelmed awe at the burning towers, shiny and horrifying, and every step from the school to the tunnel.

Long before the ferries arrived, we watched one tower fall and cover us in inescapable dust and debris. Coated and bewildered in the tunnel, I realized there was no way out and wondered if we were trapped. I questioned jumping into the river to avoid dying there, though knowing the spontaneity of water and the rivers of New York City, shuddered at the thought. I remember witnessing the good, bad, and very ugly of human nature that day. Facing the surrounding death, I spoke to God in disbelief my life would end there. Details such as these rebloomed in my emotional retelling to the Green Haven Correctional Facility prisoners.

At a certain point, I greatly wanted this storytelling moment to end and, unintentionally, partially checked out. I was out of my body, watching myself tell the story and hoping I'd hurry up and finish. However, emotions I'd tucked away were rushing out in public in a room full of grown men I'd just met. I felt myself speed racing through the tale, embarrassed with a broken voice and all. I couldn't face the audience anymore. I felt naked and distressed. I'd put my head down, talking into the lowered microphone resting partly on my chest for stability and clutched by both hands for most of it. Finally, through tears (not even realizing I was crying), I crawled past the finish line and finally reached the end of my speech.

"... and I thought I would die right there—I saw it, I saw our bodies, I saw me lifeless, and I just couldn't believe it! But there was no way out! And suddenly, there *was* a way out! And I knew God wanted me to be here, and I'm still here for a purpose, and I'm really thankful..."

This is essentially how it concluded.

I felt pathetic, to be honest. This may have been my first real cry about it since that day. I sniffled and wiped my eyes, preparing to look up at the crowd, which had once again fallen completely silent. Then I felt a few other members gathered around me, which I appreciated because I was going through it.

As I recalibrated the present, I saw another sight I never saw before nor have seen since. A room full of grown men—hard looking, institutionally hardened grown men at that—crying. Some even sobbed. One shouted, "You DO have a purpose, girl!"

and applause began erupting *again*. More began to shout encouraging things to me and the gang. I was humbly overwhelmed and at a loss for action!

The humanity, hope, human warmth, and unconditional love were potent in the room. Jamal came back out, being the masterful chief of ceremony he is, remarking about the story again. They stood again, applauding resolutely as though a decorated soldier had come home. I was incredibly grateful for the support and how meaningful (and bigger than me) the moment was. It was like they were thankful I'd lived just to be a part of performing for them. And, in turn, I was thankful to live just to come be a part of performing for them.

I hadn't before voiced parts of the story regarding what I thought were my final moments and the apparent purpose in my life being saved so miraculously. Yet, the ordeal made me feel weak, vulnerable, mortal, and lost. Especially since life following that day was a whirlwind for the public and numerous youths who went to schools in the Twin Towers area. Life would truly never be the same, and many educational tracks were utterly disrupted.

Telling the story on this day, however, for the first time, I felt strong again. I was emboldened to speak from my heart and push through the proverbial fear of *feeling*, even when my voice was shaky and my tears uncontrollable. Standing at the top of the stage with a microphone in my sweaty hands, I felt an enormous duty to uphold. As scared as I was and as much as I didn't know what would come out of my mouth exactly, or if it would make sense outside my brain, I felt anything was better than silence. A part of me also felt I was *trusted* with the moment and, thus, capable of meeting or exceeding it by default, which was reassuring. "The called are qualified," I often tell myself. Finally, I felt this courage and breakthrough in large part was due to the collective consciousness and support of these fully engaged, appreciative, and energetically connected men of the Green Haven audience.

Y'ALL (NOT) GON' MAKE ME LOSE MY MIND

They continued standing ovations after every piece. I thought they'd get tired of doing so, but they never did. At the show's end, we sat facing them at the edge of the stage, and a few introduced themselves. Some explained they were fighting their way out of wrongful sentences or innocent of their charges altogether and were inspired by what they witnessed us perform. Some knew they were in for life and would likely never see outside of these walls again, yet were equally inspired by what they witnessed us perform. It was truly a pleasure to hear them speak for themselves, from their own hearts, to connect about the show, and feel like we really made an "impact." They urged us to keep doing positive things and thanked us profusely for coming. I got "You go, girl!" cheers even as we left the auditorium. Other than putting on a powerful show, it was surreal to be celebrated for being alive. These moments and this perspective never left me.

About ten years later, I met a young man while hanging out with members of Impact on a boozy Saturday night. He was seemingly the new boyfriend of one of my sisters in the program. He offered to give us a ride to a spot and then home. I introduced myself in the car, and he stopped me immediately.

"I already know who you are. Actually, my brother knows who you are. He's talked about you quite a bit."

I was intrigued. Paranoid and anxious, but intrigued!

"Really? How so?"

"My brother was locked up in Green Haven when y'all came to perform there years back."

(Full stop! Full gasp!)

"Nahhhh. Don't say that! OMG, are you serious?!"

"Deada**. He told me about your story, how you started crying and s***, how the whole room started crying—all that."

I was shook-eth to my core.

"Wooooow. This is wild. I'm humbled. Thank you. Thank you for telling me this . . ."

The news of his brother doing well and remembering our show after ten years put my heart at ease in many ways. It marked another reason never to forget the Green Haven performance and audience. This also constituted a universal confirmation that was too perfect to be coincidence and surreal, to say the least. A decision inspired by the show way before this ten-year mark, which set off a completely different chain of events and was directly related to my suicide survival, had turned out to be the right thing to do. This too had fit the plan of my life like a puzzle piece.

Six years after Green Haven marked the two-year anniversary of my suicide attempt and stint in St. Vincent's psychiatric ward. While I usually don't mark anniversaries for anything, I noticed the timing because I had a noticeable challenge staying emotionally stable in the first year and had beat myself up about it. I didn't consider it may have been a type of post-traumatic stress disorder (PTSD). I learned later about the profound effects of coping and trauma stored in the physical body. How even if you forget the event or move on psychologically from what you experienced, the body and unresolved thoughts can resurface stored away feelings. They can release these energies in you as the cyclical timing rolls by, year after year.

I realized a spike in mental spirals paralleled the months of the initial events by the second year. I was objectively alert while painfully aware of a new season of resurfacing PTSD looking to intensify. This time, I was determined to avoid, destroy, or transmute this misdirection of energy by any (safe and sustainable) means.

Desperate for substance-free distractions to get me through a particularly hard and sleepless night, it came to me to try what seemed like a cliché tactic "just crazy enough to work." I decided to take the focus entirely off myself and put it on someone else. I looked to uplift, spotlight someone and their experience, let them know I was making it through the night, and reaching out in support of them making it through theirs.

I decided this couldn't be anyone I knew because they'd be hyper-focused on my PTSD or judging the details of our shared experience. I'd learned you couldn't really say or write the word "suicide" to most people. Ironically, it was a trigger for them as civilians, almost more than for you as a survivor. People seemed not strong enough to have conversations about dark or empty places without focusing on negatives or a perceived state of mind of the person, rather than the incredible humanity of being able to go there, understand, and be . . . the humanity of being able to "see in the dark," to triumph in energetic or spiritual darkness.

I thought back to the powerful show at Green Haven. Those faces, their stories, the applause, tears, and spirited shouting. The love I wish I could have bottled and kept for "Nights Like This" ***The Five Heartbeats voice*** Also, their openness to all aspects of light and dark we touched on in art, speech, and poetry—the mutual elimination of judgment which connected us and made us bigger than the circumstances over us. The incredible amount of fighting so many of them were doing in their own lives every day, away from every comfort, everyone, and everything they loved. I decided this powerful example of humanity was resonant then and could be resonant now. So, I decided I'd focus on someone else and make it through the night by writing letters to people in prison. *Boom!*

This "project" certainly got me through the night and then some. I found the *responsibility* of doing it right and how I wanted to mean days and even weeks in the making. As I wiped my anniversary tears on the first night and began searching for how to start, I found a propagation of pen pal programs and was delighted to see Green Haven had one! I excitedly scrolled through and quickly realized a huge hurdle. I couldn't remember any of the names of those we'd met that day! *Ugh!* My heart broke about this. It'd been such an emotional roller coaster. I'd been so emptied and poured into but could barely remember.

This is also why I damn near cried being told I was remembered clearly and fondly so many years later. We just hadn't exchanged names like that, which spoke to how much more everything else mattered. I made the executive decision to bypass the Green Haven program altogether. I wouldn't feel right connecting with people who weren't at the performance that day and not with those who were. It felt out of order in my heart. I preferred starting fresh at another institution to avoid the risk of sidestepping someone who'd been so gracious to us. So, thankful for the Green Haven inspiration, I took this show on the road.

I spent the rest of the night and the next few days combing through a dozen different pen pal programs from facilities nationwide. Not to belittle the perfectly valid idea of the programs themselves (which obviously set technological precedents for the evolution of online companionship apps), but I was amazed they existed. Thankful and surprised at how many men were putting themselves out there, communicating, and looking to connect from behind the wall as well as numerous women with equally, if not more, amazing stories looking to do the same, though mostly with men only. I respected this, took the hint, and discerned I needed to be very selective.

I read through hundreds of profiles with laser-like intention, filtering for standout details and choice of words. I didn't know exactly what I was looking for and understood the issue of safety involved in opening myself up to people I didn't know. Yet, I knew this idea was clearly put on my spirit in a late hour of survival. And like Green Haven, there existed good people who were just in bad situations. I knew I had skills for reading energy, motivation, and character, and felt it was a perfect time to lean on my sensitivity as a superpower.

I moved forward, reading through profiles, knowing I would know when it was right. I would just know! I made the rule that

ANY inkling of "ehh" or not-rightness meant a firm no—keep looking. I did this repeatedly until I arrived at a list of ten men of various ages in various states covering the map. I'd craft and mail a handwritten letter to each of them.

I introduced myself, what inspired me to write, that I was working through this intense PTSD, hoping our humanness through captivity was a connection, hoping they were uplifted through another day as a result, and encouraged them in their respective situations. I'd comment on what I saw in their profile pictures and what stood out in their descriptions. I didn't want anything but for them to make it through their night. I didn't expect any to write back. I thought they'd think I was "crazy," random, distrustful, and coming from *wayyy* left field! I didn't expect to develop meaningful relationships with any, and this wasn't even the point.

Every single one wrote back. I continued to build a letter, email, or phone-based relationship with most of them who had long sentences. As years passed, cases, statuses, facilities, and dynamics changed, and some lost contact. However, a few remained my close confidants throughout college, encouraged my solo career as a creative performing artist, and continued sharing their lives, thoughts, growth, and humanity. Some continued to send me gifts, art, poems, pictures, and handmade cards.

Two of these men continued to stay connected in a manner that felt deeper. They unexpectedly suited my energy like yin to yang and yang to yin. We remained consistent in letter writing and phone calls over the next ten years. I learned so much from them about life, love, pain, masculinity, femininity, how to love and be loved, knowledge, wisdom, and understanding. I continue to appreciate their raw survival in the bellies of prison facilities and their ongoing spirit to really and truly live. I'm proud to have secondhand witnessed and applauded them through numerous accomplishments, feats of inner strength, and graduations of the heart as they have me.

I traveled out of state to meet the family and visit the facility of one known as Kasim O. Gero. The day I met his sweet mother, Ms. Cheryl, outside the prison we'd enter together, she embraced me with a big hug I didn't expect. She thanked me for coming and warmly said "I had to be an angel." She'd go on to host me in her home, cook for me, talk with me about life and love, and be an example by continuing her education, fostering children, and running businesses. On the few occasions Kasim and I had disagreements, she made sure to highlight my fair reasoning, right-doings, and defend me behind my back. I'm proud to know she truly loved me and I'm grateful to have experienced her love. At the time of this writing, she and her youngest son, Kasim's bright younger brother, Delonté, who'd confided in me, gave me wisdom, and made me laugh, are no longer here physically. They remain two of my most loving spirit angels.

After what seemed like "love at first sight" to boot an already booming chemistry from letters and calls, I'd continue to visit Kasim and develop an intimate relationship with him. I met his young son and more family members along the way. We'd engage in positive activities like studying, fasting, exchanging training tips, funny stories, and poems. We talked through many dark things and connected human experience dots for the better. We grew through growing pains, individual achievements, and some of the most challenging times in our lives.

Sometimes he'd put me on to books, music, pro wrestling, and cultural things I didn't know about. He also introduced me to the revolutionary practice and monthlong commemoration known as Black August. We noted the difference in his prison experience once he left his "gangster" existence behind and embraced one of greater purpose and social uplift. He began tutoring other inmates, running workshops, making speeches, and describing his desire to preserve land and work in youth empowerment upon release. I'll never forget his story of being a little boy and deciding he wanted to create homes and homeless shelters as his profession in life. He reminded me of Jamal in this, children with the vision and desire to heal the world. That such spirits can grow up and find themselves in prison seems to beg more questions about society.

We both outgrew our old and unserving selves at respective paces. When able to touch each other, we held every hug as long as possible. I once had the opportunity to be freely in a facility with him for what they called "Family Day." We cheerfully jumped rope, played kickball with children, walked in the sun, watched the clouds, peacefully held hands, slyly avoided watchful officers, laughed, and enjoyed brief (albeit unnatural) normalcy. I'm very proud of him as a person, man, survivor, and warrior. This was one of the most transformative relationships of my life, which I have no regrets about experiencing.

I continue to love and appreciate another close confidant of the unexpectedly profound letter-writing decision—an admirable, strong, intelligent man and human being. Being a bright jailhouse lawyer and very accomplished student, he'd successfully cleared his case of 100 years of inaccurate sentencing (read that again!) in headline-making fashion. At the time of this writing, he's received associate and bachelor's degrees as part of landmark university-to-prison programming in the United States and is en route to law school. Though we had communication gaps and other primary relationships, we stayed connected and conferenced for over fifteen years. Due to the greater distance, I never physically met him or his family, so the entire relationship was built on these conversations. I cherish relating, inspiring, and enjoying each other along the way.

We had an encouraging spark and intense chemistry from the start as well. The spine of our connection was debatably the tremendous respect we had for each other's intelligence, visionary thinking, energy in action, and positivity. He was one of the most consistent personalities I'd ever known, a great keeper of resolve and grounded-ness. Our mental adventures covered great ranges, and we watched each other grow in divine manhood, womanhood, and personhood.

When I started writing to him, I was embarking on a challenging journey in higher education, to which he was a great (escape and) support. The tables turned and I was happy to be a cheerleader as he leveled up with college degrees. He's done more with himself from a prison cell than many do with an entire life of physical freedom. I'm very proud of him as a person, man, survivor, and warrior. It was one of the most transformative relationships of my life, which I have no regrets about experiencing.

I couldn't have expected these fruitful and loving additions to my life on the night I was just looking for a reason to stay alive. Few words can express my gratitude for how prison letters in my mailbox would brighten my mood on the dreariest days, and prison calls would ironically lift my spirit. These people, strangers whom I'd never met, became loved ones who at many points helped keep me going.

This came in handy when I hit another psychological wall two years after the start of letter writing and was detained in the Mount Sinai psychiatric ward. Terrified of reliving another monthslong stint, I was relieved it was only for a week (longest week ever!) On the first day I slept all day, which was honestly heavenly. Then just as quickly, the *not-the-spot-ness* kicked in, and I was almost hysterical about wanting to get out.

They had pay phones in the day room, so I called my big sister Dietrice Bolden from the Impact program. I remember hearing her voice and responding with maximum anxiety, "They got me in here, and I gotta get out. Please don't leave me in here, please!" For years, I've internally apologized for how anxious this probably was for her to hear. What could she do, after all? I could hear how heartbroken she was for me, though she graciously said she'd do her best.

Mount Sinai's ward was clearly a step up in attributes though, which was a relief. I was no longer in a dark dungeon in the belly of the West Village (respectfully). Instead, I was on a high-story panoramic floor in the hills of the Upper East Side. They insisted on group therapy sessions, which felt intrusive, unproductive, and annoyed me, but I appreciated the intention of holistic structure. They even had a schedule! Though my words were still generally treated as untrustworthy, the staff didn't flinch or look to intimidate me when I walked by. The paint on the walls was brighter and had more life to it. Everything was much cleaner, sleeker, and of better quality. It made a difference.

The facility's building overlooked East Harlem, a place I'd roamed through a lot as a child. I'd played sports there, had my Impact audition there, training boot camp and boot camp graduation there, met my first boyfriend there, had a favorite pizza shop and thrift store, performed in various venues, and had close friends in the area. Now a world away in yet another ward, I'd often sit by the windows and peacefully watch the neighborhood play. Students excited to be out of school, nurses on smoke breaks, buses following routes I knew well, and restaurants I'd never been in. My heart felt so close yet so far. Like the St. Vincent's experience, I'd visualize myself free, on the street, engaging in the outside I could see but not touch. I remember a few sweet moments and colorful characters I crossed paths with.

On the day I was admitted, an older American-Black lady was in the waiting room with the brightest, longest, firetruck-red nails I'd ever seen, and fading, frayed, kinky, natural, lime-green hair. I thought I was hallucinating her. As her story unfolded, her hair was green because of a chemical reaction while escaping a

horrible fire and losing her home. She'd clearly been through a lot. She couldn't contain how not all right she was or the anxiety of not knowing what she was going to do. I greatly felt for her in this, empathetically knowing what it feels like to lose everything I owned and not know my next move. Also, she could've been my grandmother, and no elder deserves to wake up with no security or support to live. Still, she carried herself like a queen and was very nice to me. She was very sane, courteous, and polite between venting. I prayed it worked out for her, and I'll never forget her depiction of "the red, the black, and the green."
X Clan voice

During my stay, a very serene, mean-looking, mute, thick-bodied Mexicano was also in the facility. He dressed every day like a character straight out of the West Coast gangster movies of the 1990s, which I loved. A living embodiment of the *Vatos Locos*, *Chicanos*, *Blood In Blood Out*, *Mi Vida Loca*, and iconic *Lowriders* (who have excellent taste in music). He wore dark Ray-Bans, rocked piercings, bandannas, flannels, white tees, khakis, metal accessories, and hard stares. Apparently, his rap sheet was long, and he didn't have words for anyone. Though some things are good to be aware of, I wouldn't judge him either way.

I often sat near him in our tiny art class (yes, to my delight, they had an art class!). I found his energy peaceful to be around and would often compliment him on his drawings, to which his focus was so intense yet so relaxed. Though he shrugged off every piece like it was nothing, he was talented, and I could tell drawing brought him a lot of peace. He'd graciously nod at my novice doodles and share pointers and perspectives. Close to my release, I saw him cutting something out like an oval, which he handed to me. It was a yellow flower, a tulip, which he'd drawn for me, and signed. I gasped and thanked him. He bowed from across the tables and said sternly, "It's been a pleasure." Again, some of the hardest "gangsters" have the sweetest hearts. If I could've framed it, I would've. I carried this flower home and put it on my wall.

Y'ALL (NOT) GON' MAKE ME LOSE MY MIND

In hindsight of my ward and prison experiences, life was closely paralleling art and vice versa. Following them, my open-mindedness to the experiences of prisoners, prison families, political prisoners, health facilities, and various mental health topics increased. This expanded consciousness led me to explore these topics in my independent study, college papers, community activities, art, media, and music. The way dots connected in real time wasn't linear. Not much in my life has been, nor am I a linear thinker. Though years out, it all looks somewhat fitting, methodical, and intentional.

There's irony, for example, in the overlapping time frame of the Darnell Martin-directed movie *Prison Song* reaching its heightened popularity. This feature film starred Hip-Hop's own Q-Tip from the legendary group A Tribe Called Quest alongside fellow music legends Fat Joe and Mary J. Blige. While a few members of Impact and I were all abuzz about seeing this film, we soon (and unexpectedly) were making our way upstate to perform at Green Haven, exposed firsthand to some of the experiences of incarcerated people. Google Reviews describes the *Prison Song* plot as such (spoiler alert!) —:

Life has dealt Elijah (Q-Tip) a tough hand. His stepfather is sent to prison, and his mother (Mary J. Blige) becomes institutionalized. Elijah spends time in foster homes, but his talent for photography leads to a college scholarship offer. Soon, however, events spiral out of hand, and Elijah finds himself behind bars for accidentally killing a man (Fat Joe) during a fight. Assisted by his understanding lawyer (Elvis Costello), Elijah fights for his dignity and prison reform.

Much like the "Elijah" character, life had spiraled for me too. I'd continue to meet a host of meaningful people and utilize my art and passion for human interest as a means for survival and social change. I'd choose my political science major to complement my exposure to social systems, the full caste of people affected by them, and my interest in power, access, relationships, information, and control in any industry.

I learned from adjacent peace, reconciliation, and justice studies that dignity and lack thereof are the crux of most human rights issues and even some in business. I realized the main thing I was acting out of when I wrote the first prison letters *was* dignity. Simple dignity. I was determined not to die in surrender that night but to live and connect to the dignity of living and birthright in others. I found exemplary dignity in good people in some of the lowest places of our society. Even though PTSD can still loom, and triggers are an ongoing mastery, the spirit of this often helps me make it through the nights now.

My life would be drastically different had I not performed at the Green Haven Correctional Facility. Had I not done so enthusiastically and tearfully told a survival story to a room full of "lifers." Had I not let detainment serve me and stayed open to growth in repressive habitats. Had I not taken the emotional initiative and reached out to uplift complete strangers. Had I not dared to take risks in love, challenge my mind, share my gifts, and open my heart. Had I not let people show me who they are, trusted my strengths, and remained true to my growing authentic self. This strange, multiyear course of events may have stemmed from almost losing my mind, but in their own bold strokes, contributed to me never losing it again.

CRITICAL THINKING

CHAPTER 10
DMX, ALL CAPS WHEN YOU SAY THE MAN'S NAME

THERE ARE CURRENTLY *TWENTY-LEVEN-UMPTEEN THOUSAND* ***Usher voice*** products sold online branded with the phrase "y'all gonna make me lose my mind." A classic lyric (however bastardized by many) giving only a cringey cross-cultural wink back to its prolific Hip-Hop originator and one of my biggest inspirations, Earl "DMX" Simmons. This lyric—penned from a genius work, a song named "Party Up" which made no reference to a party nor spoke on themes of any happy celebration, further solidified the magic of DMX's artistry and the magnetic humanity of his ragingly subversive energy.

He was on a three-album streak of platinum number-one-selling bodies of work from a major debut. In a 2016 interview by *Fader* titled "Bring Your Whole Crew," X stated generating upward of $144 million for his Def Jam record label back in 1998. Such a run for a new artist was previously unheard of in music, let alone Hip-Hop.

His unique quality of groundbreaking performances, infectious live prayers, vivid album art, cinematic music videos, video games, and movies such as the Hype Williams-directed visual masterpiece *Belly* also created long-lasting influence. Little do many know, but Dark Man X was on a mission to be memorable for over a decade prior. According to the Songfacts.com account of the record:

> [Party Up] was released as a single from DMX's third album . . . And Then There Was X. Like his first two albums—It's Dark and Hell Is Hot and Flesh of My Flesh, Blood of My Blood, both released in 1998—it debuted at No. 1 and quickly went platinum. But it was a long time coming. He got in the game in the late '80s and had a career setback when his first single, "Born Loser," stiffed when it was released in 1992. On "Party Up," he felt like he still had something to prove and was sending a message to anyone who thought his success might soften him up. "It took me 13 years to get a record deal," he said. "You're going to get more than a couple of albums out of me."

In this stride, he was on to something energetical and not just about chart-topping music or cutting through industry politics. In our modernized growth-hack, life-hack, and bio-hack-obsessed eras, few seem to understand (out loud) how meaningful maintenance and methodical alignment are to growth. As Dr. Dre told Kendrick Lamar on "Wesley's Theory," his uberfunky and psychological romp of an opening for the *To Pimp a Butterfly* album, "Anybody can get it. The hard part is keeping it." We often hear sports commentators note athletic accomplishments signify not only the culmination of seen and unseen experiences but also the onset of a new level of being. Keeping unwanted weight off or making addictions tamable, if not obsolete, requires different habits from initial losing or quitting. Money management, financial vision, and planning are arguably more important than having money itself. Staying a champion or repeating a championship requires a new level of training, performance, rest, or recovery.

What levels of being was DMX tapping into which made him bounce back from what could've been a fatal career setback, and instead, stabilizing, redirecting his gifts, fulfilling his heart's desires, and generating over $100 million out of the gate, uniquely?

Let *that* marinate!

In any unique experience, achievement, or simply living happily, a magnifying glass can be held over the question . . . Is success from our ability more than our perspective, or our perspective more than our ability? Should they even be segmented? Could they be the same thing? Are they hand-in-hand taking a Jill Scott "Long Walk" in the park when all is well, getting clearer, or "Slowly Surely" on their way to clarifying each other?

Social media megastars, nonreality-TV-housewives-turned-moguls (like the single mother who needed childcare support and ended up creating the billionaire "Barney" children's series empire), popular spiritual leaders, well-known niche podcasters, and small-batch wellness entrepreneurs give us intriguingly modern examples of people who have varying amounts of ability and perspective. The answers to who they are, what they can do, how they want to live, and resolving obstacles from self to scale is also the basis of their businesses and success. In these cases, ability may not be about a unique talent more than organizing a set of skills, recreating an experience, or directing a passion. Likewise, perspective may not be about making sense of the crowd or claiming, "A Seat at the Table" and, instead, uncomplicating one's desire and sense of a feeling. This, in turn, may create new talents, a new crowd, and new tables.

DMX arrived at his unique stroke of voice, heart, energy, and creation and seemed to nurture them with every accomplishment. It's likely every time he was seen or heard, despite his personal challenges, he was operating from this unique stroke, from a whole spirit or clear sense of one. While often speaking in raw poetics about shadows, internal conflicts, and the negative undercurrents of society, he was also living vibrantly and truer to form than many. He seemed to resonate as intensely alive while personifying the darkness of human existence. With an energy that wouldn't deny itself, DMX gave life and musical therapy to millions of listeners while lifting the culture of Hip-Hop to new heights.

I find it fitting his spirit animal is the dog, which he was often lovingly seen with, had heartfelt stories about, and vocally emulated. Also, often calling out with joy, grit, and carefree power, "Where My Dogs At?" One of the most apparent associations of the depth of this connection and the omnipresence of Hip-Hop energy is within the Indian, Sanskrit, and Hindu cultures. According to Prabhu communities, the reverent, potently present, all-birthing vital force referred to as prana energy is sometimes also understood as "the bark of a dog."

CHAPTER 11
ACT LIKE YOU KNOW THE SEQUENCE IS KOLLAGE

I BEGAN WRITING this book under a multihyphenate title to be narrowed down later. The short version (!) was called "Gave My Last F*ck: Notes from a Hyper-Creative Hip-Hop Unicorn, Curious Athlete, Social Entrepreneur, and Sensually-Awake Suicide Survivor." I was obviously tuned to several things, but it was more a selector or soul algorithm than a marquee. I planned to open the introduction by quoting myself, saying:

It's very freeing to know that and let that go . . . to the misery, drain, dysfunction, disorder, damages, and disappointments of life, I gave my last f*ck.

This title came to me while thinking about how many times I've faced a fear of doing something meaningful and yet, how many other things I've let myself be held back from doing. Looking in the mirror at the cyclical condition of being undermined or overlooked, and yet, how many things I've kept to myself and never said. I have little experience with memoirs or self-help books. Though this might seem like a mashup of the two, this wasn't my aim here. Not necessarily my thing, respectfully. An unpretentious approach was the feeling, but the profane title header wasn't quite what I wanted to say. Especially

Y'ALL (NOT) GON' MAKE ME LOSE MY MIND

since a lot of people seemed to be saying it already, and I wasn't sure if they really moved me.

Eye-opening meetings of the mind, speeches, interviews, documentaries, tweets, memes, posts, and pins that colloquially speak my language have gotten me through several challenging periods. They've made hard-hitting wisdom digestible, opened my mind unassumingly, or affirmed little things I could easily take with me, absolutely. Books that aim to extend this type of impact in long form, through branded verbal stylings of no-nonsense "real talk"—I mean with profanity *all* in the chapters . . . *all* in the title *Suge Knight voice* for some reason just never made it to my shelf, respectfully.

Digital sites like *Mashable* and *Book Riot* call them "sweary self-help books." Self-help for people who hate self-help but still want to read self-help books. (Did you stop to think about that because I sure did?) What I find interesting (and maybe totally unrelated) from being outside this readership (though an understanding ally) is "real talk" as a tone and public profanity as linguistic subversion. While not exclusive to Hip-Hop, they have certainly been gifts that keep on giving from Hip-Hop culture to the mainstream. Between 2015 and 2022, multiple book titles donning this style have sold double-digit millions of copies. Creatively, I applaud what's being done here. Even with the advent of mass self-publishing, not anyone can sit and write a clear and moving book, let alone create a niche audience from it. It's just that . . . I don't know. Something else. Maybe it's nothing . . .

There are endless numbers of brands using iconic strokes of Hip-Hop energy, song titles, lyrics, colloquialisms, and wordage in their footprints like "oh snap" (which I wouldn't have even noticed if not for a Biz Markie "oh snap" counter popping up on Instagram years ago. They documented every use of "oh snap" across non-Hip-Hop mediums, and the results were far-reaching). Also, "yo," "chill," "in the house," "in the building," "crib," "fam," "crew," "gang," "squad," "hits different," "fresh," "dope," "drip," "bad," "flow," "beef," "game," "like a boss," "word," "hustler," "what's up," "what's good," "joint," "fire," "sauce," "juice," "it's your girl/boy," "trap," "thug," "gangster," "streets," and way more! All with the aim of cultural fluidity, a more approachable brand voice, authenticity, and selectively streamlining language while generating unshakeable brand equity and financial empowerment as a result.

There was a time when rap albums were seen on primetime news being trampled by politicians because they contained explicit lyrics. There was no holding back about how this was poisoning society, lowering moral standards, and how the ballooning sales of Hip-Hop artists were cause for attention. Maybe Hip-Hop crawled, so sweary self-help books could fly? Maybe. I also observe the drivers of this bestselling niche are not the Snoop Doggs or Ice Ts who survived the "Parental Advisory" sticker era. They're scholars of their own mediums and, in most cases, barely Hip-Hop adjacent. The social rebellion or ingenuity in their backgrounds is usually neatly confined and lends credibility but isn't always the core of who they are.

Oddly fitting ironies, social studies, and political economics aside, this is an effective example of how free we are to create our own realities and master creation as the world changes. (I still believe there should be a Hip-Hop institution attentive to the leverage of its distinct cultural creativity and, where tangible, its intellectual property. Many architects and communities are not sustainably independent in contrast to inspired-by creators who become exponentially prosperous. I don't know; there's just something off about this to me!)

Nevertheless, for months I considered the freedom of using my own version of a profane title. I said *Gave My Last F*ck* with glee throughout my apartment, while walking down the street, in cadences on the treadmill, as a mantra to close out my yoga. While sidestepping stress, missing calls, avoiding social media, watching birds fly, visualizing my desires, investing in what I wanted, looking in the mirror, resolving issues, clearing out confusion, or brushing my teeth. *Gave My Last F*ck* was going to be everything. Saying it with my chest, getting my literary rocks off while reclaiming cultural rebellion, and prosperously staking a flag in the soil as someone directly of the culture with something new to say. It gave me new life. To quote pro wrestling's Bullet Club, "Too Sweet!" Alas, maybe it was.

As I did more research on entering the sweary self-help field, one thing became flaccidly clear. The number of books mirroring this style was more than a few, it was no longer uncommon. This meant for a unicorn like me, "The Thrill (was) Gone." ***BB King voice*** Additionally, my research brought up a very coherent point alleging if not painting a socially accurate picture that, essentially, I'm not really "supposed" to write such a book, succeed on a large scale with it, and because of market saturation, be in a position to match the successes generated to this point. I'm pretty saturated on the word "privilege." But even if we go around it, there's still very applicable cultural fluidity going on. *Book Riot* said their mouthful as such:

What's missing from all of the punchy, in-your-face advice? The fact that these people come from a place of immense privilege. All of these authors are white. Most are college educated. Jen Sincero is "unapologetically rich." When Sincero says, "if my broke ass can get rich, you can too," she conveniently leaves out the fact that her "broke ass" grew up in a wealthy suburb of New York and attended a private college. Even considering his hardscrabble upbringing, as a white man Gary John Bishop has a lot of social privilege. Our perception of Scots as champion swearers doesn't hurt either. It's hard to imagine a Black woman breezing past the "angry black woman" trope in order to pen a plainspoken, profane bestseller the way Bishop did.

I've seen sweary titles written by Black authors and authors of color since. Perhaps their lesser popularity is more about timing and market saturation than their ability to leverage cultural fluidity to scale. And maybe I shouldn't have done this research; perhaps I discouraged myself. Still, all signs pointed to shifting off a punchy, blunt, and stylistically profane title. I also asked myself, "What if I could just do better?" The research proved empowering in this regard. It gave me an informed place to decide how I wanted to represent myself in the world. For one thing, uniquely.

Also, I've learned from being in the minority on several occasions, when you simply observe, you freely receive valuable information. What you think you're missing out on may not even deserve you.

My hesitation wasn't about whether I could make it work but whether it would feel good, proud, and freeing to dive into a crowded, questionably diverse, and uniform pool of authors. Rarely have I ever been one to follow a trend or do what everyone else was doing, to my delight and only temporary discomfort. There's peace in successfully thinking for yourself, which you'll never get from others. Knowing the real fun of what I can have that's right, better, and perfect for me can begin at my authority at any time in my mind.

Also, the allure of profanity as a sign of fully realized, unapologetic free will (not always a true sign) has severely underrated and misjudged how free will operates within boundaries. For example, having "clean" versions of your music as a recording artist, especially in Hip-Hop, where it's almost essential to your advantage in so many professional mediums. This principle extends to the cultural reach and prosperity of one of the pillars of the craft of rap in poetry.

I vividly remember reading Langston Hughes describing—just as I'd heard Eminem describe—about their clean, censored (or, as I see it, mobile and marketable) works being available in multiple countries and languages beyond their active careers. These two are fully embraced, industry-leading, culture-shifting, award-winning, generation-spanning, beloved poster children of their crafts, even in places where English isn't the "Native Tongue(s)." This is largely due to choosing to make their respective art "clean" and more accessible.

The widest hips in the world couldn't straddle the range

between Langston Hughes, who spoke of "rivers, dreams deferred, and a raisin in the sun," to Eminem, who spoke of "spatulas, mental health, trailer parks, and pistol-whipping" having the same business strategy almost a century apart. In this, I see voluntary censorship as an extension of artistry and strategy instead of a limitation. Many believe life is inherently abundant, and we create limitations and false beliefs. I'm open to being available for all audiences who would love to hear my voice, feel my energy, read my words, and be part of prosperity that betters things beyond me.

The last thing which came to mind before I made my title shift was other people saying this title out loud. Outside of my chosen soul tribe would be my indigenous, African, immigrant, and predominantly Catholic family saying, "Her book is called what??!" Cue the "here we, here we go . . ."

Maybe that was the real last f*** I gave.

My usual thoughts on courage prompt me to ask, "What Would Malcolm (X) Do?" This time, with the shadow of profanity on the impact of creatively inspired words as the bottom line, I asked, "What Would Rakim Do?" and the decision was crystal clear. Ironically, he wouldn't give a f*** about the allure of a profane title. A brief conversation with my father sealed the deal. We went from discussing perceived limitations of prosperity concerning salaries and hiring practices at the corporate level to him casually suggesting I should write a book. I hadn't told him I was already writing one. (The way I smiled!) So as much as my ego wanted to disrupt this disruptor's space, I chose to believe in freedom from limitation and having better, more unique, and more effective inside me.

(I still reserve my right to not give a f***, of course.)

At the time of this writing, I still hadn't read the popular *Subtle Art of Not Giving a F*ck* by Mark Manson or any likewise sweary titles of the niche. I'm glad I didn't read them, respectfully. Much like the legendary Hip-Hop supergroup OutKast recalls counterintuitively not listening to any Hip-Hop music around the time of creating their 2000 masterwork of an album *Stankonia*. Or when Oscar and Grammy award-winning performer Jennifer Hudson informed *Entertainment Tonight* she didn't listen to predecessor-legend Jennifer Holiday's version of the showstopping song "And I Am Telling You I'm Not Going" before she went into the studio to record her monumental remake for the 2006 *Dreamgirls* movie.

She'd heard it before, knew of the rich and colorful history of it which it existed, and this was important. But what I gathered from her admission was the vibrant energy of the original recording would be too much of a fixed idea on her natural imagination and fluid readiness, weighing unnecessarily on her consciousness and coloring her approach. Thus, also obstructing the transport of fresh inspiration from her heart, being in the moment, and the "do *my* thing with it" of it all. I believe this is a metaphor for life and explains why I'm touch-and-go with social media and entertainment news. I've learned to take people lightly and to value presence and connection as highly as discernment and detachment.

In this all-inclusive universe where millions of things can latch onto you with the promise, illusion, or valid proposal of making life better, easier, or more fulfilling, it seems the stronger you are in being better, easier, and more fulfilled in yourself. In the evolution of your nature and approaches with everything, the better returns you experience, and the more unique, pleasurable, and à la DMX—resonant your living is. Foregoing the example before her enabled Jennifer Hudson to unlock her truer talent, ability, unique success, and most importantly, her own worthy exhilaration, which, in turn, inspired many beyond her.

One could argue singing it as it was sung before would've been easier, especially since she has range and ability as a performer, which is essentially boundless. But for a true artist, this denial of creativity and expression can be incredibly frustrating. When you know you have your own light inside you or have been on a long journey to the fruition of it, living with yourself and the varied returns of a mindless copy-and-paste may not be easy at all.

You may also end up stumbling through the creative process, trying to match what was already done, which may mean more than wasted time. Shrinking and stretching in inappropriate places for your instrument may handicap your growth and make a habit of a divided mind trying to be in multiple places simultaneously. Being practiced at singular focus, trusting herself, and being positively curious about this blank canvas allowed Jennifer to make a clear decision. Channeling her own interpretation of the song in new and unique creative heights flowed beautifully with the use of talent she already had and believed in. As a naïve observer, *this* seems easier.

There was likely deliberate practice and training leading up —but she simply went in and did it from start to finish. This created a pathway for a lot of good to meet her authenticity, uniqueness, audacity, and centered power in continued momentum without the hurdle, speed bump, or gate of an inner conflict. This breakout role and performance put "J Hud" on the map, as they say, and furthered the life of this song, musical, and classic story to new generations. Respectfully, thank goodness she didn't give a f***.

My awareness of connections like this is part of what makes my life worth living. I've learned to love certain things about my mind, the way I think, the way I *can* think and do things. Things I used to hate or be disconnected from in myself, I got more curious about and realized more purpose or appeal in. Season six of the HBO series *Sex and the City* featured a character suffering from mental health imbalances. In an episode titled "Boy Interrupted," he stated, "I'm figuring out . . . why certain things seem to be harder for me than everyone else." I related to this a lot. After a young life of hard work and the conditioning to constantly question if I was still working hard enough, my question shifted to why I was working so particularly hard at all, at anything, people included?

Getting fractional results from this grind when I saw so much more for my life as well as not feeling well, excited, or valued as I am, was depressing. Had I been "hustling backward," as they say? I made a point to go to the drawing board as much as possible.

Only a blockhead cudgels his brains on his own, or together with a group, to "find solution" or "evolve an idea" without making any investigation.

—Mao Tse-Tung, No Investigation, No Right to Speak (1930)

Gradually and in some cases instantly, I became enamored with the ideas and results of ease, order, peace, clarity, and harmony. Life with less of (and then without) what I call the "second skin " . . . without an identity revolving around pain and pain management, exhausting reversals of self-sabotage, and the proverbial "chip on the shoulder," which life convinced me was a good thing always to have. Routine heavy lifting, always the consummate underdog, the constant struggle ideology—a belief of always coming from behind and maybe even off to the side! Why was this such a go-to if it wasn't helping me?

Life without this suddenly seemed exactly right, with rich examples growing everywhere I could look. DMX decided to be the protagonist of his own story, darkness, and all. Jennifer Hudson decided finishing seventh place on the third season of *American Idol* wasn't the last of her. Where was the magic I knew I had and always saw in life around me? What had I been erroneously looking for within which made life so anxiously inconsistent and predictably miserable?

21st century wisdom has linked smartphones, smart homes, cars, products, and "working smart" to the non-stoppery of the information age, on-demand era, and knowledge economy. With varying results from all this smartness, how you *feel* is sometimes the only way to know if you're truly "working smart." Unfortunately, with all this new strategy, technology, and exposure to new generations of successful individuals has come a new crop of what some call "ambition hustlers." People who are pounce-ready to take advantage of anyone looking to "level up" in the upgraded matrix. The words "energy" and "manifest" have also been hijacked and commercialized across pop culture and social media, hash tagged to death, and thrown around incessantly by people known as influencers and healers without completely forthright intentions.

Powerful principles like the law of attraction have also been "pimped" by many a lackluster shock-jock book, personality, or paid online course. Likewise, the power of affirmations has been cheapened and considered a flimsy ploy of fake-deep positivity marketing. There's even a wave of thought about positivity as a negative thing, as in people using positive thinking as irresponsible avoidance and essentially being ticking time bombs of under-the-rug-swept issues. (I do see validity in this. The phrase "honesty over positivity" comes to mind.)

Still, sometimes we only know the truth *by* how it feels. Where I used to curse my deep-feeling heart and emotional intelligence, I now embrace its superpower of sensitivity. This made me think, "Is there more I used to hate about myself, which is actually excellent?" Even when I'm not feeling my best, I'm aware of momentum and know what not to do to escalate bad swings. Not knowing exactly what to do has also become satisfying because I know I don't always have to know. I can just go with the next logical step of every moment, every easy or inherently good thought I can arrive at. Without forcing, rushing, or shrinking, my trust-myself muscles can become strong enough to see things to a desired result in almost any situation.

Contrary to the sappy reputation of *feelings* thanks to pop music, reality TV, genre shaming, and Hip-Hop's disapproval—to be able to feel is very important. The negative ego-machismo connotation of "not giving a f***" covers the truth that curiosity is a trait of genius, and care is a demonstration of strength. I'm unafraid to feel numerous things, be curious, and deeply care about what I care about. A lot of excess energy is freed up for those things by knowing (or feeling) what no longer moves me, what I no longer want to feel, what feelings I no longer accept as an identity, what I no longer care about, and no longer have fruitful interest in.

These things are not of my attention, focus, or living reality anymore because they're obsolete, thanks to what is. My choice, my vote, my venue, my life and living—starting with what I want to feel about anything. When I decide and start practicing the decision, even where I stumble, new habits and expectations form to phase out the old. The best part is when the evidence begins to reveal itself.

Many spiritual teachers note mastery in any one thing is a template for mastery to be had in all things. Prolific, prophetic, and deliciously controversial 1970s evangelist Reverend Ike once stated, "The ocean doesn't care if you approach it with a spoon or a bucket." Denzel Washington once replied to an interviewer who asked about people being informed versus misinformed by lies spread by the media, "You practice anything, you'll get good at it." One of my Hip-Hop mentors, Hassan El-Gendi, also known as the hassinian, donned me with the name "EMMA LEE" and once told me, "There's no such thing as conscious rap because everyone is conscious. It's about where their conscience is and what they're more conscious of."

Say word.

CHAPTER 12
IF YOU'VE CRIED ON YOUR BIRTHDAY, MAKE SOME NOISE!

"You can plan a pretty picnic, but you can't predict the weather."
—OutKast, "Ms. Jackson"
:ratio:
"Wherever I sit, son, that is my throne."
—RZA, GZA & Raekwon, "Destruction of a Guard"

I DIDN'T GROW up in a birthday month, birthday week, birthday = big day = big plans, house. I did receive a few cakes, kickbacks, special outings, nice cards, and gifts. Still, I was an only child of divorced parents, one who moved out of my state and the other who traveled a lot, so I was alone or without a noted celebration on many occasions. I've worked on several birthdays and had many which left me feeling so horrible I took a step back and questioned whether this was a feeling I ever needed to feel again. (The answer was no.) Alternatively, I've read childhood trauma can move people to a willing distortion (or negation) of age and time.

Beyond existing on your own anniversary, I've routinely wondered why there's so much "pressure" around making this one day "special." Many often go against their better judgment to do what looks or sounds good instead of what feels good or truly pleases them. Sometimes, it's the plans people force which makes the day go horribly. Other times, it's the people (planned or unplanned) included in the celebration. The forced appraisal of your social circle, friends, and family can be sensitive or a blind spot to begin with.

There's a lot of expectation surrounding this day. Those with routinely eventful or adventurous gatherings often feel the need to somehow "top" themselves each year. It can become more about event management than enjoying oneself and another year of survival, thriving, maintenance, or growth. Often, people throw elaborate meals or parties *for* their social circle, friends, and family, insisting their birthdays are to celebrate *them*. Many wish for a special person more than an event, gift, or edible treat, so this perspective has a lot of validity.

With the influx of reality television, vlogging, and digital content consumption, pop culture has acclimated to ways in which people with production teams, marketing budgets, and verified social media accounts organize the coverage of a birthday. Sitcoms laughably remind us of "Murphy's Law" while offering neat optimism in everything working out by the end of 22 ad-free minutes. Some couples celebrate each other and enjoy creating their own traditions. Some have one partner who celebrates and one who doesn't. Some like to sleep in, some "Wild Out" **The Lox voice*** Some make plans, and some keep plans to themselves.

Some people care deeply about their age; some are proud to have it. Some are just enjoying themselves, some are defined by this number, and some will lie about it for the rest of their lives. Ageism, youth-obsession, and impersonal projections of success have added anxiety to whether people feel they're enough or where they want to be as another milestone eclipses. "Quarantine life" during the COVID-19 pandemic showed many having to contend with low-key and singular celebrations. Many low-key and singular people are always contending with this. (Some aren't contending as they're very much at peace.) Some can pamper themselves, catch a flight, or make or buy something special. Some highlight the day with a particular meal, dessert, harmonious ritual, or simple act. For some, it depends on their mood that year. For others, it's an inherently flawed and losing game of good-on-paper or esteem-on-screen activities unsuitable to their true desires or authentic selves. Some would love company. Some would love to be alone but can't be.

Some *did* grow up in a birthday month, birthday week, birthday = big day = big plans, house. Some grow up in very collective and celebratory environments, as dope in their public adventure as in their siloed privacy. Some live with or communicate with families who ask, "what they want to do?" like clockwork each year. Some are part of families which set a standard of making simple desires magical affairs for the day. Some people only have lackluster birthdays because they give their families lackluster ideas to run with. Some families won't accept lackluster ideas. Some families *are* lackluster ideas. Some would love quiet and solitude but are insisted upon by their families, friends, and social circle to have a communal experience.

Some are bound by tradition to have a cultural or communal experience such as rites-of-passage, healing circles, or coming-of-age ceremonies. Some spend the day cleansing, clearing, and balancing. Some must be among nature; some are in enclosed spaces. Some are on assignment, some are deployed, and some are coming home on this day. Some are on parole or probation, and some are in prison. Some will seduce; some will be seduced. Some will have sex, some will abstain, and some will masturbate. Some will receive affection; some will be touch deprived. Some get closer to a higher power, and some get more in touch with their lower selves.

Some will use the whole day to get ready; some haven't showered or even gotten out of bed. Some will go to a concert and be acclaimed by a featured musician. Some will get shouted out by a DJ or put-on-live. Some will go to a restaurant and get sung to by waitstaff, who may or may not have their hearts in it. In the same restaurant will be those having birthdays but not being sung to because no one was asked. In the same restaurant, it's a staff person's birthday. Some don't want the attention. Some wish they didn't have to ask for it.

Some people cook, some get cooked for, some order food in, some go mostly hungry, and some will go on a spiritual fast for the day. Some go on private dates and enjoy "royal treatment." Some are treated with one of the most novel and calculating of all social inventions: the surprise party. I remember being heartfully wide-eyed while helping plan surprise gifts or parties for others. Seeing organizers be so concerned with this and that to unequivocally meet the goal of wholly intercepting a life to celebrate it and bring someone sheer, memorable happiness. That's a different kind of love! I've surprised a few with handmade or unique offerings for their birthday or a meaningful experience. I do love this feeling. I've been surprised with thoughtful gifts, which made me feel like it was my birthday even though it wasn't. I love this feeling too.

Now into self-care more than ever, the subject of birthdays in contrast to what can or should constitute self-celebration year-round is something I've continued to examine, if not debate with myself. (At the time of this writing, I'm still in a research and development phase.) I've made some exciting private plans, gifted myself something I desired, or engaged in a personal ritual to bring myself order and acknowledge, at the least—gratitude. But until further notice, I've stopped making public plans, posts, or statements, making my birthday digitally visible, or sharing with coworkers and anyone who doesn't already know or remember. I've wiped the slate clean. I've reclaimed my self-celebration to reset it as I see fit for the rest of my life. As this experiment of sorts progresses, I continue my inquiry into the general fascination, celebration, indifference, disappointment, and depression around the singular birthday.

Y'ALL (NOT) GON' MAKE ME LOSE MY MIND

I once saw a Facebook status that moved me about a young woman whose mother and sister made heart-wrenching transitions at young ages. To her, every birthday marked living beyond the physical limits of those nearest and dearest. She made sure to celebrate every birthday because, in her mind, she was defying odds and, in essence, carrying their spirits. I found this quite admirable and loved this for her. For some, birthdays are communal experiences that represent the bonds of a family, making it another day to uplift "one of our own" and, therefore, us too. This is beautiful. Some people have friends who are more family than their families and function as such for year-round celebrations. This is beautiful too.

With few exceptions, I'm a firm believer in "I'm gonna do this differently" energy, especially when something isn't working for me. My "breaking generational curses" board on the relatively anti-social media app Pinterest started with funny posts, memes, book titles, and meditations on how to assess, heal, unlearn, and move forward from family ties, childhood conditioning, and lingering trauma bonds. It evolved to include media about modern parenting, family roles, ancestral perspectives, psychology, therapy, family planning entrepreneurship, childfree topics, relationship ideology, having a vision, and challenging norms. I've dated men who were executors of their family estates and seen how their vision and those before them can powerfully affect so much. This also plays out in every family or group where the chosen culture of a household determines how the individuals within it see, treat, or celebrate themselves, as well as their future friends or partners. This is absolutely reflected in the variations on birthdays.

Internet commentary on the topic of birthdays (and birthday depression) includes:

- "Cus it's my birthday."—@rihanna

- "Surround yourself with people who are more excited about your birthday than you are."
—EnchantingMinds.net
- "What's your birthstone? Mine is rock bottom."—@imskytrash
- "The fake love on your birthday is the worst thing."—Internet Commons
- "Birthdays are sad. Everyone suddenly gives you so much attention for one day and then again ignore you when the day ends."—@StupidThoughts
- "You think you can hurt me? I don't even celebrate my birthday."—@wtftush
- "Most people who hate birthdays don't actually hate their birthday; they just hate having expectations and no one to fulfill them."—@BAECHARA_
- "The way I get excited about my birthday a month in advance only to do nothing and cry on the actual day."
—@mscriesalot
- "Y'all ever get birthday depression?? That ~~shit~~ is real."
—@1kxavier
- "My birthday dinner table is going to be very much empty, and im okay with that."—@Jamir Banks
- "My birthday is coming up, and I'm trying to decide where I should go to celebrate. I've narrowed it down to Kitchen or Basement."—@matchu_chutrain
- "People who treat their birthday as a normal day think they're more mature than everyone."—Internet Commons
- "We are just miserable; leave us alone."—Internet Commons
- "Might have to celebrate my birthday in the strip club on GTA."—@Raenelle Castillo
- "Deep down, I really want my birthday to be nice this year."—@Brilliant

- "I'm going DUMB on my birthday omll."—@Dee Rip Niaa
- "Birthdays will be a huge deal in my household. i don't want my children to EVER refer to the day they were born as just another day. that breaks my heart."—@_slimarella_
- "Girls can never just celebrate their birthday on ONE day. They need the whole month, 6 outfits, 2 dinners, a holiday, and 3 cakes."—Internet Commons
- "I wanna be so happy on my birthday I cry."—@triracial1
- "I've realized with age you have to make your own birthday special if you care about it. Don't let yourself be disappointed by people; take control of your day and plan it how you want it!"—@Chaantellie

---

One of my persistent qualities (which I had to learn to balance for sanity) is the urge to put "special sauce" or "go the extra mile" for whatever I'm engaged in or devoting attention to. Even in silence or humbled invisibility, if I'm involved or leading something, I have to do it with great intention. I normally inquire or act on how any person, place, or thing could be better. Having had some horrible birthdays and the way my heart is set up—I never wanted anyone who cared to have a good one in my presence to feel worthless, a disconnect, or despair. And so came an era where I used to do this thing . . . *Exhale*

I used to wish multiple people a birthday greeting on Facebook every day. I mean, *multiple* people EVERY DAY. I don't feel-a-way because I cared. I'm at peace with having a big heart. It's a blessing to have care. It's powerful to be strong and smart enough to discern where to put it. You also never know all of what someone goes through in their everyday world. After a while, I felt-a-way because it seemed I'd wasted a lot of time or could've used some of it and my energy and attention wiser. Perhaps there were more deserving people and places for my heart. But it's cool. I did it out of love, it's over, and I learned. To this day, I marvel (at how I really made the time) and how I really cared. I was really that girl.

It started innocently enough—one greeting here, one there. Then regularly, and soon, every day, I was on there. This was a mission (to be clear, an *unpaid* mission). Due to always being on the go, I felt it kept me connected to people in my growing network, and it was good to let them know they were appreciated. And not just a regular "Happy Birthday." Oh no, regular just *wouldn't* do! Even if it was brief, it had to be a special set of words for *that* person. So many of my birthdays sucked so badly, often to tears, I was clear that no one deserved this. I knew many might never have a surprise party like the ones I was a part of giving. I wanted everyone to feel uplifted or good about something on theirs. So, before maturing about my energy and using social media differently, I was hopping on there to do this EVERY DAY. I'd also marathon-text people on holidays and major celebrations. Thinking of everything else I was doing in life, I'm exhausted just thinking about it! "We make time" is an accurate phrase about the power of choice because current-me wouldn't believe it if previous-me hadn't lived it myself. *Oh nah!*

I recognize other people's birthdays a lot less now, though I've continued to have the heart and sense of what people should feel worthy of experiencing. As I said, I've also totally reconsidered celebrating my own. At one point, I completely abandoned it and all the carefully orchestrated industry around birthday sociology and commercialism. For me, the reclaiming and cleaning of the slate experiment felt *really* good.

There's undoubtedly an extensive range in the schools of thought on birthdays. The fact of even thinking about it *is* a school of thought since many people don't acknowledge the day or its numbers. The prospect of birthdays being a social construct was brought to my attention by a prolific and profoundly intelligent artist, "The Artist," actually, still known as Prince.

While on the seesaw of my decision to experiment, I heard Prince say to a crowd at his *Rave Unto the Year 2000* concert, "How many birthdays have you had?" The highly engaged audience went into a frenzy shouting all types of remarks and numbers back at him. In typical Prince-fashion, he took a timely pause and responded in an ultracool, punchline-esque, deep bass voice: "One. You've only had one birth-day." Ha! Genius. The fact-ory, though!

My mind was blown, and I cried with laughter. A gong was rung. I could instantly free myself of the whole birthday-ism, which I really didn't care for and truthfully didn't resonate with me as a fruitful positive. I could feel Prince's approach since he was also one of my biggest inspirations. A legendary and prosperously boundless creative connected to millions of intimately appreciative people worldwide. I also couldn't ignore how he never appeared or seemed to carry the burdens or limitations of age. I recalled him speaking about the illusions of time and how we reinforce the illusion to the point of stress and disease. I found a lot of sense there. I also decided I'd like to improve at taking care of myself and celebrating myself throughout the year because only *one* day for me out of 365? I don't feel those numbers. I don't dig that math!

It was a while until I got good at practicing these new thoughts, and I'm still a work in progress with their application. (The phrase "just a masterpiece trying to master peace" comes to mind.) But with the freedom to make any number of my days special now, f*** a birthday! F*** any stress about making this day or its recognition "memorable." I can make my whole life memorable. I can create a moment for myself at any time and share it with people who reflect this energy on any given day. I can recognize my growth cycles and celebrate small victories as they happen. I treasure memories of great birthdays with others, helping throw those surprise parties for people who weren't always celebrated, and making special gifts for those I love. The energy of the singular birth-day which gave us life, which still excites us to be here, *is* what I celebrate, support, and cosign the goodness of. I allow this energy whenever I want, and however I choose. I honor others the same way in my mind and am tuned to more opportunities to show this throughout the year, with zero drain and maybe even more meaning.

Not caring about Facebook-backed measurements of validity has been lovely for me, let me tell you! From this one seemingly trivial decision, I've had so much more time, energy, and awareness for things that make me happy, make me money, make better connections, and add to my peace. It's been a small reinforcement of the life I desire. I can create, unlearn, learn, free up space, work with the energies present, and discern in every area, just like I did with this one idea. All the little things for your peace, harmony, and sanity really *do* add up. For someone who was once willingly suicidal and "connected" to so many people, there are more things than ever in my selective and private life which are a blast for my body, mind, and spirit. In many ways I'm able to have more fun than I did as a child, which is something my inner child and I deserve.

So many things used to keep me in a choke hold about how I saw myself. How I (mis)understood the world and how it (mis)understood me. How to live, think, engage in relationships, and interact with society. How to deal with what I don't like and get what I thought I wanted. I've systematically kissed all these void-reinforcing question marks goodbye—unnecessary noun by unnecessary noun—gone. Banished from my kingdom, joked on by my jesters. Should these choke hold intruders of life find ways to return, they're flagged immediately à la when Chris Rock would yell "SECURITY!" in his 2003 self-directed movie *Head of State*. All you hear after this call is the yoke of a frame or the snatch of a collar!

The term "contrast" in color theory makes something distinguishable to the eye. It's a complementing opposite, an overall difference in visual impact from one color being surrounded by or in proximity to another color. This is often attended to in detail by graphic and visual artists, yet untrained eyes easily pick up on it. Contrast in life—as in negativity, shadow, frustration, conflict, or confusion—does occur in proximity to our best attitudes. I still have contrasting moments, days, or nights. *Oh fasho.*

Many spiritual teachings interpret this happening to habitually give us distinction about where we are in relation to what we want and what's right. After many battles with this so-called distinction, I've learned it's not really the battle I think it is, even if I just need to be angry, etc., for said moment. When something negative lingers in with a burst, sight, word, situation, stranger, or someone I allow close to me—for a moment, mood, day, project, or season—I know my job is really ease . . . to ease my plane to a safe landing to my best ability. No crashes or casualties as a policy, but a well-trained cabin crew, prompt cleanup team, and investigative core ready to roll if it goes there. No forcing, rushing, chasing, shrinking, begging, or overplaying. Just ease, clarity, or harmony into the next logical step, the next best thing, the next best present.

I've given enough of my life to nouns and thoughts which didn't deserve me or my best. They also certainly weren't ready, capable, or responsible for giving me the life I deserved. It's very freeing to know this and let it go. To reopen to a world of positive possibilities, increase, and enjoyment with anything stimulating. To have the infinite power to create my life as I choose to experience it and for the right nouns to meet me in stride of my good thoughts every single day. To become an effortlessly equipped positive attractor, a victory vacuum, success magnet, accomplishment absorber, peace pipe, a happy person (who's not terrified about being happy) and *still* enjoy honesty, sarcasm, and all types of humor if not even more. The phrase "When a woman leaves anything for herself, she won't be back" is a bold statement on what we must sometimes bravely leave behind. And so, it is.

To the misery, drain, dysfunction, disorder, damages, and disappointments of life, I gave my last f***. I just decided. Y'all (not) gon' make me lose my mind. UP IN HERE! Up in here.

ARTS, CULTURE & ACTIVISM

CHAPTER 13
WILL THE REAL AFENI SHAKUR PLEASE STAND UP?

TUPAC AMARU SHAKUR, also known as 2Pac, is ranked 164th in the "top 500 poets" on AllPoetry.com, respectfully ahead of international greats such as Du Fu, Hafez Shīrāzī, and Anaïs Nin. Among his top poems on the website is "When Ur Hero Falls," reflecting on his mother, Afeni Shakur, and her trials with drug abuse. Afeni was known by many to live dedicated to better vision, community uplift, and strength. As an organizer and speaker for the historically groundbreaking Black Panther Party for Self-Defense in the 1960s and '70s, she contributed pivotal leadership to keep revolutionary progress alive. Political targeting by the FBI government agency and its covert and illegal project known as COINTELPRO led to a mass indictment of her New York chapter. They were violently raided in their homes early in the morning, imprisoned, and dubbed the "Panther 21" or "New York 21." With her track record of capability, she was elected by the group to utilize their bail money and, upon release, stabilize the organization, arrange legal defense, and make public statements. She was also one month pregnant with her son, who would further immortalize her in art and become a global Hip-Hop icon.

On the Poetry Foundation website, Tupac Shakur is described

as an American rapper, actor, and one of the bestselling music artists of all time, with over 75 million records sold. Their brief description ends with:

His unpublished family photographs, intimate stories, handwritten song lyrics, contracts, scripts, poetry, and other papers were published posthumously in Tupac Shakur Legacy (2006), an "interactive biography" by Jamal Joseph.

This same Jamal Joseph, also of the Panther 21, former political prisoner, brother to Afeni, and godfather to Tupac, emerged from prison with two degrees, creative production experience, and more fire for real change. He would eventually become a professor and chair of the film department at Columbia University, director and screenwriter of the *Chapter & Verse* feature film, an Oscar- and Grammy-nominated songwriter, Def Poetry Jam-featured artist, and author of *Panther Baby: A Life of Rebellion & Reinvention*, among many more accomplishments. He would also unofficially become my mentor after I joined his youth arts and leadership program, Impact Repertory Theatre. I approached him a year or two into my thirteen-year membership with a small group of young people, a document of points, and a speech about how the organization could be better. I believe it was this instance in which he first took note of my spirit. We began having one-on-one talks for years to come.

I found myself drawn to the interconnected history I was immersed in. As the "Hip-Hop police" became a more known issue, I got deeper into researching the intersections of the US prison system, pop culture, and music artists. I'd seen the very eye-opening cover image of *The FBI War on Tupac Shakur and Black Leaders* by John Potash (foreword by Pam Africa with Mumia Abu-Jamal, afterword by Fred Hampton Jr.). I'd also gotten my hands on a copy of the actual T.H.U.G. L.I.F.E. code of ethics for the streets, which Tupac once envisioned while in prison, structured on paper, and eventually rapped about. Fittingly or ironically, the rebellious and unapologetic "Thug Life" persona became exponentially more famous than this written code of honor and better business protocols. It dealt with creating safer, more unified, and more humane environments in a network of enterprising urban neighborhoods.

I discussed my findings with Jamal, and he told me of some of the talks—rather, debates, Tupac would have with him about his T.H.U.G. L.I.F.E. code and the approach of his larger vision. He felt passionate that uniting the streets, pushing the persona, creating successful leadership, and having the ability to make more effective community investments from the success of his entertainment ventures was a winning formula. However, Jamal had his doubts, questioning the approach constructively and critically. Apparently, it was an ongoing hot topic of their one-on-ones. Knowing Jamal for being strong-minded, strategic, and wise, as well as his experience with social politics and government surveillance, I could clearly envision and almost feel them having such debates. It was also surreal knowing I sat with Jamal discussing life, art, business, and politics just as Tupac did as a spirited young man with ideas. I appreciated these car rides, lunches, and dinners with him very much, wishing we could've had a few all together.

This relative closeness added fire to my curiosity and self-image as a young person with visionary thoughts about the world. It also made my inner Tupac "fandom" blossom to new heights. If you've ever seen the "conspiracy Charlie" meme from the *It's Always Sunny in Philadelphia* series, a man intensely describing a situation by pointing to a bulletin board filled with documents, thumbtacks, cross-connected strings, and inked-up photos—it's a close depiction of my level of energy for why I loved Tupac Shakur. Fully present, intelligent, artistic, poetic, and, to me, defined the Dead Prez's definitive line, "It's bigger than Hip-Hop." I felt a connection also through the spiritual and interdimensional nature of art. Like many, I was inspired by his vibrant energy, rich vocal tone, character, expression of manhood, sensitivity, humor, and sense of integrity. Reciting

2Pac songs was always about coming from your gut, saying it with your chest, or sincerely from your heart.

While public focus was on his arrest record, antics, and controversies, I focused on what he offered in interviews, music concepts, and poetry. I'd heard him speak numerous times about his passion for great writing via deep, gripping, and emotional storytelling. This spoke volumes to me as I was fascinated by deeply moving art and had carried a composition notebook for creative writing since the third grade. This also reminded me of my mother, who rarely spoke about my art or creative talents yet apparently named me after famed British writer Emily Brontë after reading her deeply passionate novel *Wuthering Heights*. Tupac seemed to have a very open channel for creating human experience art and feeling all that comes with such a gift, as well as the courage of conviction, a very resonant voice, ability to project and articulate clear perspectives. I could relate immensely and looked to him as a generational model for navigating light *and* darkness. I would soon realize that everything I was admiring, respecting, and learning from him was his mother, Afeni Shakur.

A box of books sat conspicuously in the middle of our rehearsal space one Saturday morning at Impact Repertory Theatre. Word spread weeks earlier about senior members and directors going to Atlanta, Georgia to establish a like-spirited youth program with Afeni Shakur. It would be named Amaru Kids and accompany the opening of a six-acre Tupac Amaru Shakur Center for the Arts in Stone Mountain. Not yet senior enough, I stayed behind; however, I was thankful to be present when a shipment of *The Rose that Grew from Concrete* poetry books by Tupac Shakur arrived. I snatched two, keeping one at home and one always with me. In the acknowledgments section was a list of youths

Tupac wanted to highlight. Though we'd never met, the name "Emily" was there, and I felt closer than ever.

In this book were several poems inspired by his mother other than "When Ur Hero Falls." It pointed my spiritual compass more to Afeni, and I became increasingly curious about her. The traveling core returned from Atlanta with glowing things to say about her, her fully present energy, unashamed honesty, and radiating love. Sometime later, she would visit our rehearsal space in Harlem, meet the rest of us, and watch us perform.

When she came through the door, she was happily beaming in my eyes, though quiet and respectfully not wanting to interrupt our workshops. She greeted those she knew, waved, and took the seat Jamal set up for her. During the show, she sat attentively like a proud mother, riding each emotional wave, clapping for extended seconds after almost every number, graciously exclaiming "wow!" and "my God." When we finished, she jumped up for her definitive applause and insisted on thanking us for the performance. She hugged several of us, saying, "The children, MY GOD, the chillldrennn are *so* goodt!" To my delight, including me.

The hugs she was giving were fast, so when I saw her approaching, I told myself to really soak it in. She motioned my body swiftly into hers with great intention. She was soft yet firm and electric. I felt the feeling of true motherly love in those few seconds. As she pulled away, she stopped moving elsewhere and looked at me. She said, "And you. YOU! You were dancinggg and RAPPING, honey! Oh! I loved it, and I love you. Don't stop. *Please* keep-doing-THAT." I stood there in her alpha feminine gaze with my heart wide open, speechless. She pulled me back in for one more hug, this time with a squeeze. I closed my eyes and held her tight, receiving the loving energy of her pure belief in me and joy in our existence. I didn't want to let go.

She stayed for a bit to talk to us from her heart and confirmed all the positive things I'd heard about her. She was frank about how she'd done drugs before, that they ruined a lot of good in her life, and how thankful she was to be redeemed from dark places. She was so clear and forthright about it that it made me question all shame I was holding onto. She spoke highly of our talents as young artists and the importance of what we were doing, with our original material aimed at real-world storytelling and positive change. She encouraged us to enjoy ourselves but not take lightly how powerful we were. She praised Jamal and wished she could bring all of us down to Atlanta to meet with the youth she worked with, hoping it would be possible one day.

Years later, I was requested by another founder of Impact, a community, film, theater, and production legend named Voza Rivers, to attend the Tupac-inspired Broadway show *Holler If Ya Hear Me* and report back on my experience. Honored by this request, I took it very seriously. I employed my best attention and noted a comprehensive rundown of everything I saw, heard, and felt. I'd also auditioned for this show months earlier and, sadly, was not selected, so I had high hopes the talent would be exceptional. The cast was incredibly talented, committed, and executed the script to their best ability. I was not as fond of how the inspired-by music resonated, how the decidedly "nonbiographical story" unfolded, and the authenticity of the depiction of street energy. I was of the posture that since it was Tupac, it had to be of a certain realness, rawness, feeling, and artistic quality. I was thanked for my review and told it was very thorough and helpful.

Days later, I saw media headlines about Afeni having been in town to see the show. A couple of nights difference, and I would've met her again. *Damn!* I just wanted one more hug. My heart almost melted when I saw a picture of her backstage with a huge smile. She was sincerely happy the show existed. I shifted to think about how it would feel to be Afeni Shakur. To grow up as she did, go through all she went through with the Panthers, give birth to Tupac, raise him (and his sister Sekyiwa) as a single mother, watch him battle controversy and become an abundant success, receive the bitter news of his murder, receive no real justice on his prolonged case, having to move on with your life and the organizing of his estate, all while grieving. To be at the opening of a Broadway show in his honor had to be an encouraging and joyful reflection of how resonant and ongoingly appreciated they both were. I realized in the gleam of her backstage smile that my critique didn't matter so much. It was a reflective miracle the show existed at all. I was happy to see her happy.

I was right in my instinct of knowing one more hug from Afeni escaped me. We were reunited again only after she made transition, at her New York homegoing service in Brooklyn at the House of the Lord Church. Jamal hosted the proceedings. I'd been away and not doing many shows with Impact, so it was my first time being with the group and program in a while. I arrived early in case help was needed. I walked through the sanctuary and into the main space where video playback was being tested. I sat and watched, then saw Jamal break a momentary stride of pacing to greet me. He lit up a bit when he saw me, which was pleasing. He did his signature washcloth wipe off his forehead, embraced me, and asked how I was doing. Then he put his arm on my shoulders and walked me through the space, engaging in conversation.

Many alumni members of Impact know what it is when Jamal is in what we call "director mode." On the one hand, I've learned a great deal from it in preparation for the larger entertainment world and the benefit of my own projects. On the other hand, routinely, if I'm slipping midtask or coaxing myself through conflict, I'll hear a loving (or deada**) memory of him yelling the likes of "use it all!" or "get the shot!" or saying sternly with Malcolm X hands punctuated by villainous laughter and a sharp mental pivot, "we needed that like yesterday." In director mode, no debates, fidgeting, or complicated ideas are allowed, and there's minimal time to "get it right."

This scenario was unique because it wasn't a scene, rehearsal, booking, or public event to direct. It was a homegoing, a funeral service for his loving big sister who was a legend in her own right, a pillar of her community, and the mother of a superstar who was also his godson. Yet, it was *still* an event, *still* a program, and thus, *still* a show to be directed. Thus, he was rightfully still in director mode. Much softer in the role, but definitely still there. I felt the vibe almost immediately as he broke down the situation in our walk-and-talk.

"You've seen the program?"

Intentionally stepping lightly, I replied with an aloof, "Yes, looks lovely."

As I'd done many times since shifting forward from Impact and only visiting a rehearsal or supporting a show from the audience, I'd pre-pep-talked myself about not performing under any circumstances. (Results varied.) This was a known scenario with alumni, especially those who'd had principal roles in the repertoire. To be fair, sometimes being spontaneously asked to perform was great. A beautiful welcome, an excellent option for exercise, and nice knowing you'd always be wanted and seen as valuable. Alternatively, it was often past the timing of your willingness to be used. Ratio: you didn't come to perform, you wish you weren't needed, or upon being noticed you just wanted to disappear quietly. From then on, you knew, especially if a special guest was due or Jamal was in director mode, that you could and would be pulled in. Have a solid defense ready or don't show up at all, just pick a different day to come around.

I was feeling pretty strong in my defense that day until he handed me some papers, his version of the program. It was packed with added notes, cues for the audio and visual engineer, and more. He pointed me to a section that featured a stocky couple of paragraphs. I read some lines; it was bold and very passionate.

"What's this, Unc?"

"This is a transcript of Afeni's closing arguments in court during the Panther 21 trial."

"Wowwww" I exclaimed, reading back over the words. In my hands were the final words of the eight-month trial, after which the Black Panther Party and New York chapter were never the same. Exposures of false claims by police, infiltrating members, lack of evidence to support testimonies of fraud, and Afeni's impactful representation in the landmark legal defense led to the acquittal of all 156 counts of conspiracy and violent attacks. *156!* What became a national news story, a cross-cultural media storm, and pivotal disruption to the Black Power movement ceased its story with a judge reading aloud *"not guilty"* 156 times.

Throughout the trial, several photographs were taken outside the courthouse, including those by Roz Payne. Some of these photos have since become available online through the Payne Sixties Archive, published by the Center for Digital Research in the Humanities, University of Nebraska-Lincoln. The accompanying description shares rarely expressed details:

Ultimately, 13 Panthers, including Afeni Shakur and Dhoruba Bin Wahad, stood trial in a case that became a cause celebre among black militants and the broader New Left. For ten months prior to the trial, the jailed Panthers were held in solitary confinement with lights on 24 hours a day and denied reading materials, recreational facilities, and family visitation. Several were not given mattresses, and the two female Panthers were limited to four sheets of toilet paper per day. It was also reported that prison officials harassed Panther attorneys. Famed composer, Leonard Bernstein, helped raise bail money for the "New York 21." During the court proceedings, District Attorney Hogan referred to the Panthers as a "terrorist organization," read from Mao Zedong's "Little Red Book," showed jurors the film "The Battle of Algiers" and attempted to introduce political posters from one of the defendant's apartment into evidence. In what was, at the time, the longest and most costly trial in New York state history, the Panthers were acquitted of all 156 charges on May 12, 1971. In the wake of the failed prosecution, local law enforcement and the FBI continued to target the New York Black Panther Party.

Afeni was eight months pregnant with Tupac by this time. It was setting on me that a woman just like me (but eight months pregnant!) was in such an extraordinary position, with her comrades' lives and a whole history and future on the line, to will to victory.

Tech rehearsals for the homegoing service continued in the church, and another video was projected on the large screen to the left of the pulpit. It was an old "home movie" or video diary of a women's retreat Afeni used to organize. It showed several women enjoying peace, construction, joy, and self-care in nature and talking about community improvement. Many noted her anonymous work supporting young women, formerly incarcerated women, single mothers, and domestic violence survivors over the years. Whether it was the retreat, food drives, health and beauty supply drives, housing, education, or more, Afeni did what she could for countless others. I was full—of how much more amazing she was to me.

Jamal reapproached, gently and with hugs, but about his business and to lower a boom, of course.

"I want you to read her words from the transcript as part of the program."

"Say what?!" As my face twisted, he advanced immediately.

"Em, I know you can do this. You know I wouldn't ask just anybody to do this. The thing is, there's not much time, and I need a decision, like, now. So, will you do it?"

Whew, chile!

My head was still tilted to the side. When I woke up that morning, I took a stretch, drank water, washed up, and picked out a lovely blouse. I thought about getting to the train on time and ensuring I knew where the church was. I questioned stopping at the bodega for a little snack and fruit juice for the long train ride. I went over my game plan to stay lowkey, not perform, support my family, and dip. I wondered what pictures of her they'd display, what stories would be told, and if I should pack extra tissues. What I didn't think about was formally reciting Afeni Shakur's history making words and doing this on a live film feed in front of people, many of whom were there when said history was made! I couldn't have imagined being asked this. This was huge and different, reading her actual words at her actual homegoing in front of her actual community. I *definitely* didn't have an I-won't-be-in-the-show defense for this kind of ask. If the situation was a chess game, I was in check with the very real threat of checkmate soon behind. An emotional fourth-and-inches on the field! I took a breath, wrapped my head around doing it, and simply accepted.

He said we had enough time for a couple of cold reads; then, he'd have to tend to the rest of the service. He gave me a few minutes to reread it then returned, sitting in the front pew directly opposite to watch me recite it. The first read projected well but was stiff. My nerves clearly weighed it down, my cadence was awkwardly searching for a rhythm I couldn't quite find, and I stumbled on a line. He stopped me, and I exhaled, apologizing.

I began feeling overwhelmed. I absolutely had to come through on this. First, he told me to relax, reassuring me I was right for the job. Then he shifted gears and asked me what I remembered most about her. Once warm from a memory, he told me to look up something on my phone. It was a recorded speech she gave at the Dream Reborn Conference in Memphis in 2008. He made sure it was the one, then walked away and left me to listen alone.

Afeni's speech touched on everything from her hindsight of the Panthers to the spiritual uplift in her life, the importance of organic farming, land ownership, entrepreneurship, and executive training of minorities. Her larger vision was infused in everything. She poignantly distinguished when she spoke the words "my community" that she was talking about the world and being part of a global community, that "her people were everywhere." I loved this. It resonated with my experience of feeling like a cultural bridge and connector of African, indigenous, and diaspora peoples. She was once again opening my mind and heart and emboldening my soul to better action. She was "not impressed until she saw the work!"

When I thought I'd gotten all the highs she had to give, she suddenly emphasized:

And whereee are the women? WHERE ARE THE WOMEN? Don't play with ME! Where are your STories? You all, FIND those stories and TELL EM! They don't HAVE to be cute! If you don't tell them, we will be E-RASED! ALLA-READY, these children don't know that we were there. Allll-ready. They don't know, that had it not been for us, there wouldn'ta BEEN no Panther Party!

The combination of her vocal tone, projection, preacherlike cadence, verbal emphasis, truth-telling, queen-mother-warrior energy, and her life flashing before my eyes induced a flood of tears down my face. I really missed her. I really wished she were here. I wished I'd had more time with her. Yet, she also spoke directly to me and my life through this speech. All I was juggling, all I was fighting for, all I was settling for, all I could no longer compromise. In my hands were her powerful words, power used to free numerous bodies, minds, and dreams. These were the words of a giant. Jamal saw me crying and embraced me. We took a few seconds for these tears then exhaled.

"All right. Now let me hear it again."

Touché, I thought. Masterful! Director mode energy had never left the chat. I energetically agreed this was not the time to drown in the sensitivity of grief. I straightened my posture, sniffled up snot, wiped my tears, and took my mark. I hit the second read with a distinctly different fire, in a pocket this time, riding the wave of my interpretation of her cadence in the Dream Reborn speech. I also did my best to imagine myself as her, really giving the speech in court while pregnant. I finished, and Jamal sat back on the pew, legs crossed, Malcolm X-thinking man's hands, and eyes closed. He stayed like this, silent for more seconds, slightly rocking. I started to worry it wasn't good enough. I knew I could do better. Suddenly, he exhaled, opened his eyes, uncrossed his limbs, and slapped his thighs.

"You got it. I'll introduce you."

He walked away. I finished wiping my tears. *Whew, chile!* Two cold reads, and I was in the program with a huge job. It would also be filmed, livestreamed, press was gathering, and actual Black Panthers would be in the audience. But no pressure!

An hour or so later, after I gave the reading and walked offstage, Jamal retook the podium. He joked how I sounded just like Afeni during a lot of it, and several elders cosigned with laughter, reminisce, and commentary. I did feel like I'd tapped into her spirit on delivery. I did feel I channeled her, or she channeled me, for a precious moment. This moment and the words of both speeches never left me. I went on to write my first song as a solo artist, titled "My Life," and penned these opening lyrics:

Silent decisions, 2Pac-isms, a rapping general
Facing ciphers like Afeni facing federal
My heavy eyelids adorned with emeralds and petals rose
Playground crack vials, drug schedules, and social codes

I knew firmly from then on everything I loved about Tupac was really her. I appreciated them both for their respective journeys and activities. To me, they live on as two distinct people of two different generations and two sets of unique accomplishments. I'm clearly expressing Tupac energy when I'm reciting "Thugz Mansion," "Ambitionz Az a Ridah," "Brenda's Got a Baby," "Changes," "Letter to My Unborn Child," "Until the End of Time," "Part-Time Mutha," "So Many Tears," "Me and My Girlfriend," "Do for Love," or "Keep Ya Head Up." Yet, even in these songs, one can easily recognize the root of Afeni's energy. As Muhammad Ali once said, "me, we." The apple truly never fell far from the tree.

The effects of her love, honesty, vision, soul, and power continue to inspire me as an artist, woman, global citizen, and spirit. When I second-guess or feel coerced to be less than myself, I often think of women like Afeni, Nina Simone, Josephine Baker, Lena Horne, Eartha Kitt, Miriam Makeba, Hazel Scott, and Winnie Mandela—who remained themselves, embraced their true identities, stood against odds, and influenced generations beyond them. They found the courage to create life in the face of unthinkable pressures, and so can I. They were hard, soft, bright, dark, and seemed to permit themselves to be at every step of reinvention. They accepted their gifts and created new molds of personhood. They commanded their full instruments from wherever they were. And so, must I. And so, it is.

CHAPTER 14
VALENTIN, A HIP-HOPERA & SELF-CARE STORY

"STOP SINGING."

"Say what? I mean, excuse me?"

"You must not sing."

"Umm . . . I thought—"

"There is damage on your vocal cords. I can hear. This can fix, but you must stop singing for *at least* three months before we work together. Completely rested the voice, this is how must be. When ready, we start then. Remember, please. Do-not-sing. OK? Bye-byeee."

With his decisive dial tone resembling the flat line of a heart monitor in my ear, so went my first conversation with world-renowned classical vocalist, producer, and educator, Valentin Peytchinov.

Stop singing?

As a robust and highly accomplished bass from Bulgaria, he was used to filling rooms with his vibrant energy, fully present voice, heavy accent, and big, warm, actively purposed body.

Stop singing?

A student of highly reputable teachers, he was also a multiple award-winner in vocal excellence, a trained pianist, composer, and masterclass instructor across numerous countries. Being the first singer admitted to The Juilliard School of Music from the then referred to as "Eastern Bloc Countries," he was given a full scholarship on credentials and recommendations alone. He went on to grace the likes of Carnegie Hall, Lincoln Center, numerous opera houses, conservatories, international festivals, public radio, and chair various arts programs. In solidifying his own teaching techniques, he began training artists and speakers of all types, founded a studio school, produced his own shows, and gave students opportunities to perform.

In the art world and in my eyes, he was a "made man." And for me to train with him, he wanted me to . . . *stop singing*?

STOP SINGING.

In angst, I wondered, or rather, worried. My inner monologue spiraled like a gymnastics ribbon into a vent of confusion and frustration.

"Could this simple instruction be oversimplistic? Don't before you do, stop to start, break up to make up—What are we really doing here? *Pointing fingers and clapping hands* I came here full, well, and ready to sing! What can he hear? How can he be so sure? A little tired, sure, but *damaged*? I can't have damaged vocal cords! I just *can't*. You mean all this time, all this practice, I've been *damaging* myself? And how do you fix singing-damage with singing? How am I supposed to not sing for three months? Not even a hum? Rapping too? What about my music? Is this a riddle? Is this a test?!"

This was *not* a test. This was me avoiding and complicating the truth of his perceptive and instant appraisal. The words echoed and bounced in my mind like a handball court of sharply recoiling thoughts. In my honest and deepest thinking, I could feel the vocal damage he was referring to in my upper register. My high notes had become rougher and streakier from their smooth and soft normal. I'd assumed it was usual fatigue, normal wear-and-tear, but I was also calcified in the rhythms of high pain tolerance and convenient bodily ignorance.

Since I was no longer in groups, choirs, or sessions with

rapping friends, I'd been practicing voice by myself for months, hours a day, multiple times a week. The sudden shift of no structured rehearsals, packed show schedule, or routine release of performing left me with a multidimensional anxiety I didn't know how to healthily address. I was mostly oblivious to my withdrawals from the stage. I hadn't been exposed to discussions about stage withdrawal and its physical and mental health effects in formerly active performers.

As I craved more active learning, I also didn't know what I didn't know. I took my best guesses from curiosity, then reached and pulled from what I knew. I strung my makeshift lessons along between songwriting, envisioning, and visual mapping of my solo career. Meetings came and went with people connected to various parts of the music industry, mainstream, and independent underground. I performed at several open mics, flirted with a few professional offers, and wrote some songs for people, but nothing was happening definitively, positively. I saw a need to get my creative fundamentals in order and identified goals within this goal. While resources organized, the one thing holding my art together (or so I thought) was I kept practicing.

I remembered my previous Impact group members, Jonathan Hudson and Jarrett Parker, who respectively became music directors and vocal educators, telling me my voice was "deceptive" because it could do more than they thought it could do. I believed in their belief I had more to offer as a vocalist. This justified years of being moved around the vocal sections of choirs and times when I wasn't content in only letting the established "sangers" (not singers) "sang" (not sing). Also, after a bleak period of "dumbing down" my raps, my Hip-Hop lyricism was fully circling to regain its more intense, resonant, poetic, and flowful traits as an instrument. I was eager to perform in a way I hadn't yet vocally, but I felt a disconnect in my soul. It became almost psychological—sort of a psych-out, like I had a song in my heart but didn't know how to sing it.

Encouraging me to open into my voice, Jonathan and Jarrett

pushed my boundaries with gospel, musical theater, and classical selections I never considered singing, like "And I Am Telling You," "O Mio Babbino Caro," and LaShun Pace cuts. As I sang them, I was wide-eyed at hearing what I could do, yet my time with their formal instruction was eventually over. I took this spirit into a self-medicating creative phase. I filled my days after work with activities in any direction which felt productive. I had no idea exactly where my voice was regarding formal classifications. I didn't have any musical instruments and could barely play them if I did. I didn't have a comprehensive plan or vision for my voice, nor did I think I needed to stop to make one. My only plan was to keep going.

I did whichever exercises were most familiar, convenient, or at my disposal. I'd squeeze out the last bit of my active energy for the day, often to the limit of exhaustion. So, Valentin's call to "stop singing" gave way to reason. It wasn't a crazy leap to think unsupervised I'd pushed myself too hard, misdirected techniques, was consistently singing out of my range, or followed routines not ideal for my voice.

I'd foolishly feared that my talent's ability would somehow slip away without all this pushing, without my normalized overworking. It wasn't just about building the vocal strength and endurance I thought I needed. According to my gut, it was also time to learn more about what my voice could really do on its own and what it really *wanted* to do. I needed to experiment, listen, and feel out new places, different scales, moods, colors, and approaches. I underestimated my need to prioritize health amidst this and the direction which would come from a whole new understanding of the voice itself.

I soon found myself excitedly working with a young music producer out of Queens, New York. As a former personal trainer who kept himself in top shape, he had an affinity for self-care, correct technique, and honing crafts. Working mostly on Hip-Hop, R&B, and dance tracks, he became a thoughtfully willing partner in me taking firmer steps in the music industry. We ventured into making an album from my growing vault of reference songs and a few of his original productions. However, with no team, no strategic plan, and a lot to figure out regarding budget and marketing, things mostly stayed in experimental stages in the studio.

Remaining productive with the ability to record, experiment hands-on in his musical range, cowriting, workout sessions, and the influence of his "straight edge" (no drugs, alcohol, or tobacco) lifestyle, it was a good place for me to be. I hadn't been in routine proximity with a young artist of his level of discipline in a long time. It often felt more constructive to take the two-hour trip to Queens to listen, write, talk, and watch him practice piano or work on mixes, than to stay home. My interest in audio engineering and producing sounds also deepened from his passenger seat.

He also reintroduced me to pro wrestling in our leisure time after many years of not watching. This prompted conversations about performing, audience engagement, entertainment psychology, and immersive art in larger contexts. We shared and encouraged our individual industry adventures, and he advised me against "wasting time" with certain people, places, and things. He sincerely believed in me and my talents, and I never forgot how this belief was lovingly expressed. I told him about conflicts I felt regarding my vocal progress, and he suggested I consider a consultation with Valentin. From this lead, I made the call.

"Stop singing. I tell him too; you must."

Not gonna lie, I was f***** up behind this instruction for a while. Discouraged mostly because I'd worked so hard for someone (who knew better) to tell me I'd been working against myself. I would also need to raise the money to pay for the intensive classes. My producer understood my angst but reassured me this was coming from a master teacher who'd changed his vocal life for the better. I knew there were plenty of good reasons to trust this scenario and do something different to get a different result. I needed a direction, and this was a direction. If I allowed it, this was having a vision for myself, this was a personal investment opportunity, and it felt right. Finally, after throwing dart after dart and feeling like a hamster on a wheel, I was ready to get off and really go somewhere in construction. So, I followed the order.

Vocal rest did me very well, and the three months seemed to melt by. We began training in classical and bel canto operatic techniques, the anatomy of voice, and vocal dynamics. Too nervous to start in the group classes, I insisted our first session be one-on-one. My mind was blown as we discussed fundamentally how to sing and how the body supports (or hinders) this process in various ways. Then with his encouragement, I joined the classes of two to five other students at a time and received the immense benefit of learning by listening. With few exceptions, everyone was an operatic voice singing standard classics, yet every voice was utterly unique.

While I'd sung traditional hymns in a cappella choir, arias in private sessions, and various styles in contemporary gospel choirs, this method, precision, and intensity of vocalizing was different. This was a world-class vocalist and renowned master teacher in front of me with his educated ears and hands on the keys saying, "let's go." Also, standing there by his piano, my body was positioned in a way it hadn't been before and was relearning how to use itself to support the voice I was generating in this new way. I ached from this full body singing engagement in pronounced posture, but things began to click and anchor inside.

It was work, and the work was working. I was singing like never before. I also felt more confident about my ability to do the exercises in front of veteran students. Valentin pinpointed my accurate range almost immediately and quickly stopped me from pushing past its fluctuations on any given day. The damage on my upper register was also suddenly nowhere to be found! I was singing from a new place entirely. I careened through notes in class I used to struggle with alone in my room. I now understood and could feel the difference between healthy fatigue and unhealthy strain.

He was strict about correctness but very encouraging about my progress. Along with his clear piano playing was his stern, amplified, and colorful voice providing commentary and jokes throughout the class. I still often practice with my old recordings of our sessions for the lifetime of valuable lessons, no-nonsense instruction, and his unforgettable warmth.

"I love smart people like you. It's going so fast. Do you feel how fast you're learning?"

"No, no, no. The top is flat. Again!"

"You hear that? Like a bell, the voice. Perrrfect! Every tone in the range should be like this."

Valentin believed "there is only one voice" and trained in a very successful method of his own universal mastery. To him, it didn't matter about the singing style or the type of singer. It was about the source and support of the voice itself. In following this principle, he treated me with just as much care, support, and discipline as his veteran students, though I so clearly and awkwardly felt cut from a different cloth.

While I was the only "rapper," no rapping was done in class, though this wasn't intentional. He expressed absolute interest in working on things I'd perform on stage, which was exciting and hilarious to think about. I was intrigued by applying these techniques to transitions of rapping and singing within the same song. Much of my music involved this, and I wondered how it would come together in the Hip-Hop setting where my rapping voice carried intensity quite differently from my much softer singing voice. I also envisioned more vocal possibilities for the

Y'ALL (NOT) GON' MAKE ME LOSE MY MIND

future when performing longer sets and creating full concerts. We discussed incorporating this thinking in our next level of intensives, but, alas, life, his tours, schedules, and eventually, the COVID-19 pandemic put things on pause.

Though completely unique, Valentin was no different from several professional elders in my life who (to my honor or embarrassment) loved to use me as an example to make various positive points to others. As I grew to enjoy singing more freely, he grew to enjoy stopping suddenly at the piano and turning to the rest of class with a coy look on his face to say:

"You know she's a rapper?"

"She's a RAPPER??? No!!!"

Black-girl-blushing! The whole room would be shocked, and I'd just laugh and nod. I was honored he was filled with so much pride at my artistic camouflage and the evident success of our training. I was honored to *have* such an artistic camouflage (apparently) and was beyond grateful for our victory. It wasn't just about the singing. He'd put years, maybe even decades, of life back on my voice. I now also had confidence in my own instrument and a deeper understanding of *how* it could do whatever it wanted, whether singing, rapping, or even just speaking. I knew better, and I was doing better.

One of my smallest group sessions included an affluent Russian vocalist who flew into New York just for the lesson with her young daughter at her side. After practicing in rotation for two hours, Valentin did the "breaking news: she raps!"—to which, on cue, the lady was shocked. She exclaimed to her daughter about the news, to which the little girl looked confused, then smiled a big smile and quickly hid her face.

"She sounds very good, right? Wow!"

"Thank you so much. Valentin is the man."

We finished up, and I was told the little girl, who'd barely said a word wanted to share something with me. As it turned out, she loved to rap! They played me a video of her back home in Russia, perhaps in their backyard, spitting some "yo, yo, yo's!" and doing some very B-girl things. I was as shocked as they were about me.

"Woooowwww. Look at youuu, Hip-Hop!"

She blushed and hid her face again, then brought it back out, nodding. Ain't that something!

Further inspired by the knowledge I was among the *truly* cultured (ha!), I kicked a rap freestyle. I started flowing, simply recapping the day's events, encouraging our love of art, and finished by incorporating the girl's name. She was so lit up with happy energy she seemed not to be sure she should be so happy, especially in front of her strictly classical mother. But it was all love. They were all wowed, all smiles, and very appreciative. I felt a very heartwarming sense of connection. I also remembered what it was like being a small child like her, roaming around with my mother, doing whatever she was doing, and being in grown-up places which had nothing to do with me. To make this girl feel good and seen in a way that validated something in her felt good.

On their way to a plane ride home, I felt extra thankful to be geographically close to Valentin as others were booking flights just to see him. Also, at the fact my art, Hip-Hop, and rap roots were never devalued in this space. In fact, they were encouraged after the affirmation of my voice for its own sake. Where such a mutual artistic appreciation can lead is limitless. I value moments like this so much.

As they left, I told the young girl, "Keep rapping." She replied gleefully, "Keep singing!"

The body, voice, mind, and more make up our instrument. You must care for it as the musician must care for their strings, horn, guitar, or drum (machines). It's the literal vehicle of our living experience. It requires fuel and upkeep, listening, freedom, and fine-tuning. The thoughts and training within will always surface, so make sure these are as constructive as possible.

Had I not been open to investing in myself, learning something new, vocal reprogramming, and being completely different from other students yet learning from them, my life would be very different. Had I not been open to an entirely different culture of people, art, and professionalism, I wouldn't be the artist I am with the ability to enjoy global experiences. Above all, following the initial direction of three months of vocal rest was vital to my growth, health, and ability, let alone the success of the training itself. Never mind not being able to sing effectively without this. I may not have a voice right now without this!

Training with Valentin allowed me to allow myself an openness to what this world and life positively offer. Betterment, culture, greater vision, valuable understanding, enjoyment, health, confidence, connection, and genuine love—for starters. Had I not focused on the fruits of this challenge, I would've been racked with anxiety and insecurity, and it wouldn't have been nearly as much fun. Freedom of choice and freedom of attitude continue to be some of our best tools for transformation and meaningful success.

And as it turns out, when it comes to world-class experiences, creativity is a passport, and Hip-Hop is a universal stamp.

CHAPTER 15
REBEL SOUL BURNOUT & MEETING THEE KATHLEEN CLEAVER

I'D BEEN A PERFORMER, creator, and staff at the Harlem, New York City-based Impact Repertory Theatre for twelve years since the age of twelve. While many of us weren't full-time producers, teachers, artists, or entertainment professionals, our seven-hour workshop rehearsals, creative meetings, and at least fifty shows annually made balancing our regular lives a full-time occupation. While many other reputable performing arts groups and youth programs existed in the city, Impact had unique grassroots energy, polished original material, and consistent bookings. Esteemed guests were brought in routinely to watch us rehearse or teach guest workshops, and our monthly show list was ever-expanding. Performances via foot, subway, packed rental van, charter bus, and even plane took us everywhere, from block parties, basement churches, and community centers to music landmarks, Ivy League universities, arts institutions, sports arenas, and high-profile corporate events.

While expected to perform our original or commissioned repertoire as young professionals, we were also expected to be "youth ambassadors" wherever we went. This included supporting the organizing at a venue, managing ourselves backstage, promoting the company, and speaking on record with the media. On several occasions, I was also responsible for introducing the show, and in a few cases, gave structured original speeches as part of themed events. For example, a speech on the connections of youth, Malcolm X, and Dr. Martin Luther King Jr., for the Blue Nile rites-of-passage program at the renowned Abyssinian Baptist Church in Harlem. And in fittingly contrasting fashion—a speech for Mosaic, the diversity, equity, and inclusion staff at PepsiCo corporate grounds in upstate New York.

My time in Impact was a wildly dynamic ride of knowledge, cultural exchange, and self-discovery with a range of world-class talented people. I still remember the first time I saw the group perform a one-hour show at Pace University, where I'd coincidentally become a student years later and perform the same program in the same theater with the group annually.

Back in sixth grade, we'd arrived at this unnamed field trip oblivious to what we were about to see, and I'd been in a foul, hopeless mood about everything. I'd already decided whatever this show was, it did nothing for me, and I hated it. By the end of Impact's performance, I was stripped of this prejudice and internally speechless. As the room was in an uproar, I sat quietly and wide-eyed about what I'd witnessed. I was forever changed. I looked around my fellow audience of once jaded and bitterly judgmental teenagers, suddenly free and giddy with childish excitement. Through music, purpose, movement, poetry, and undeniable energy, our hearts were moved, and our minds opened. The entire energy of the room shifted permanently.

Cofounder Jamal Joseph screamed over our thunderous applause as the show closed. "Do you want to do this?! Do you want to be a part of this?!"

My only answer was YES!

I remember my audition and being informed I'd made it . . . into a training boot camp. On my first "Training Day," surprisingly, I walked into a martial arts workshop taught by some of their best dancers. My fellow classmates, trainees, and I went from embarrassment to pride in wearing our boot camp shirts throughout the neighborhood. (Sending misbehaved teens to sensational boot camps to be made fools of was a big trend in popular '90s television talk shows like *Maury*, *Ricki Lake*, *Jenny Jones*, and *Montel Williams*.) I soon learned our "Boot Camp 2" was the first incoming class of nonoriginal members in the young history of Impact. Room for growth was ongoing as the company expanded for the first time. I relished taking advantage of everything this free program had to offer. True to its Black Arts Movement and Black Panther roots, they even served free lunch! It became my air.

Sundays through Fridays were cool, but my fellow trainees and I lived for the excitement of training day Saturdays at Impact. The day we felt we could really breathe, feel, and learn. We'd happily exhaust ourselves over the seven hours of workshops, spend all week talking about it, practice for practice, and hungrily anticipate the next rehearsal or show. Our boot camp was slated to be a six-to-twelve-week process but continued for four months.

Once we graduated into the company, I realized there was a whole new level of work to become a trusted and reputable performing member, get on the dance line, be considered for vocal solos and theatrical monologues, learn technical support, or be a core part of creating new pieces. Veterans received a wider variety of apparel and show opportunities. Elite guest instructors also frequently taught only small subgroups of the most capable members. This kind of unspoken challenge to the rank-and-file excited me. So did the powerful words and insights of the six founders and senior staff. Whatever Impact was serving, I wanted and was soaking up with enthusiasm. I began a slow and steady trek of "working my way up." I also tapped into leadership by discussing with other members ways to make the program better and bringing this formally to the staff's attention.

With the success of our "Boot Camp 2" experiment, boot camp classes continued into the double digits. I indeed worked my way up, relating at every level though being distinguished alongside the most reputed and capable. I also became junior staff, then senior staff, a program coordinator, and a company captain. Racking up years of loving commitment, I journeyed from childhood into adulthood with wide eyes and a full plate. I willingly represented a living history, its transformative ideas, a traveling show, and an organization, often more than I represented myself.

As I eclipsed over a decade of membership, cofounder Jamal Joseph prepared for an event at Columbia University's Miller Theatre for the release of his autobiographical book *Panther Baby: A Life of Rebellion & Reinvention*. There'd be legendary speakers, press coverage, a book signing, and Impact as featured performers. The event was a symbolic full circle as decades prior to becoming a professor of screenwriting, directing, and chair of the School of the Arts film department at Columbia, Jamal passionately encouraged people to burn down the college during a protest as a member of the Black Panther Party. This poetic example of limitlessness in life's offerings has since been highlighted even by the university itself. It's been the opening line of his bio on the Columbia alumnus website for years.

With Impact's reputation for having a dynamic live show and being one of his pride and joys, we were, without a doubt, slated as the event's headliners. Typically, every performance was different for us, which meant routinely "putting together a show" based on the desired show length, venue, event purpose, season, theme, or intended audience. We'd pull from our repertoire, improvise new pieces, pull from classics, and collaborate on creating special content. By the Miller Theatre show date, a new and quite large boot camp class had also graduated into the membership, and it was desired by executive staff that they be quickly worked into performances. With the existing regulars, returning alumni, and eager new graduates, at least fifty of us were rhythmically preparing to rumble on stage that night.

Rehearsals were a bit intense, getting new members ready and simultaneously filming the book trailer for *Panther Baby* around Harlem. Veteran members and staff felt the weight of emphasis this show would be livestreamed, have revolutionary legends in the audience, and the order to be "on" for roaming press. I'd kept to myself. As I neared twelve years in the company, I was also going through a "mid-youth crisis" (for lack of better words).

The repetition of weekly workshop demands added to the expected antics of big show processes, coupled with the clueless nature of the most novice members needing support, topped with work-life balance and now college schedules, put a spotlight in my mind about suddenly being one of the eldest in the group. I uncomfortably felt the proverbial "10,000 hours" rule. Could it be the program that saved my life via that fateful sixth-grade field trip was now my crutch? I wasn't sure, but something was off. While my love for our traveling family was immense, I was worn out, and my joy was changing. I repeatedly questioned my purpose, direction, and desire in life. The years of willingly representing everything but myself, "getting lost in the work," so to speak, perhaps affected my ability to see my whole self clearly.

I was always genuinely happy when the *real* Black Arts Movement, Black Power Movement, or Black Panther elders would come around, be at our shows, or greet us. I remember one of the most bluntly honest, highly revered, eldest of elders being honored at a Black Panther anniversary event uptown on the City College campus. Numerically, he was in his 90s, maybe even 100s. But energy wise, he was snap-crackle-popping with youth and spirit! They called him to the stage as we finished performing, and he made his way up while yelling at us *not* to move.

When he got on stage, he looked around, gave some hugs and high fives, then turned and exclaimed to the room, "I don't give a s*** about y'all old a****. THESE children right here, THESE is who I care about! If it ain't about them, I don't care!" The room exploded in laughter and affirmation. Up a few rows, dangling her feet in childlike delight, was a giggling living legend in poetess Sonia Sanchez. She'd go on to perform with us and lovingly ask me to accompany her to buy popcorn at a nearby supermarket. It was always family cookout or family meeting energy. Whenever such elders were "In the House," there was a lot of grounded, clean, "old school" love, and we were treated very well. A consistent embodiment of this was Cyril Innis, former Minister of Cultural Propaganda for the New York chapter of Black Panthers, whom we called "Uncle Bullwhip."

Rehearsals and filming for the *Panther Baby* book trailer carried on and brought Bullwhip to the proceedings. As caretaker of official merchandise, archives, banners, posters, and artwork of the Party, he came to decorate the storefront being filmed and our rehearsal space to recreate the looks of the Panther office headquarters. Several of us dressed in the signature all-black with picked-out natural Afros, berets, and political buttons. Uncle Bullwhip coached us between takes using his memories of the live action of the '60s and '70s. Then with a few of us at peak attention, he decided to teach one of the chants they used while community-patrolling the same Harlem streets we now stood on.

It was rich fun in the moment, and Jamal saw us performing it and put it into the film footage. Then he had us teach it to the rest of the membership and dictated it be put into the book release show. The simple call-and-response (with added choreography) would now become part of the repertoire and thus subject to be called upon at any show. I was made lead chanter for the Miller Theatre performance, which would be our first time doing it in front of an audience, let alone revolutionary elders who were there for the *real* thing. The night came, and knowing a few songs preceded this moment on the set list, we filled the stage with bated breath. Spreading out almost wing-to-wing and front-to-back curtain with our packed crew, we began the show and warmed up the room with exuberance.

Though we did our best to warn against this in rehearsals and our preshow rundown, many new members excitedly jumped into preset dance lines, rearranged blocking, and fumbled their way through numbers, just ecstatic to be doing their first show. While frustrating, to say the least, I sensed the pool of enthusiastic young people around me was reflecting and signaling my more profound sense to shift. Not just on stage but in life, as I'd been questioning. As other senior members took note and maneuvered themselves back in place, I felt this wasn't my battle nor something to stress. Knowing I also had a few solos coming up, I decided to move to the very back of the dance line and blend into the background vocal choruses.

As I scooched back with play-it-off movements and facials, subtlety motioning and communicating with veterans to shift the lines (while dodging arms, elbows, knees, and feet), I felt a little defeated. I looked at the smiles on the new members' faces, enjoying themselves, and the agitation in the veteran members' bodies, composing themselves. As cameras busily captured footage from far corners, the hot, bright stage lights blinded our view of faces in the audience. I could only perform, I couldn't see in front of me, only what I was in and what was behind. This was now beyond my control. I'd done my best, but I wasn't sure I had enough to continue giving to this whole new class of membership, fellow veterans, executive staff, and myself.

Feeling a bit useless and wanting to lie down, I remembered where I was, who was in the audience, and one of my greatest stage lessons from Jamal echoed once again: *"Use it all!"* Of course, this wasn't the time to lie down. This was *showtime*, on film! There were at least fifteen minutes of high-energy show left, and I had to deliver this chant—and deliver it well.

Thankfully, it went smoothly. As we began stomping in unison and melodically singing about "the people's power," elders called out from the crowd with glee and pride. A few were astonished we even knew about the chant. I imagine it must've been a surreal reoccurrence for them, hearing this decades later "out of the mouths of babes." I could feel their genuine excitement. Their applause lingered, and I was relieved.

With no time to rest on said relief, the next musical cue hit like the green flag of the Indie 500. We went immediately into a movement-heavy, four-rap verse and dance break Hip-Hop piece called "Politix." I went from holding the mic for the completion of the chant to spontaneously riffing the song's introduction and opening hook while dancing to the opening group formation. Knowing I was holding one of the better mics, I strategically crossed the stage to pass it to the first soloist, and we were off. Finally, we concluded with our bright Broadway-like inspirational finisher, "Happiness," eking out the last of our fuel before bowing and exiting the stage. I walked away, dripping with sweat.

The adrenaline high coursed through me as I caught my breath in a hallway backstage. I'd gone hard. I felt heavy and emptied. My chest burned, and my body whispered about the soreness I'd feel the next day. I hadn't invited anyone to the show, no one was meeting me after, and I wasn't in the mood to chill. There was just too much on my mind.

Jamal and senior staff went to greet the press and finesse the book signing while some veterans headed back to the hood or hit nearby spots off-campus. Lingering back, I let being on the lookout for kids waiting for parents to pick them up be my scapegoat. Many new members' parents were just as excited to see their kids perform as their kids were to jump in the show. Whether they understood or respected the professional aim of all our rehearsing and rank-and-file or not, I appreciated their excitement.

Parents thanked me on behalf of Jamal and the program. *"If Only You Knew"* ***Patti LaBelle voice*** I thought, thinking of the unseen build and stress to this point. I also thought about how sweet it was for these parents to come and be enthused about their children's ongoing public activity. I greeted, thanked, gave quick feedback, and encouraged. Exhaling, I felt the inner tug to head out but saw Uncle Bullwhip coming and paused to pay my respects. Still profusely sweaty, he greeted me with a firm pat on the shoulder.

"You did good, youngin!"

"Thanks, Unc."

"Really, now! Aye, dahling! I'm proud of ya. You didn't hear us screaming for y'all?"

"Ha! I did. That was great. Thanks, Unc."

We hugged. My depression was palpable. He tilted his head and began chuckling.

"Aye, pick your head up! Somebody wanna talk to you . . ."

He motioned behind me. Exhausted at the thought of greeting another show-hungry parent or explaining the importance of rehearsals and membership processes they needed to respect, I took a breath and got my attitude ready as best I could. Deeply dreading this, I turned my shoulder with another exhale—but was silently startled aback. This wasn't a member or a member's parent. It was author, law professor, former leadership officer, Communications Secretary of the Black Panther Party, and all-around icon . . . thee Kathleen Cleaver.

Just . . . there.

There. Standing there, here. Out of the legacy and history books, out of the classic videos and images, out of the myths and real realities. Standing, glowing, waiting, here, right here . . . for me? Just in my face, beaming with a big a** smile. Uncle Bullwhip's chuckle turned into belly laughter.

Y'ALL (NOT) GON' MAKE ME LOSE MY MIND

"I believe this is who you wanted, Queen. I'm outta here! Catch up with y'all! Head up, youngin! Love y'all!"

She thanked Bullwhip and affirmed she'd catch up with him and other elders who were congregating. Their jovial energy was pleasing, the comradery had never changed. It was also endearing to be addressed with the same love despite not living through what they lived through. She turned back to me and exhaled, resuming a big, warm, excited smile. I was gently frozen in her golden aura and light gemstone eyes. Neither of us said anything for a few more seconds. But she just kept smiling and now, was nodding side to side.

Suddenly, she blurted out her first words, unexpectedly, boldly, and brightly.

"I LOVE YOU!"

My head, neck, blinking eyes, and shifting eyebrows all said, "*Excuse* me?"

I had to be dreaming.

I was still standing, but I was floored. Wow . . . asf! A million words came to mind for this pioneer woman I'd admired through stories, books, and the internet, from generations afar. What do you say to a living legend you admire, who's filled your whole heart? Who, in essence, fought for you and your ability to live wholly? Who wasn't too proud to tell you she loved *you*? I didn't want to leave her hanging, but I didn't know what to say or how to process what was happening. I moved my soul-searching eyes into hers and suddenly, from my heart, blurted out the best and truest thing I could say back.

"I LOVE YOU TOO!"

We exclaimed and hugged, with my sweat and all. This was really happening.

"Ha! I know that might sound weird."

"No, please, I seriously love you too. Thank you so much."

"Ha! I'm like your biggest fan right now. I was sitting in the audience, just watching you go. I said, *wow, look at her.* So, I told Bullwhip I gotta meet that sister. You are just . . . I just love you!"

My entire being was lifted in (!!!) and "Oh My God" energy. She proceeded to recall details of the show and my performance in it. I zoned out midway, thinking, *damn, she was really watching. She was watching wherever I went on stage.* She noted specifically how I moved to the back and made way for younger members to occupy the spaces ahead of me while still giving a show from the rear. The fact this was being said to me was astounding in my formerly depressed mind. To Kathleen Cleaver, I was this good, this memorable, this powerful, and this worthy. To living history, a changemaker, warrior, true queen, and a bada**, I was more than enough.

I thanked her for coming. For watching, seeing, and saying this to me. For going out of her way to find me hiding out backstage just to tell me this. It meant so much. I thanked her for being her, which meant so much. Now, in person, I saw the consistency with who she really was as a woman and nurturer, as well as her lifelong work in the Party, civic leadership, and underlying principle of love for the people, "mind, body, and soul."

We hugged again. I was blown away that my sweat didn't bother her one bit. It was real love; it was a real hug. She encouraged me to keep doing what I was doing and follow my heart.

"You got it, girl! Thanks again! Just wow!"

Speaking like *I'd* done something for *her*.

I stood there for more seconds now in the empty hallway and quiet backstage area. It was as if "Glinda the Good Witch" had just put the ruby slippers on my feet and reminded me never to take them off. *Toto, I don't think we're in deep depression anymore!* The trunk of my mind had been lightly rearranged. I gathered my things, moved through the doors into the book-signing crowd, motioned my leave to a few, and quietly dipped from the building.

The following year would be my last in Impact. It was a hard but necessary departure and sowed the seeds for a bold new chapter in my life. Kathleen Cleaver saw something in me, lovingly watched me from the back of the back, and made it her business to tell me she loved me. It was time to shake down my internal "crisis" and start questioning its mental health imbalances for validity. For right now, though, I'd stay high, off living-legend-love. Taking it easy, I continued my walk off-campus deeper into Harlem, floating all the way home.

CHAPTER 16
LADIES WHO LUNCH (WITH IMMORTAL TECHNIQUE)

I SHUFFLED down the stairs of the 127th Street entrance of the A-B-C-D train station in Harlem, hurriedly walking the platform while looking through my bag. Midway, a composed, unassuming, and slightly broody figure stood before me. Though seemingly in deep thought, poker-faced, and wearing all black and dark earth tones, I sensed a brightness and comfort about the carriage of this weight. I was drawn to look closer.

"Brother Immortal?"

He snapped to attention, squinted, and searched my energy. I briefly reminded him of the Constitution Center in Philadelphia, Pennsylvania where we'd met. He and his two-man crew shared a green room with our performing arts youth group Impact Repertory Theatre while waiting to take the stage at a community rally for well-known author, journalist, and political prisoner Mumia Abu-Jamal.

Mumia's latest book *Jailhouse Lawyers* had been released and received much praise by the revolutionary community. The book also greatly impacted my decision not to go to law school, so I was happy to be at this live event celebrating it. He'd be calling in from prison to speak, and the likes of Cornel West (and his scarf) were also there. Armed anti-Mumia protesters lined up outside the building and tried to intimidate incoming guests. Police cars stood by with sirens on, silent but rotating to suggest balance yet imposing an authoritative light show on the streets. African drummers, local dancers, Immortal Technique, and our group were charged with raising the morale of all those inside through music, culture, art, and powerful words. It was a beautiful, world-class venue and a full, neatly packed audience.

I never forgot how patiently and graciously Brother Immortal and his mans-and-them went along with sharing a room with twenty young people, including our youngest, who were loud, running around, and playing after the long bus ride. Though I knew he was deep into community activities, he was also a major music act and one of my favorite emcees. He was from Harlem like me, an immigrant like me, knew darkness like me, loved passionate writing like me, and was a knowledge nerd like me. I'd been listening to his music for years and knew of his low-key legendary climb to global success as a completely independent artist. He consistently made bold statements in his art with detailed, informed, and unapologetic political commentary. Some minimized this as "conspiracy theory rap," but I knew his catalog offered much more.

"Dance with the Devil," "You Never Know," "Peruvian Cocaine," and an album skit where he talked about being conscious but still eating chicken wings continued to live rent-free in my mind. He also owned a strikingly unique stage presence. Moody, commanding, and intense yet warm, energized, and polished. He seemed to share much love with his audiences on a human level and perform from a real place. While strategically prosperous, he was clearly driven by more than money, and in my eyes, he was a "made man" on his own terms. Meeting him was an unexpected honor.

I'd felt a way that thee Immortal Technique had to share a room with us and not have his own space, though I was grateful to cross paths. It was my first time meeting and sharing an intimate space with him. Gestures of warmth, focus, and humility told me a lot about him as a person and a man, as well as who he surrounds himself with. They treated us respectfully, stayed to themselves but acknowledged us with smiles, and kept cool heads as our kids played freely. I was relieved they were so level-headed and pleased not to be disappointed in meeting a hero. Now suddenly, we were reunited—with no groups, crews, show, or audience.

"Brother Immortal?"

He paused and seemed to think back on the night at the Constitution Center. Then after some anxious seconds of God-I-hope-he-remembers-otherwise-this-is-embarrassing agony, a huge smile took over his face. He almost immediately leaned over and embraced me with a warm hug. I hugged back.

"How you doing, sister?"

We exchanged pleasantries and recapped the evening. By the smile, hug, and eye contact I got, I discerned he regarded me with a certain respect, especially because of the revolutionary community we shared. Somewhere in the conversation, I cordially asked if he'd be willing, interested, and available to guide me on business building and being an artist. I knew I was asking a very busy man for free game . . . (I've always had audacity.) To my delight, he said he would and that we could do it over a meal and be thoughtful about it. As quickly as he gave the invitation, he qualified he wasn't looking to intrude on me sensually, sexually, or romantically. I could tell he meant it, was relieved we could be straight-up about things, appreciated the consideration, and safety.

He explained his commitments and instructed me to contact him when he returned to town. We exchanged numbers. I really hoped this man would keep his word because, for one, the music would never sound the same, ha! We'd unexpectedly run into each other once more in Midtown and seal the deal on linking up. On the day of the rendezvous, he asked, "You like sushi?" and I knew this was going to be a meal I'd remember.

For the record, at the time, I did *not* like sushi.

Ha! To be accurate, I didn't know if I liked it. I'd never had it before. Nevertheless, I trusted his lead and, with an open mind, met him at a Japanese cuisine and sushi restaurant around 122nd Street and Amsterdam Avenue in West Harlem. I told him about the cherry to be popped, and he laughed, saying, "We could've gone to a burger joint; it's cool." It *was* cool, though. I was there for good company and guidance; part of this meant the experience of his expanded palate, intellectually, professionally, culturally, and—culinarily.

He explained some basics and what would be "safe" orders for me to try, then proceeded to request some very exotic choices for himself. He and the waiter spoke a language I knew nothing about, and I loved it. There was only one thing I didn't love about this lunch and moment I'd never forget. Thee Brother Immortal, who'd graciously made time to share space, break bread, and compare life notes with me, had peacefully and truly shown up.

But I didn't come as my whole self.

I was a fraction. I was not my whole truth, making it less enjoyable than it could've been. In hindsight, the guidance he offered and questions he asked may have remained the same. However, I know I was not my "authentic self," as pop culture often says. This seemed to impair my reception and interaction with the unique and meaningful experience at hand. It put anxiety and insecurity in places they didn't need to be.

I was knee-deep in founding my transnational nonprofit organization to be named Ottoo Brand Artivism-PADER at this time. It would focus on the arts, community advocacy, and financial empowerment in my two homelands of New York City and

Uganda, and I'd build it with my father. I was doing fewer shows with Impact and less artistic training for the trade-off of more business strategy hours to get the organization off the ground. I also worked full-time at a high-volume Starbucks coffee location, networking, and constantly seeking more knowledge. None of this was unusual as I was no stranger to intense research, supporting myself, and simultaneously building on ideas. What was out of the ordinary was I was in a committed relationship (I had only experienced a couple), which was slowly consuming, draining, and transforming me beyond my better judgment. I'd shown up pretending to be the girl who wasn't in an abusive relationship.

My partner at the time was a bright, cultured, charismatic, and staunch businessman who fairly used the opportunity of me founding a nonprofit to provide fundamental input and encourage both our activities. It was to him I spoke the idea out loud in the first place. With his positive nudges to explore my vision and trust my unique experience, I began fleshing out the organization on paper one night at his house. He had a flexible, entrepreneurial schedule and routinely made time to accompany me to the library, share documents, plan meals, and school me on how to handle networking events. As a stylish clotheshorse, he also insisted on coming with me to shop for business clothes and looked over my outfits when we had big meetings. In many ways, this was a great help.

We first met after a show in Harlem at the Dwyer Cultural Center. He introduced himself while offering perceptive compliments about my performance individually and with the group. He was nearly twice my age and very savvy, so I stepped carefully as we engaged in a series of intellectually stimulating conversations. Eventually, an intimate trust was established, and we found ourselves gelling very well. I was very closed-hearted initially but gradually let him do more things for me and enjoyed staying with him. Outside of this, I worked my exhausting five a.m. shift forty hours a week while living in a gunshot-adjacent rented room where I couldn't use the kitchen or have company. Large doses of satisfying quality time with an exciting new man in my life (who could cook) while building a self-determined business and experiencing the different nouns of New York through our combined adventures became a relieving escape.

I logically but mistakenly thought because he was older, loved me, knew of my vision, and was significantly experienced in the fields I was diving deeper into, he also knew better what was right for me. I learned a lot of valuable perspectives and information from him and his network. Yet, I was also suppressing my true self in a misdirected effort to stay open, positive, and understanding of this new world. A lot was coming at me fast, and I was doing more absorbing than discerning. I was also using a lot of determination to bring this big idea to fruition, yet not quite honoring who I was at my core and who I really wanted to be.

I didn't know exactly when and where to take the reins of my own identity while building something bigger than myself. This is also after being in Impact for thirteen years, and for thirteen years, Impact being my representation. There was a period even before the height of our Oscar- and Grammy-nominated popularity where people of all ages would see me in the street and call me "Impact," not even my name. I became company captain and was routinely thinking about the program, members, families, shows, rehearsals, repertoire, meetings, and being a point person at events . . . to the point of burnout. I was also aware I'd outgrown a lot and felt unsure of whether I was walking away with a solid foundation for myself.

While I was happy for courage, peace, and mental increase in leaving the group, I was in a fluid space of new growth, and identity rebuilding could've gone several ways. Now also in a committed relationship, my partner's influence progressively became more than supportive. Red flags became inconveniences and malicious transgressions were challenging to address. I felt isolated as our interactions became psychologically and emotionally abusive, financially draining, and damaged nearly all my other relationships with friends and family. While we had a sincere connection, performative warmth, fierce defenses of my honor, and love-bombing interspersed in all of it distorted the reality of ugliness, questionable intentions, potential trapping, and me still living out other people's versions of me.

The fact I'd shown up to this lunch in a suit my partner picked out for me was already making me sick. The fact that most of my wardrobe was now suits and conservative power dresses I realized weren't exactly my style made me sick. I looked myself over before Immortal arrived and wanted to run home, rinse my spirit, and change, but it was too late. I tried not to think about my discomfort and appreciate that this was happening.

Then there we were. I was about to lose my sushi-virginity to a waxing poetic Immortal Technique while wearing a gray and black suit, black turtleneck, gray and black herringbone pumps, and a tapered Afro haircut on a sunny weekday afternoon in Harlem. I looked like a cross between Nino Brown from *New Jack City* and Steve Jobs, and I felt lost in the translation.

I did my best to focus on the moment.

I enjoyed Immortal reminiscing about his time in the neighborhood. It turns out we'd been geographically close for years. He recalled his first arrival in New York and exposure to Hip-Hop expressed everywhere, which I heavily related to. With the graffiti, all types of music blasting, all types of people and action everywhere—it was like a gritty wonder world, a ghetto Disneyland. I imagined this time in his life before he started moving more independently in the streets. Before any legal trouble or studies during his eye-opening prison experience. He spoke of community service work with incarcerated young men, about sharing knowledge and breaking cycles. I thought about the commonality in our vulnerable experiences, love of writing, enterprising attitudes, and visions of betterment.

I felt my not-wholeness affected the conversation when he

asked me what I wanted to do. I thought it was a trick question because we'd met performing, and creativity was my biggest love. I was ready to embark on being a professional solo artist. Yet, here I was, sitting in a business suit as a businesswoman, insecure, and totally *not* on my artist wave, so it was a good question. He seemed to just *not* entertain visualizing me as an entertainer. This tickled me as I realized it was likely on purpose.

"Why don't you become a teacher? You seem like you love kids and would be a good one. We need that. I know the pay is wack, but you could finesse it a certain way . . ."

It wasn't the first time an experienced professional would try to talk me out of being an artist. I was aching to convey my enormous appetite for life, creation, alchemy, autonomy, and mobility, but sadly, I didn't have the words to communicate it. Nevertheless, he provided a good read and a good lead from good instincts for the limitations at play.

We got around to discussing music and he offered firsthand insights on "The Industry" ***DMX voice*** How he could do prosperous business for himself as a manager or A&R but why he didn't want to. He advised knowing who I was as an artist before pursuing it any further. He explained some of what women are commonly pressured into, especially Black women. He read me up and down in a manner of seconds.

"Do you want to sell sex? Or you wanna be a teacher, like KRS-One? You wanna be like Beyoncé? What are you gonna do if . . ."

I listened, thinking rapidly, barely having answers but not caving in. I felt some questions were limited, but I understood his aim. These were real terms in which people thought and made decisions from daily. He also didn't want me to go through certain things and at least have my head on straight if I wanted to go through them. He left my life up to me. I was grateful for the perspective, pressure, and candidness.

It was time for him to go. He slurped up the last of his soup, paid the bill, and walked us out of the restaurant. I mentally reached for a grip forward as my herringbone pumps clicked past the bamboo fountains across the tiled floor. He got himself together as we stood outside, then looked at me.

"You all right?"

I knew less at that moment than when I'd arrived, and I'm sure it showed. We both smiled.

"You're gonna be OK. It's a lot, I know. But you clearly got something. I wouldn't have had lunch with you or spoken with you like this if you were a piece of s***."

I laughed, thanked him, and we hugged goodbye. He'd be leaving town again, and I wouldn't see him again for many years.

"It's a beautiful day. You better enjoy it. I will!" he yelled walking up the block. A part of me wanted to scream, "Take me with you!" or "Help me!" but really, he already had.

Looking down at my waist and legs at the fallacy of the Nino Brown-Steve Jobs suit, I wondered if the suit was telling a whole truth and I was the one denying myself. Though my body felt trapped in the fabric of a question mark, my mind felt enlightened. I slightly dreaded walking back to the house to meet my boyfriend in such a fluid mental state. He'd want to know all the business advice I got, whether Immortal tried to push up on me in any way, and likely go in about what I should've said, asked, and did. I exhaled and pulled out my phone.

While Immortal was in the bathroom, I'd taken a picture of the table setting before the food arrived. The glasses, clay bottles, his chair, the Japanese calligraphy, dark mode décor, wood, rice paper screens, wildflowers, and green plants. I enjoyed how simple and elegant it was and how different it was for me. It had also been a while since someone just spoke to me, for the me in front of them. This was the only picture I took or was interested in taking that day. I was pleased with the platonic intimacy of the moment.

Inner conflicts aside, I was encouraged. I smiled because it happened. I had a lot to think about, but it was indeed a beautiful day, and I'd do my best to enjoy it. I was a tad bit lost, sure. But we'd both found realness in each other. He'd kept his word wholeheartedly, and I now had business knowledge I couldn't get from a book or paid course. I'd had lunch with one of my favorite artists and was able to take a deeper look at myself. I'd also never left Harlem and somehow learned way more about sushi and Japanese culture, all thanks to a raw poet from Peru.

SPORTS, FITNESS & RECREATION

CHAPTER 17
TOUGH GIRL: A MINI-CAREER IN TACKLE FOOTBALL, PT. 1

IN MY ROOKIE year on the Harlem Giants football team, the iconic video game *Def Jam: Vendetta* for PlayStation 2 hit stores. Creatively merging outlandish pro wrestling matches with some of Hip-Hop's biggest names and hits, it was a favorite among my best foe turned best friend on the team and me. We routinely found ourselves in his mother's project apartment rotating between it, *Madden*, and *Mortal Kombat: Deadly Alliance*. The latter featured a new eye-sharpening mini-challenge unlocked in arcade mode named "Test Your Sight." As our highly skilled middle linebacker and defensive captain, my friend excelled at it frighteningly well. I didn't get the correlation of the contrasting mediums reinforcing each other until I closely watched him play.

The quiet, stillness, and focus he employed to successfully outwit the unassumingly difficult shuffling cups was mind-boggling. Being physically explosive, vocally boisterous, loudly comedic, very in touch with his anger, monstrous on the field, uncontainable, and with the street name "Reckless," watching him silently train his eyes was like watching MMA and pro wrestling superstar Brock Lesnar lead a meditation. Determined to become a better player, I followed his lead in opening my mind and using everything around me to excel.

Exposure to these video games contributed to my affinity for cross-culture experiential products and storytelling. In doing so, they proved a pillar to my unique strengths in art, Hip-Hop, live stage, media production, and the vision necessary to succeed in business. On and off the field, this inspiration from my teammates, coaches, and community support system proved foundationally meaningful to an unforeseen path. I was about to go from amateur player to scouted for semipro to an assistant, coordinator, and coach in three years, and I'd need all the vision and support I could get.

"You've got a lot of heart" was one of the most meaningful things said to me and among my biggest takeaways from being a tackle football player. I was one of two girls in a community league covering New York City and Newark, New Jersey in the early 2000s. Our barely grassy field was just off the highway in East Harlem, which made dodging exit ramp traffic part of our regular exercise. At the time, gentrification hadn't set in this part of the neighborhood, so our view from the field was abandoned buildings. We didn't represent a school; we weren't a Pop Warner league team; we weren't sponsored by anyone. We were in the hood, doing our best with the best our money and love could produce.

My positions were defensive end, defensive tackle, outside linebacker, and both sides of special teams in the 13-15 age range. On rare occasions, I was running back in practice. Once they accepted how serious I was about being there, my team decided to train me extra hard, so I'd be toughest and fearless no matter who was in front of me. Word of this got around and when the league commissioner found out I existed, he banned me from games. He reasoned the insurance policy didn't cover girls, and I was jeopardizing the entire league. The soon uncovered truth was the policy covered "players" and didn't specify gender at all. His repeated bold statements and warnings against my participation raised many eyebrows. Those eyebrows became vocal, and it turned into quite a thing.

Parents, neighbors, and random people began staging small-scale protests on the sidelines. It resulted in heated arguments, threats, a rumored lawsuit, and thus, a preemptive community legal team assembled, all over me even stepping on the field. I remained in practice faithfully, but I was benched for most of the games in my first season. Our local cheerleaders even made cheers about putting me in games (ha!). I was more embarrassed than anything about this attention because, to me, popularity meant nothing from the pine of the bench. (Also, we didn't have benches. They didn't want me so close as to sneak into a game, so I had to walk the sidelines and sit by the fences. I was fenced!) Privately, I felt the commissioner was more scared I'd be good than scared I'd get hurt.

It still surprises me I wasn't more adamantly resistant to him trying to stop me. Me, a.k.a. "Emilia X," who commonly assumed the role of a new-age Nina Simone, tightfisted with "the red, the black, and the green." Ms. "Fight the Power" herself chose to quietly suit up, maximize practice, and stay mostly silent about it. Perhaps because, by then, there was already a lot of tension in my mind, home life, and transitions in puberty. Being ignored while standing out, feeling punished for being different, seeing more for myself, and fighting for normalcy became an emphatic standard in my life. I was sick of everything being an underdog fight. I joined the team because I loved the game, knew I could do it, needed a release, and was emotionally drawn to the feeling of power. I wanted to feel my power again (preferably as I tackled someone to the ground). *This* time, I wasn't interested in starting a revolution. I just wanted to play football.

I'd be avenged as the season went on.

Y'ALL (NOT) GON' MAKE ME LOSE MY MIND

On my first day of tryouts, Channie Allen (known affectionately as MaChannie) from my arts program Impact Repertory Theatre personally brought me to practice. She was a mother figure to many, an excellent cook, and homemade Impact's free lunches every week. I stayed with her and her two daughters, Niger and Nadiyah, in Central Harlem, while disconnects with my father were reaching all-time highs. After almost four years of a dramatically bitter separation and joint custody, my parents' divorce was finalized, and my mother had left the state. Being a young girl, MaChannie supported me through this very sensitive time. I told her I was interested in playing tackle football and had heard of tryouts in the neighborhood. She was taken aback but didn't judge or discourage me, which I really appreciated.

"Are you sure this is what you wanna do?"

I affirmed, and this was all she needed.

When the day came, she traveled with me to the park and surveyed the scene. We walked up and saw several boys being segmented for tryouts. She gestured me off.

"Go 'head, Emily; get on the field, baby."

I lightly jogged out to the small group. Almost immediately, the eldest coach, Coach Bovain, yelled out through his dentures like a spewing firecracker.

"And *where* is SHE going?!"

I heard him, as almost everyone did. I slowed my hustle and turned. Coach Bovain was old school, but MaChannie went to that school too. I braced for whatever was about to happen.

In the calmest and most assertive manner ever, she turned to him (head and neck only first), put one hand over the other, raised her eyebrow, and looked him straight in the eye.

"*She's* going to try out. Now, do WE have a problem?"

(Can't forget about the slight head tilt!)

Meeting his match, Bovain backed down almost immediately. She motioned for me to keep walking.

"Mmhmm . . ." Bovain continued, disgruntled by the unexpected psychological defeat.

". . . but if she gets hurt, that ain't our fault! OK, now, LET'S GO!"

The first whistle blew, and so it began.

Three days a week, every week, in the sun, rain, sleet, or snow, on our community field of mostly dirt and rocks. As far as mental learning and physical growth went, I loved every minute of it. My emotional and psychological experience, however, was another story. I can't say the practices were horrible, but they weren't exactly warm, welcoming, or enjoyable to start, either. When I wasn't being picked on, joked about, or yelled at, I was being "taught a lesson" by someone who seemed to wish I'd run all the way home and never return.

I always returned.

I quickly devised certain rules and mantras to make it through every practice. One of them was the "three-second rule," being, when I was tackled to the ground, I'd take no more than three seconds to get back on my feet. This ensured no one would feebly ask me, "Are you okay?" and question my ability to be tackled or withstand the rigors of the sport. While it may not have been the safest activity for me, it's what I felt I had to do. This strategy seemed to work in my favor, as people routinely saw me getting up—tackle, after tackle, after tackle. There was no physical lesson any player could try to teach me greater than the mental and energetic one higher powers were already moving me through.

There *were*, however, plenty of tactical and athletic lessons to learn. I was used to dynamic movement in dance for stage and theater, but this was my first time on an athletic team that required straight running across hundreds of yards a session. In essence, I had to relearn my body and become a newer athlete than I'd ever been. Due to physical imbalances likely from unaddressed issues of performing since childhood, the act of sprinting long distances and making sudden stops felt slightly unusual. I didn't have comparable amounts of power for giving tackles like the boys until further along. Learning to resist being taken down or forcibly moved off my center also took time. There was a lot of special hand and arm leverage, like Sumo wrestling techniques, which also had to be learned.

The most significant adjustment which *every* new player had to deal with was learning how to hold our heads inside the tightly weighted football helmet. The neck muscles must adjust to this gradually, so this process can't be rushed. For this, players are typically required to practice with the helmet as soon as it's available and do their best never to take it off. You'd be required to wear it even on conditioning-only days (no shoulder pads or tackling). Often, guys wore their helmets at home just to get an edge.

Stamina, endurance, footwork, eye contact, angular mobility, ball handling, and even peripheral vision all had to be trained. In the beginning, I struggled with almost every drill. In contrast, I was well coordinated, attentive, coachable, and in my mind, clearly understood what was supposed to happen even if it hadn't clicked yet. My physical body also seemed to have a presence that suggested something solid. I was clearly strong, withstanding the training (barely!), and soon became stronger. However, with so much talent on the team, I still had a long way to go to impress anyone. I wasn't a standout by any means other than being female.

Tackling drills were intense and often made more difficult, specifically for me by all the coaches. If they weren't more difficult, I was asked to do multiple or match up with some of the toughest guys. On numerous occasions, I had my "bell rung" by hard, stiff, crackling tackles.

A young Dominican nicknamed "Bebo" was once called in to match up with me. Surprised, he'd been missing in action and wasn't even aware I'd joined the team. Bebo was said to be fifteen years old and sincerely might've been, but his body was at least five years his senior. He was lean but ripped, solid with six-pack abs and a growing mustache, and to me, looked like he had a wife and three kids at home. He possessed a very traditional macho attitude and a very pretty, feminine, delicate girlfriend who was usually there to watch, drool, and be in awe at his strength and athleticism. He was handsome, skilled, one of the team's elite veterans, rightfully arrogant, and for all intents and purposes, a "big man on campus."

He was visibly *disturbed* when he saw me standing on the field in the drill line with gear on. He remained disturbed and would never speak to me, just giving polite, awkward head nods. It seemed to him I was an alien for playing tackle football, and the coaches were crazy to let me. I didn't mind this opinion. I knew he was a tall mountain to climb, but I looked forward to every opportunity to get better and eventually put him on his a**.

They set up a drill with me as running back, heading straight into linebacker tackles from several players. When Bebo arrived and was told I'd be running the ball against him, he responded, "Her?! Coach, I can't do that." They pulled him aside and spoke privately. I don't know what they said, but when he returned, he looked me over, then in the eye, smirked, shook his head, exhaled while putting on his helmet, and said, "This is no good for you. But OK."

My heart raced as I clutched the ball into position. As important as taking the tackle, it was also vital not to drop the ball or be stripped of it. We lined up as teammates stood by, watching intensely. The whistle blew, and Bebo ran at me at full speed like a bull in Pamplona. His tackle hit and cracked. Our equipment clashed loudly, making the first loud smack echo into the cold night sky. Bebo's hit was hard, and my body went up high as the first set of "*oooh!*" erupted from our onlooking team, also echoing. Additionally, the hit was so explosive, that I had enough time to think several thoughts while airborne.

Among them was, *damn, I'm up pretty high . . . that means the ground is about to hurt.* There was no reason for me to be this freely high in the air, unless to knock the ball out, as his arms should've been wrapped, and weight driving me downward to dead the play. I figured this was another tactic to get me to quit. It was a damn good try! There was another loud smack when I finally met the earth, erupting the second set of *"oooh!"* and followed by the impact of coming down on the football, closing the sonic boom. As the ball slid out from my arms, I writhed in pain. Knowing I couldn't stay down for too long, I literally saw stars like an old cartoon. I'd always thought the phrase "seeing stars" was exaggerated, but nah, it's true! I blacked out for a few seconds and then came back to stasis.

"She's all right; give her room!"

Though we all knew it was an expressly brutal hit, the coaches insisted nobody help me up. They came over and ensured I was good, then congratulated me on taking the hit and not fumbling the ball. I did my best to cover up how much I was still reeling from agony. I knew they knew it was a big hit because they let me take a break. Bebo stopped on his jog past me, unapologetic and unremorseful. Shaking his head at my existence, he said, "I told you, NO GOOD!"

Soon, however, I did get good, and things began clicking between my brain and body. My hand-eye coordination increased, and I caught more throws. I may not have been as fast, but I started running routes with more precision. I may not have been as powerful, but I began wrapping my tackles better and using people's weight against me . . . against them. I was very focused on continuing to show up and execute to the best of my ability.

Though the desire felt mostly subconscious, I still also wanted to show I was something more. Not being a star player nor being groomed to be one, my persistence was seen as admirable but still treated as nothing special. I was no longer miserable and now was as good as the mediocre boys, but so what? The personal victory of going from sore outcast to one with the crowd wasn't enough. In many minds, it was still very possible that one day, I'd simply stop and never return. I was expected to ride the bench (well, the fence) if I made it further into game season. I knew I had to take myself seriously if no one else did, but *how* to make this happen, I had no idea.

A unique opportunity to show what I was made of fittingly came during a simple group exercise. Early on an overcast Saturday, the coaches combined all age levels into one practice. Scores of us filled the field and contended with the raised level of demand and competition. Of course, the most elite athletes and skillful players shined. Captains at every level were also called to lead by example and organize the ranks. Toward the end, before a scrimmage game, the coaches corralled us in the middle of the field to form a big circle. We took a knee, and with chime-ins from all the coaches, head coach, Coach O'Neal gave a speech comparable to any rousing sports movie. Of course, it was about giving more than what we were currently giving and the attitude it would take in practice to win games and become champions.

Our group was not without its rebels, clowns, and the behaviorally challenged, so we soon found ourselves on the wrong side of a discipline lecture. Sensing we still weren't taking them seriously enough, the coaches decided to reprimand us with exercise. Specifically, with an extended round of an isometric hold and abdominal strength drill named "six inches." With the body laid straight, arms at the sides or under the pelvis, the legs are held tightly together and raised six inches above the ground. On command, they're instructed to open, close, crisscross, or do any number of shifts. We did this every practice; it was a source of dread for many.

On this day, they instructed us to hold the regular position indefinitely. Fifty or sixty of us with helmets forming a human crop circle and legs reaching into the air resembled an old Busby Berkeley musical or the spokes of a bicycle. The coaching staff walked around to heckle, hinder, ensure we kept our feet at exactly six inches, and count out whoever gave up. Seconds turned into minutes, and quickly, one player dropped after another.

You could hear the agony amidst the merciless yelling of the rightfully smug coaching staff. Soon, the skies also opened to a drizzle, and being faceup on the field in our helmets, water began trickling into our eyes, noses, and mouths. One could barely address this without affecting the six-inch hold, thus causing more to give up instantly behind the added challenge of nature.

Another minute went by, and I was still holding. Indescribable was the pain burning in my core, the energy raging through my pelvis and lower back. Occasionally, a coach would walk by, get close to my face, and try to talk me into giving up. I wouldn't.

"She's still in it! I don't know, but she's still in it . . . Who wants to give up?!"

We were now way past our usual couple of minutes of this exercise, and it truly seemed like an eternity. It was the longest I'd ever held an isometric exercise in general. By then, all my bodily processes were devoted to holding up my legs, so I dared not even peek at who was left. I only concentrated on maintaining the hold and keeping my eyes closed against the downpouring rain. Then suddenly, I heard "RAISE IT UP!" and all the coaches echoed the call to lift our legs inches higher. I'd never put so much energy, focus, and will into anything in my life.

We elevated and held there in torment. The coaching staff remarked how there were only a few of us left. I thought, *a few of us left? That means I'm one of the last few standing!* I was almost delirious with fatigue, but this gave me something to believe in. "I'll show them. I won't give up." Suddenly, I heard "RAISE IT UP!" *again,* another call to lift our legs inches higher! The pain and burning became unbearable.

I'd never commanded my body like this. I saw a quote in a gym poster stating, "Tell your body what to do," and found it supremely enlightening. But I'd never applied it with a conviction beyond what I already knew how to do or thought I could figure out. Holding "six inches" indefinitely wasn't something I thought I'd ever have to do and was not what I expected to experience on this day.

More dropped out in an instant. I heard "Higher, HIGHER!" and felt the energy of the circle change. I squeezed my eyes tightly and held on as long as I could. I felt bodies moving around on the other side of my eyelids. Mother Earth also slowly devoured me in her mostly muddy, wet grass. I began to yell out as I couldn't contain the ache anymore. "Nothing and no one is gonna make me drop my legs," I told myself. I was partly astonished because the fight-or-flight felt so extreme, instant relief would've been easy to obtain. But it would've meant giving up, and this I wasn't interested in or willing to do.

I became delirious with body shock. I'd pushed past my limit and gone far beyond any conceivable measure of a limit for regular exercise. The parts of me which weren't on fire grew numb. I communicated with them. "I understand. Do what you need to do. But I don't care what happens. We're holding up these legs!" I began squirming to compensate. In the middle of my physical inventory check, I felt hands touching my shoulder pads and tapping my helmet. A voice spoke out to me.

"It's OK, Queen. You can put your legs down now."

What? Queen? Strange . . . I thought. I must be dreaming fr.

No one there had ever spoken to me with such regard. Thinking I was for sure hallucinating, I continued feebly holding my shaking legs, which were now probably at two inches. More voices and yelling in my direction grew coherent.

"It's over. It's done! Stop! You're the last one standing!"

Whatttttt?! I thought as tears began running down my face. I finally let my legs drop to the field and exhaled, panting.

"Are they serious?"

I continued to rest in the mud, which now framed me. Even if they were lying, I'd done way more than I thought I could and made it pretty damn far. I considered defeat, and I was still incredibly proud of myself. Then as I reoriented to normal breathing and bodily functioning, I noticed a faint, growing noise.

It was applause. It came through a murmur until it registered. It was for me.

"Can you get up?"

I responded affirmatively. Way past my "three-second rule," but it was OK. I felt bodies helping me up and started opening my eyes. I was indeed the last player standing. Whoa!

When my eyes cleared, I saw Coach O'Neal standing in front of me, holding his clipboard and a wealth of approval. Many came to pat me on the back and dap me up.

"Good s***."

"Nice job, young lady."

"I can't believe you beat me!!!"

"I'm impressed. Respect."

"OK! OK!"

"Nahhhhh, you wild out!"

"I ride the bus with her!"

"Yoooo!"

I was still delirious in recovery, but everyone stopped to give me credit for the triumph. On my feet, I gestured gratitude and that I was OK. One of the defensive and special teams coaches, Coach Rob, had been among those who taunted me the most and was now smug about knowing all along I could kick everybody's a**. How I also had more to show them.

Coach O'Neal gathered everyone back into order. He made several honorable comments about how "a girl had more guts than anyone on the field" that day. Then he walked over, looked me in the eye, engaged my hand in a handshake, and said, "Now *that's* what I'm talking about." His whistle blew, giving us minutes to collect ourselves and break into sessions with each coach. Everyone moved swiftly into the next thing, though I was still being greeted and congratulated. People who never spoke to me before were suddenly making speaking to me their business.

Everything changed from then on. In the following practices, Coach Rob took me aside during team drills to train me one-on-one or with a few other guys. I ran his drills till I couldn't stand it, or until *he* was tired.

"You're tough, I'm not gonna lie. But for what you're gonna face out on that field, you gotta be even tougher. Guys from other teams will find out it's you, and they won't hold back. In fact, they'll go harder! This is to prepare you."

The entire team was also instructed to look out for me as I'd be a known target. They weren't lying. Players from opposing teams would utter some of the meanest and borderline disturbing things to me during games. Especially between plays, when they saw me lining up, and after tackles. Thankfully, extra training proved successful as I withstood it all, and no one ever tackled me harder than my own team.

Speaking of tackles . . . drills intensified again. The hardest, named "the nutcracker," involved the same setup as the Bebo scenario but additionally being blind to start. Two players lay on the ground opposite each other and flipped over at the sound of the whistle, athletically got their bodies up, ran full speed ahead, and tackled the player across from them. The rest of the team huddled narrowly around the tackle zone, amplifying the concentrated feeling of a head-to-head battle. The expressly loud "CRACK!" from the intensity of said tackle usually meant it was done right. Because you'd lay facing away from your opponent, you wouldn't see them until right before the tackle. This forced you to rely on technique, override fear, and adapt to spacing, body language, and positioning in the moment.

Coach Rob called me into the drill one night and kept me in. Even though the element of blindness slightly terrified me, crack after crack, I held on. I was getting cheered too, with teammates saying, "This next one is tough, Em, but you got it! Don't be scared." Then one round, Coach quietly brought *two* players from the 16-19 age level to line up opposite me. No one else was going against two, let alone from drastically different weight classes. I couldn't see anything but heard, "Coach, you're gonna kill her!" and knew it couldn't be good. After that, things got eerily quiet, and I began praying through my mouthpiece!

Some whispered for me to stay calm and run straight. A few walked away and said they couldn't watch. I squirmed for some seconds, then closed my eyes and took deep breaths. I looked above the field lights into the night sky and waited for the whistle. It came. I got right up, swiveled to stand, and saw two big bodies (and their shadows) approaching me. One had been lying down and was running up the dirt like *Sonic the Hedgehog*, while the other was somehow in the air already, double-teaming the hit from high as the other went low. Adding to the demonstration, they stayed on top of me, which was excruciating, though they did ask if I was OK and seemed to mean it.

The team digressed to work on something different, and Coach Rob took me aside. He spoke about my experience so far and his motivation to toughen me up, which I appreciated.

"So, how you feeling?"

"I'm pretty good. I know this is what I signed up for."

He walked me to the far side of the field, where a large, old, rusty soccer goalpost leaned in its elder existence. He led us to it and looked up.

"OK, get up there."

"Excuse me, Coach?"

"You ever done a pull up before?"

"No, Coach. I wasn't very good on the monkey bars, though I wanted to be."

"Well, we're gonna fix that. You're very short, so I'll help you up. But once you're up there, it's all on you. You got it? You've gotta hold yourself up. Got it?"

"Yes, Coach!"

I exhaled, unsure about what was to happen. Dark night had fallen, and fatigue set in. I could see our neighborhood transgender prostitutes handling their regular business by the over and underpass tunnels on the far edges of the field. The rest of the team was behind us, some deep in learning plays, some lazily passing time by. "Everything was everything," I guess, and this was my charge, to hold myself up off a cold, rusty, ten-foot goalpost. This was my whole life, right here, what I had to do to get further and become better. I dreaded it and doubted my ability, but I trusted Coach Rob, and knew he was doing with me what many others wouldn't.

I got up there and quickly registered the thickness of the bar as a challenge to my small and soft hands. The rough texture from its chipping paint and chillingly exposed metal was unforgiving from years of a neglected outdoor stance. Its cold rigid metal seared into my flesh like a freezing iron. I was instructed to literally get a grip as he held my lower body steady.

"You got it? Can I let go?"

"Yes, Coach!"

It didn't take long for my smooth skin and lack of upper body strength to work against me. I struggled as he told me to remain "by any means necessary." I hung on.

"Whatever you do, don't let go!"

We did this a few more times with a few more exercises, concluding with five-ish solid pull ups. Though my palms were blistered and gnarled, and my chest burned, I was exhilarated to have done full out pull ups for the first time. We moved on to defensive lineman drills, handwork, and balance work. We continued as such for several days before he brought me back into the fold with the rest of the team. Short of harmful exhaustion, he pushed me past what I thought I could do, and we built a great rapport. I'm very grateful to Coach Rob and all my coaches, whom I worked with to learn every part of the game. I'm happy they saw me become a better player and the legitimate threat on the field they knew I could be.

Y'ALL (NOT) GON' MAKE ME LOSE MY MIND

The Harlem Giants made it to the championship game that year. The week before it, all the coaches huddled during practice. I was called over and quietly let in on their decision to put me in the game. They made it clear they didn't want to get the team disqualified; however, they believed I was more than capable and wanted to give the biggest middle finger possible to the league commissioner. After all, there was nothing legally documented that said, "no girls," so we could fight pushback if necessary. We planned.

Game day came. The whole team was hyped in knowing we could win it all. Everything felt like a movie, including the moment when the signal came for me to complete a substitution which put me in the game. I got the signal, quickly checked myself, and ran to the coach's side. I listened to the whispers of the head coach's instruction and the play the defensive coach told me to run in with. They snapped my helmet into place as I collected myself and put my mouthpiece in. I was more than prepared.

As I ran in, our beloved East Harlem crowd cheered. Though I wore a decoy jersey and different socks to hide my identity, our regular crowd knew it was me. They were ecstatic and almost blew the cover but, thankfully, didn't shout my name. I joined the defensive huddle, to the surprise and joy of my teammates. They reassured me they had my back. I relayed the play, our defensive captain relayed it again, called for the break, and we marched out to position.

I took a deep breath, put my hand in the soil, and took my stance. I'd been waiting to feel this in a game for too long. I was happy to take out all the injustice on this opposing team. I looked into the eyes of the offensive lineman across from me. He looked into mine and began chuckling through his mouthpiece and face guard. He realized it was me and loudly noted, "It's the girl!" I stayed calm (and started chuckling too!) then immediately went to work. He had me a few times, but I still racked up several tackles, sacks, and assisted plays. At one point, I heard them complaining to their coach about not knowing what to do with me. Ha!

Our defense completely shut them out in the second half, and we won the game. All the cheers put volume to a million types of victory. I was greeted and given respect by everyone on my team *and* the opposing team and their fans too. Their very talented quarterback came over to greet me and personally lift me up. This meant even more because he was killed in a shooting in Newark a few months later. (Bless up, young king!)

Alas, we were champions.

Happiness overtook us on the field. Our coaches were elated, and teammates cut up about how proud they were of me and how good it felt after such a crazy season. The commissioner, still pressed to deny it, bitterly handed over our championship trophy.

After the game, I went to stay at MaChannie's house. She and her daughters had seen me through numerous practices and prejudices. They knew the awards ceremony banquet was coming up and regarded it a must "Stunt 101"—an opportunity to "show up and show out" one more time. They felt making a statement visually and energetically was important.

Thanks to their support and feminine guidance in shopping with me, doing my hair, pep talks, and walking in my highest heels to date, I arrived at the banquet "glowed up" in formidable style. My hair was laid, my red, white, and royal blue jersey tucked neatly into a black pencil skirt, hugged by black stockings inside knee-high, stiletto, pointed-toe boots, and topped by my gleaming, white, unbroken smile.

Our defensive captain and my best foe turned best friend received "Defensive Player of the Year," especially for several clutch tackles, an interception, and a special teams touchdown in the championship game. I cheered gleefully for him. Then unexpectedly, *my* name was called. I was awarded "Rookie of the Year" to raucous applause. Effectively speechless, I knew enough was said on the field and through my winning presence. It'd been quite a journey.

We never heard a peep from the league commissioner again. We gathered for photos high on comradery and proven victory amidst a sea of individual and championship trophies. Change was ahead, and the team would never be the same, but as cameras flashed, I knew this moment was sweet, forever.

CHAPTER 18
TOUGH GIRL: A MINI-CAREER IN TACKLE FOOTBALL, PT. 2

THINGS TOOK A VERY ugly turn in the off season.

One of the alumni players who'd returned midseason to be an assistant coach contacted me. He was present when I won the "six inches" abdominal exercise challenge and was one of the first to congratulate me and help me up. He'd asked me to chill, noting he lived with one of our head defensive coordinators in the Morrison-Soundview section of the Bronx. I thought it would be cool, fun, and safe, all withstanding—especially with one of my regular coaches being there. Nothing made me second-guess it.

This coach we had in common had always supported me playing during the season, looked out for me, and seemed to genuinely like me. I played under his leadership during a few games where we won by defensive shutouts, and we had a very cordial rapport. He was a mentor and father figure to several players, especially those with rough family lives. He'd done many caring things for me, and I was always happy to see him.

The plans with the alumni player were simple: reconnection through a regular chill session. I'd come over, chop it up, play video games, vibe out, and smoke some weed in whatever order flowed best. My coach said he'd be occupied but not too far from reach in the house.

I noticed an energy I didn't expect when I got there. Not alarming but slightly off and made me question if it wasn't the best day. It was "Stormy Weather" out, and I was relieved to get dry and warm inside. I found them lounging separately in the basement of a two-story house. Being late and without a cell phone at the time, the alumni player greeted me with a "Thought you weren't going to make it." When I entered, it was dark, and the hallways were narrow. The lights were on in little sections but mainly came from the big screen TV in his room. There seemed to be a weight hanging in the air. He and the coach were also very nonchalant, as though my coming was an afterthought.

I passed a room where the coach was kicking back and talking on the phone. I was excited, as usual, to see him. He paused his conversation, welcomed me, and told me to come back and see him after I was settled. When I got to the alumni player's room, he asked me if there was anything I wanted to watch or play. I said I didn't have a preference. We had a few laughs, but my attempts at conversation fell flat, and he seemed extremely reserved. Not shy but almost indifferent that I was there, which was confusing. I'd thought he wanted to chill so we could talk and have fun as teammates, maybe build on his veteran experience and me heading into my second season. He offered to spark up the weed, which was a relief as I hoped it would make him more enjoyable. I reasoned I'd smoke, get just-high-enough, and dip—to enjoy the rest of my day. I excused myself to pause and check in with the coach. *Strange*, I thought.

When I got to the coach's room, he was still on the phone, ironing clothes, and offered me a seat on his bed. This wasn't unusual as it felt generally platonic, like any friend's room and bed, and it occupied most of the space. I also had no reason to question it. I removed my shoes, playfully got up, and propped up against a wall. I tried not to be so obviously listening as he smoothly wrapped up his call—working over some lady, also not unusual. He was known to love women, and women seemed to love him back. He was a tall, big-bodied guy with a rich, commanding voice, sharp mind, humor, and remarkable ability to coach. He was a genuinely lovable person.

He got off the phone and asked how I was doing and what was happening in my life. How I felt about football and how things were going with the team. The conversation was generally smooth until he asked me if I was having any trouble with boys and if I was involved in relationships or sex. He was always very blunt with us, with everyone, especially about street life and life matters. He'd always been a bit overprotective of me as the only girl on the team, even suggesting wearing my pads differently to protect more of my body, bringing extra pads, and fitting a few on me. So, his candor or interest wasn't shocking. It was the direction of the topics which felt odd. He proceeded to make intimate comments about my physical features.

The mood shifted upon my realizing he'd also been observing me in a nonplatonic way. He lightly touched my leg on the bed, then my face. I was clearly uncomfortable. I made some combination of gestures and words to halt this and move. Instinctively, a part of me began recalling the layout of the house. An impromptu exit wouldn't be easy, but it was possible. I didn't feel an expressed danger, but I couldn't call this "good vibes" or safety anymore. Then his phone rang again. I made my way out of the room as he picked up another conversation.

"Come see me before you leave," he called out.

The alumni player was smoking when I got back to his room. By this point in my life, I'd been smoking numerous types of weed for over a year and felt a decent grasp of the process, my tolerance, and how to be high. I reasoned I was fine. *We're gonna make this mad quick,* I thought. We rotated the blunt and laughed at the TV. For a moment, I was relieved. With the mood lighter, I relaxed a bit. By the time he offered to "shotgun" me and proceeded to, I was already feeling a little funny and unable to give an accurate answer but was still in good spirits.

Soon after we finished, he left the room briefly. While he was gone, a deep wave came over my physical body. Fatigue mostly, but suddenly, I just felt heavy. Super heavy and super slow. My vision became glossy, then blurry, and the room seemed to shift. My view and hearing of the TV weren't the same. Nothing was.

I went to his bed to stabilize myself. I sat down, then tried to lift my arm and couldn't. Soon, I couldn't freely move anything. I tried to focus on where my bag was and what direction I would go to grab it later. With my feet still on the floor, I lay my upper body on the bed in exhaustion. Initially, I thought it was just a powerful high.

He returned, asking if I was okay while closing the door. I said yes. That I would take a few minutes before being on my way. A part of me internally announced; *play it cool, but we can't move anything right now, and we don't know how we're gonna get out of here.* I felt my heart rate increase but stayed as calm as possible. The best I could do was move my eyeballs around. I'd never experienced this feeling so suddenly over my body before.

He said more things that I couldn't decipher. Soon, I felt him touching my torso and around my hips. I tried to move his hands but didn't have the strength, and I was also going in and out of consciousness. Finally, I came out of a brief blackout and felt the air on my skin. My jeans and panties were down. He started having his way with me orally, and I faintly said, "What are you doing? I don't want that. Stop!" In my body, I was yelling, screaming in fact, but it was coming out of me like whispers. I just didn't have any physical strength. He did what he wanted and watched me. This continued. I felt incredibly exposed, panicked, and intruded upon.

When it was over, I felt all types of embarrassment, shame, bewilderment, betrayal, and horror in my mind. I didn't know how I would stop or get out of this. There was no weapon to grab and no vigor to defend myself with. He lifted my legs onto the bed and moved me closer to the headboard.

I unsuccessfully tried to get up again as I heard him unbuckling. Then he climbed and hovered, telling me to calm down. He covered me and started preparing to penetrate. I started squirming and pleading for him not to do this. Soon, I felt him making his way in, and I died a thousand deaths. I said, "No," "Stop," and "Please stop," repeatedly. Each time I said it was more emotional than the last. He continued to push his way in. I could feel him unjustly enjoying me. I felt invaded and disgusted. I was acutely aware of him and his shape and size. My entire being was in a red alarm. This wasn't right, and though almost helpless, I was rejecting it.

My cries and breathing got intense, my arms flailed and pushed back the best they could, I tried turning my distraught face. Continuing, he asked a cruel question. "Do you really want me to stop?" I affirmed. With more thrusts, he asked again, then finally stopped, and pulled out. Immediately, I rolled off the bed and onto the floor. I don't know how, but I put on my pants, crawled to my things, got on my feet, and left the room. I stumbled through the dark hallway and remembered my shoes were still in the coach's room.

I needed to leave this house as soon as possible, but it had been raining most of the day, so I reasoned I needed the shoes. Reluctantly, I moved into his room to grab them. He was still on the phone and noticed me making an abrupt, disheveled exit. He called my name, and I looked up, startled. He looked me in my eyes, and I could tell he knew what happened. He seemed to sense it, which caught me by horrible surprise. A part of him seemed heartbroken.

A different part of him did the talking, though.

"I'm sorry . . . but just know. Whatever he did to you, I could do to you better."

I felt horrified all over again.

I couldn't contain it and let out an angsty scoff as I left. I moved quickly, knowing I needed to make *sure* I got out. I stumbled through the layout of the block and neighborhood, still putting on my coat, shoes, and bag. I sped to the train station, up the stairs to a bench, and finally started to cry. I tightened up quickly as a group of boys spotted me going through my things and seemed to want to rob me. Then I refocused on protecting myself and making it home, moving by the station attendant's booth and staying alert with the last of my numb energy. I was still in complete shock; I still couldn't believe what happened.

My immediate thought was no one would believe me. I'd be blamed for hanging out with grown men, for smoking weed . . . all the above. But none of it was particularly unusual for me. I'd always socialized with older friends and associates. Being an only child, I was often around adults. I routinely conversed with elders, my parents' friends, and my friends' parents. I also traveled the city by myself a lot. I hated the idea of being blamed because I'd put myself there. I was mostly dismayed at being taken advantage of by people I trusted implicitly, people who'd seen me through challenge and triumph on the football field and sought to protect me there.

I was confused about why they'd do this. What had I done to invite this? I'd been to many people's houses to chill or play video games, so what made this an invitation to assault me? To sexualize and rape me? Did they think I was going to be okay with it? Perhaps. It seemed so normal to them. Maybe it was. Maybe other girls went with it. Maybe it was normal for them too. I didn't know. But I knew it didn't feel good, didn't feel right, and wasn't invited. Above everything, I'd also thought I was special to them in a completely different way. Physical disgust and emotional breakdown lingered heavily. I just hoped it wouldn't feel like this forever.

In attempting to describe it for the first time to a girlfriend, I used the words "He had sex with me, but I didn't want it," and she corrected me. "No, Em, you were raped." It didn't set in how casual normalized violence is until I heard this spoken to me.

She was right, and though I'd been through it firsthand, I still couldn't believe it.

I told my best foe turned best friend from the football team, and he was immediately *enraged*. True to his "Reckless" nickname, his first instinct was to go to the house, brutalize the alumni and the coach, and take it as far as needed. This was valid but seemed a little too much for me to handle, thinking of having to tell the story to more people, how all our coaches and teammates would then know, and the added distress if anything happened to my him while seeking to avenge me. I pleaded with him not to do anything or tell anyone; he kept his word.

I attempted to tell someone else who'd likely be more constructive, a small group of big sisters in network with my arts program Impact Repertory Theatre, who were meeting at our community center in Harlem. I was still having a hard time saying the word "raped." When my retelling attempts weren't as brave or clear as maybe they needed to be, and their responses weren't as I'd hoped, I felt incredibly awkward and like I'd inconvenienced them. I decided to be silent about it indefinitely.

Years later, while in Orlando, Florida for a gig, I sat with some girls from the arts program during a company lunch break. Somehow, while waiting for our food, the subject of rape was quietly brought up. To our horrific amazement, five out of six of us admitted it happened to us. We spoke softly about physical, mental, and emotional experiences after our respective assaults. How sensual energy and sexuality were affected, how it felt to be in our bodies since, and how judged we felt by the whole thing. We embraced each other and shared a lot of healing love which I've continued to be thankful for. I only wished we could've been there for each other sooner.

Since then, several male friends, associates, mentees, and intimate partners have also bravely confided in me about being abused, molested, or sexually assaulted. I'm grateful they felt ready to speak out and trusted me when I was also ready to listen, support them through their processing of it, and be strong enough to love them unconditionally. While keeping our respective stories confidential, I was able to lessen stigmas by empathically sharing how sexual violence has happened to some of the toughest, strongest, and most masculine men I know.

It's not uncommon for suppressed memories of assault to resurface unexpectedly. While writing this book, I realized I'd mentally blocked out being molested at ages nine and eleven prior to this rape at fifteen. A report published by the *National Library of Medicine* named "In Limbo: Time Perspective and Memory Deficit Among Female Survivors of Sexual Abuse" by Angi Jacobs-Kayam and Rachel Lev-Wiesel, states, "Trauma survivors often report time and space disorientation . . . disintegration of body, mind, and identity; and chaos, exhaustion, and confusion . . . from the conceptual perspective of 'captured in a distorted time,' which is one of the traumagenic constructs of childhood sexual abuse." My heart continues to stay positive for the resolve of all who've experienced this and navigate its effects in adulthood. It's undeserved and *not* your fault.

If you're experiencing post-traumatic stress disorder symptoms from sexual violence or need help, resources, or therapeutic support through a situation, please see the back of this book.

Psychologist Richard Tedeschi coined the phrase Post-Traumatic Growth to explain the positive changes that can arise from adversity. These positive changes are as common as the negative ones and can include increased empathy, a recognition of personal strengths, and a shift in priorities. If we continue with the example of an assault, perhaps the attack itself was meaningless and unjustified, but in healing, you now have empathy for other survivors and the courage to speak out around the injustices that cause them.

—Lisa Cooper Ellison, *"You Are Not Your Traumas. But Here's How to Write About Them"*

The following football season had its entertaining episodes but felt much less magical for more reasons. First, our beloved elder, Coach Bovain, made transition, and his unforgettable energy, old school attitude, and mind for the game were greatly missed. (Bless up, king!)

Next, practices were moved as gentrification swept the area. Car dealerships and major renovations took over surrounding blocks as our grass field also symbolically changed to turf. Many veteran teammates who were among the most talented and elite athletes also went their separate ways. This included my bestie, who, as our defensive captain, often ran switches and audibles with me. He quit the team and eventually moved out of the city with his family. Midway through my rookie season and that following year, he'd grown to also be my first love and first sexual partner, so his absence was greatly felt.

Our roster was notably thin, and with the loss of several pure position players, many found themselves filling in multiple roles. I'd gone on a vigorous weight-gain diet that summer to withstand training and contact better—one of the most challenging diets I'd ever experienced. Not easy or enjoyable, I was routinely irritated, which greatly affected my mood. I ruled my efforts "too successful" when I was called to fill in on the offensive line.

While I greatly respected and understood how crucial a good line is for an effective offense and quarterback to shine, it was the last thing I wanted to do. I got to play every game but wasn't enjoying myself. The team rapport also wasn't the same. Many didn't seem to care about dedicated practice or winning games. With the effort of a few and a lot of luck, we made it to the championship game again but lost bitterly in its final moments.

I looked forward to a visit with the New York Sharks semipro women's football team, which boasted being the longest-running and most-winningest team in women's tackle football history.

They were interested via a recommendation by one of my coaches, and arrangements were made to tour their facility. I was excited about the meeting as the only women I knew playing football were models in lingerie uniforms at pay-per-view events. I was encouraged to see the next level, especially since many said I could never have a football career.

I met some very powerful and inspiring women there. I was surprised as most players were years my senior, more than the average college or professional players, and many had children. Those who were single mothers had especially unique situations as financially, it was harder to support their lives while playing in this well-known yet still largely invisible league. Some described how quitting under pressure from family or partners was expected and how much others took on to be able to play. Everyone was polite, though only a few seemed generally upbeat, happy, and in what I'd come to expect as professional athletic shape (regardless of body type). They described drops in fan turnout and their contribution to rather lax marketing efforts. It all seemed more depressing than encouraging. A few bluntly expressed I was better off pursuing another route or a different career altogether, and I took this to heart. Despite the passing of Title IX in 1972 transforming women's sports education, breakout female athletes becoming household names, and more advancements in the field since, many standards have been slow to shift in the larger industry, including with team budgets, salaries, sponsorship, visibility, and media support. Some shifts are still yet to be seen.

Back in all-boys land, rumors proved right about the Harlem Giants' coaching staff breaking up. The bright spot was head coach Coach O'Neal was starting his own team, the Bronx Buccaneers. Upon my decision to decline the semipro offer, to my surprise, he asked if I'd assist him. We met routinely and walked through gathering administrative records, parents' meetings, organizing uniforms, and running practices. We initially held sessions in the former track and field opposite Yankee Stadium, then moved closer to Cardinal Hayes High School.

After a successful pilot season, he expressed wanting to expand the age range offerings and asked if I would stay on to head them up. So, I moved into assisting, coordinating, and coaching for ages 7-9, 10-12, and 13-15. Co-coaching were two of the best people I'd ever worked with in any field, Coach Mel, and Coach Rich. Coach Rob from the Harlem Giants and our new parent-coach Coach Mike also supplemented our rotation.

Mel and Rich were talented, pro-experienced former college players from high division schools. They were also hilarious, hood, caring, and intelligent. We gelled immediately and worked exceptionally well together. Coaches' meetings were easy, planning practices were smooth, and we genuinely enjoyed one another's company. They treated me respectfully from day one, we counseled one another on life matters, and I admired their experiences. We got along so well and were all so capable we decided to rotate being head coach, offensive, and defensive coordinators the entire season. Every game, one of us would be one for the day. We allowed each other to do what we were best at, and everything was better with all three of us. This bond came in handy because the workload was demanding.

We experienced a lot of great and coachable kids. We also had many who struggled athletically or seemed forced to be there by their parents. Some had learning impairments or behavioral imbalances, making it a challenge to remember plays or respond in real time. We sincerely wanted the best for them all. With such young ages, we had to be attentive to players with less skill, understanding, desire, or focus so the whole team could function on the field. I'm not sure if the emotion was guilt, but I felt bad for the willing, capable, alert, and coachable players who deserved to excel in the program and feel more supported in their readiness.

We did our best to give everyone constructive attention. Usually, it was just a few players carrying the team through games. I immensely appreciated the patience and maturity of the situation by the more skilled, athletic, mentally, and neurologically equipped players, as they were mostly gracious, and I knew it wasn't easy all around. The responsibility to accommodate everyone, manage egos, cognition levels, and foster unity among them was enormous. Organizing all this while dealing with parents, administration, traveling to games, and incurring multiple losses, was often draining.

We felt a lot of hiccups, but I'm thankful we were able to put smiles on these kids' faces sometimes. I hoped they'd gain something, as it was a pleasure to watch them grow and have moments, even in small ways. Also, I couldn't have picked better fellow coaches to be this stressed with!

At times, we'd observe the operation of the newly formed 16-19 age group, which I wished I could be a part of as a player but was flatly denied. (Boys in this age range were, in many cases, the size and shape of NFL players already. The concern conveyed to me was safety in their bodies, speed, and power possibly being too much, even for me.) Sad about being unable to play, I'd occasionally join the other age groups in hitting drills, to the wide-eyed surprise of our players who only knew me as "Coach Emily."

My perspective as a coach was that we weren't just teaching the game of football; we were part of raising someone's child. Understaffed and underfunded with so many players to accommodate, I was always anxious about whether I was doing a good job. Our whole staff came from championship teams and were used to winning and the right things coming together, so it was very hard watching our players lose so many games. We had to grow as coaches to resolve our frustrations and anger, inspire the players to believe in themselves, and encourage them to face another day. This was harder than I imagined it would be, and to this day, I pray my best was enough.

All the discouragement I felt was put into perspective at our seasonal awards ceremony. The coaching staff was commended throughout the program, and suddenly, I was called to the stage. Coach O'Neal began talking about when he coached me as a player and how happy and honored he was to bring me on in this role. Then someone unexpectedly walked up with a special trophy and to much applause, I was given an "Emily Award." It was a decoratively rusted silver football resting atop a dark wooden stand, with a gold plaque on the front engraved with my name in its title. It was for my achievements as a player-coach, support of all age levels, and representation of women in our community league. I couldn't have been more grateful.

It tickles me when people learn I played tackle football, and they can't believe it. They often look at me, listen to my voice, take in my energy, rationalize the tough or disciplined things they might've seen me do, rule it acceptable . . . and *still* can't believe it! It was a wild three or four-year blur of almost every part of the game. In many ways, this experience paralleled the arch of a lifetime career. Almost everything short of color commentary, though I would've done that too. I was sad to see it end but didn't want it to end sadly.

I considered getting a "sports fitness and recreation" degree for a career pathway as an NFL trainer or referee, which I would've loved too. At the time, sideline reporters and cheerleaders were the only visible women in professional (American) football. I could clearly see myself doing my part to make other roles more visible and wasn't scared of what it would take. It felt good to imagine and not be intimidated about being great or groundbreaking enough and enjoy continuing to do something I loved just for me. Even if I chose not to, it felt good to see myself as capable. Since then, I've enjoyed seeing the growth of capable and talented women in professional sports as featured athletes, referees, trainers, coaches, executives, and owners.

I can still hear the echoes of Coach Bovain yelling at us in my beginning days as a player. How much trouble we'd get into.

Being unable to contain our laughter and amusement when he'd shout so hard his dentures would slip out of his mouth. How much composure it took when he'd ask if we thought it was funny!

His favorite phrase to yell was, "Do it right the *FIRST* time!" Often getting in people's faces to say it, he'd be completely beside himself at our mistakes, blunders, and fumbles. Though overly demanding to some, I saw a lot of right in this, as many mishaps were due to a lack of simple attention or discipline. He respected hard work, focus, and execution, always striving for a high standard. I appreciated his passionate yelling because, to him, it didn't matter if we were in the hood in a no-name community league. He never doubted we were capable of being the best, and that we should strive for high standards.

Oscar and Grammy award-winner Jamie Foxx recalled a parallel to this old school counterintuitive on the acclaimed *R&B Money Podcast* with Tank and J. Valentine in 2022. He remembered playing piano alongside the legendary Ray Charles before the production of the monumental feature film biopic *Ray*. Though an accomplished musician and legend in his own right, Jamie fumbled his fingers at the keys (I think most of us would understand) and stopped, immediately apologizing. Ray charismatically stopped *him*, jokingly asking why he'd hit a wrong note? After Jamie was apparently told not to do it again, he left him with the affirmation, "Life is about taking the time to hit the right notes."

I'm a big believer in the right notes, in having the right mind for anything. Comedians, filmmakers, athletes, and entrepreneurs all talk about right timing and task management. Good people are usually good because of integrity about the right things. Success seems to be a by-product of the right things; happiness seems to last because of the right things, and improvement seems to come from attention to the right things. Even "good villains" resonate as right or operating effectively in some critical area. Coach Bovain's "Do it right the *FIRST* time!" still occasionally echoes in my consciousness. Even when I know it's not appropriate because many things take repetition to get right, I understand its intention, appreciate it, and often learn faster.

My memories of playing tackle football in the dirt, rocks, mud, heat, rain, ice, and snow remain surreal. Running a program and coaching games seems like something out of a sitcom. The weirdness of eyes and commentary I'd get while traveling with a helmet and shoulder pads in my hands. Getting hit so hard that I saw stars. Out-exercising everyone on a rainy day. Inspiring a picket line. Sacking a quarterback in a championship game while in "disguise." Meeting my first love and at first hating him. Laughing with my friends, the gleam of trophies in my room, helping other kids have their own moments. It was short, but in doing something different which I really loved, it was felt, and stretched like an eternity in my origin story.

As proud as I am of all this perceived courage, conquering, and triumph, I'm just as proud to have grown to my liking as a divine feminine woman. In "Soft Black Girls and the Reclamation of Black Femininity," Casira Copes describes, "the world seems to think that Black girls and softness don't mix." It's been my additional pleasure to shed the weight of this experience that isn't mine to carry anymore and evolve from its lessons. I wouldn't be the whole me without this journey drawn by desire and curiosity, which I didn't let fear or shame take away. It required me to give up who I thought I was to find I was already more and greater than any stigma or stereotype. Through all its toughness, tackling, and roughhousing, I've kept my soft voice, soft skin, and soft superpowers as desired. I love that for me, too.

I still have a lot of heart.

CHAPTER 19
THE REAL WORLD IS FAKER THAN WRESTLING, PT. 1

THE HIP-HOP and pro wrestling community has been quietly ballooning for decades. The *Def Jam: Vendetta* video game mashup of 2003 was a promising glimpse of what was to come for this niche audience I naturally grew into; a visionary gift of sorts for its culture nerds. I couldn't have imagined the range covered in years since, from radio shows, newsletters, blogs, and podcasts to premium content, large-scale outdoor events, in-ring debuts of rappers, and icons not just brightening up front-row seats but also participating in televised shows.

Few people know how truly happy the sport of pro wrestling makes me. First as a lifelong fan, then identifying with it physically, creatively, and emotionally. My material begging as a child was mainly about musical instruments and anything related to wrestling. I couldn't attend live events but was faithfully glued to weekly television coverage, fan chatter, and promotional materials. I got in trouble for running up my father's credit card with a plenteousness of T-shirts, posters, 8x10s, VHS tapes, autobiographies, a *WrestleMania* box set, and a life-size "Chyna" calendar. I even bought a cookbook! I can only imagine my father's perspective when he came to address me about it, walking into my room—which probably looked like an official merch shop!

Prior to this, he'd agreed to take me and a few friends to the then "WWF New York" restaurant. We ran through it gleefully like children in Disneyland, watching crazed fans imitate their favorite wrestlers, meeting the likes of Shawn Michaels and The Big Boss Man, and sipping Shirley Temples with extra cherries while Michael Cole and Taz remotely hosted the *Sunday Night Heat* show. Years later, I'd begin my start in the business by walking into the office of the same man who trained Taz and many others for the pros.

In some ways, this privacy about my deep love of wrestling made it sweeter when I embraced the opportunity to begin training. I wanted to dive into it for years, even when I became disinterested as a fan. I'd done all its adjacent elements separately: athletics, dynamic movement, weightlifting, boxing, theater, live performance, public speaking, audience engagement, creative marketing, and media production. To put it all together was an orgasmic thought. But more than my immense respect for the sport, its history, and business lived an innate desire in me to fight, to channel who I really was physically. To violently free the woman being held hostage by this nice, quiet, modest girl introducing herself as me everywhere.

Both my football and boxing careers were redirected just as I got into a groove. Actively studying dance as a concentration came and went with my degree. After leaving my performing arts program of thirteen years, not doing at least fifty shows annually plus weekday rehearsals was yet another big shift and contributed to a physical depression I wasn't even aware could exist. Though I still made significant progress, beginning my solo career as a creative and performing artist met the global stall of the COVID-19 pandemic. I was way more than just touch deprived; I had a chronic momentum hunger from way back. I needed the feeling of tackling someone to the ground, of seamless rhythm on a speed bag, of connecting with an audience, of methodically and spontaneously making art with the whole self.

The nice, quiet, modest girl really wanted to beat someone's face in. To assume my walk into life's coliseum as the gladiator and artist I knew I was. For my large amount of passion and intelligence to feel at ease in my own free heart even if it wasn't acceptable in anybody else's. I wanted to romp in a space that could accommodate me without compromise; to meet a dance with my own perfect coordination. To smoothly work, move, connect, counter, and "wrassle" someone into submission. For my rhythm, power, and uniqueness, inside and out, to serve me unequivocally. To avenge everything I never deserved to experience, one match at a time.

While motivation, a history of activity, and years of watching, studying, and consuming wrestling help, *nothing* compares to training in the ring and working matches live. I'd find this out in more ways than one. Fortunately, I went in with a "long game" and bigger vision in mind.

I chose to train with legendary WWE Hall of Famer, "The Unpredictable One," Johnny Rodz and his World of Unpredictable Wrestling Club, with an interest in learning ring psychology more than wrestling moves. Once described by Vince McMahon as "capable of wrestling on a scientific basis, many, many times . . ." Johnny was inducted into his first wrestling Hall of Fame alongside greats like Killer Kowalski, Gorilla Monsoon, Louis Albano, and Vincent J. McMahon. Hailing from the hills of Puerto Rico, he had wrestled on numerous continents, was recognized by the prestigious Cauliflower Alley Club, and received his WWE Hall of Fame induction in 1996 while I was still in my introduction to the sport.

I watched a million matches as a fan. Now I wanted the ability to see everything I'd already seen with different eyes, ears, instincts, senses, and physical adaptation to the ring. A big bonus was where the wrestling club was housed; within the world-famous Gleason's boxing gym alongside world-champion trainers, thanks to the supportive and beloved owner Bruce Silverglade. This was no Equinox—there was no EDM playing or glossy neon paint. It was a raw, no frills, communal atmosphere of betterment I desired and reconnected me to boxing.

I'd begun boxing training in my midteens in Chico, California during a very miserable time where I ended up in a juvenile delinquent program. Chico Boxing for Fitness was a gym on the list of places I could choose to do community service, which I thought was too good to be true! I signed up *immediately*. After a disciplined period of consistent attendance and quality work, I humbly asked the owners if I could begin working out. Soon, I was investing four, five, and six hours of extra sweating at the gym daily. The owner and gym founder Joe Rodriguez soon graciously began training me himself.

They had a vast library of classic boxing matches on cassette tapes to which I routinely immersed myself whenever I wasn't working or training. The gym was also full of talented, excellent, and good spirited athletes, to which training alongside them made me feel happy to be alive. Some very capable and together girls trained there, including future seven-time champion prizefighter, the "Lady of Boxing," Ava Knight-Salicka. She was being groomed for a professional career, and it was inspiring to see her train, work, and travel with a team dedicated to this goal. Meanwhile, my body was transforming in ways it hadn't before, I had a healthy focus away from problems, and the mental challenge of you-versus-you proved immense. I found boxing to be the most demanding sport I'd ever done . . . until I started wrestling.

The Power of Your Subconscious Mind, initially published in 1963 by Dr. Joseph Murphy, discusses in profound detail the origins of normal and abnormal fear. It proposes that as self-preservation tools, nature gives us two natural fears at birth: a fear of falling and of loud noises. Observe tiny babies, and this is usually true as well as logical. All other fears are acquired through conditioning, learned habits, environment, and repeated thoughts which become beliefs. (They're neutralized or made obsolete by the same means.) Legendary athlete Mike Tyson once spoke very eloquently to the press about boxers doing what people try their best to avoid every day . . . in facing confrontation. Wrestlers take this a step further in training to master, among other things, the original fears.

When my wrestling training began, it was challenging, painful, and demanding. My entire body was a different kind of sore while my mind insisted on combing through the intricacy of what I was learning even after hours. Still, it was agreeing with me, slowly, and I was having fun, even as a naïve novice. I loved it as much as I did when I was only a fan, maybe even more. A few techniques started clicking for me at the basic level. I relished watching those better than me. I was happy to practice the basics repeatedly and became addicted to improvement.

I realized I'd quickly overcome the elemental level of the two "normal" fears. Only a month and a half in, I had a very long way to go, but mentally, there seemed nothing more to be afraid of. Even if something scared me or made me anxious, I could diagnose the fear and overcome it one way or another. I used this inspiration every time I stepped into the ring, whether I was facing vulnerability in the learning process or a menacing opponent.

I learned that the pro wrestler has many athletic things to think about. Fundamentally, it's a full body sport in real time, requiring coordination of all the limbs and major muscle groups. But little is often said about the wrestling body using different energy systems simultaneously. This requires a different type of fitness, strength, control, joint mobility, and body awareness. A wrestler trains situational self-protection, spatial recognition, endurance, agility, power, rhythm, explosiveness, and above all, *timing*. This includes the ability to relax, perceive, respond accurately, and execute effectively at any moment. There is a high level of scientific improvisation involved. Beyond physicality . . . the pro wrestler must also think about how they perceive themselves and how they are being perceived.

Persona, image, and likeness are significant parts of all sports. Numerous athletes in time have sparked our intrigue, admiration, inspiration, and conversation with character and nuance aside from athletic ability. Wrestling is unique in history, being one of the first athletic activities of humankind as well as naturally found in the animal kingdom (just look at any litter of kittens or puppies). Pro wrestling as a business has centered the attraction of persona, image, and likeness from its beginnings.

In the times of the ancients, when gladiators and warriors entered pronounced, natural spaces for battle, the elements were the same. Whether it was for the love and proficiency of combat, the release and catharsis of violence, the prospect of saving their own lives, or supporting their families, every person walking through the gates, space, or ropes had a story. Athletes entering professional wrestling today parallel the ancients in this uniqueness. The legend created for themselves or uplifted by the people means as much to their careers as their physical abilities. Thus, every pro wrestler, at some point, must think about how they see themselves and how they may be seen. Black wrestlers and women in wrestling have a unique history within this history of the sport, which as reflections of me, I've been very aware of.

While it's tempting to look no further than comprehensive entertainment content such as Josiah Williams's viral Wrestle and Flow Hip-Hop masterpiece "Black Beautiful," there's even more untold, unseen, and unsung in wrestling history and, thus, its future. In the early eras, "girl wrestlers" and "lady wrestlers" like Mildred Burke and June Byers, in addition to Black women like Ethel Johnson, Babs Wingo, Ramona Isabelle, and Marva Scott, not only held titles but were responsible for moving the sport forward all over the world. Wrestling was making an all-important shift from its circus act paradigm to a major local attraction and one of the first programmatic features of the newly invented television. It also shifted from when women were banned from wrestling and boxing in the United States and color lines were being crossed in neighboring sports. Athletic, eye-catching, and distinctive Black women were among the hottest attractions recruited to build revenues and raise the profile of wrestling globally.

During their peak years, Babs, Ethel, and Marva would have been among the highest-paid Black athletes in the States. However, the negatives that came with this life were tough enough even to lead one sister to a nervous breakdown. Wrestling in the late 1950s, '60s, and '70s came at a price. Jim Crow Laws were still active, especially when the women traveled back to Southern states and overseas. During a show held in Missouri, the promoters did not allow black wrestling fans to enter. When Ethel heard this, she and her sisters packed their bags and left as a way to show their solidarity with the fans that were discriminated against. Goals like wrestling at Madison Square Garden in New York were simply impossible since some states held a ban on women's wrestling.

—*Ebony Nash for ProWrestlingStories.com*

As the television era progressed, Black wrestlers and women may not have necessarily seen more time in the media spotlight. Still, some, like the previously named women, were gaining ground in prosperous local territories. The territories fleshed out their businesses and found cash cows in weekly shows, promotions, and featured attractions. This era laid the seeds which bloomed into pro wrestling's highest popularity, attendance records, merchandising sales, and national television coverage in the United States.

Though the modern corporation era phased out the territory system, personas, images, and likenesses were already bigger, more colorful, and arguably more lucrative. Increasingly, Black wrestlers and women chose (or were bestowed) similar paths of representation, even though their stories and athletic abilities differed significantly. In looking at these nuances of evolution within wrestling's evolution, I wondered who I'd be, how I'd be perceived, and how I wanted to represent myself.

Rhonda Miller, the original head of the dance department at Pace University, once said aloud in class, "One thing about Emilia, she's always going to do her homework." This was especially complimentary because I was one of the least technically sound dancers in the stacked dance department. I was surrounded by people who'd been in dance or gymnastics training since they were single digit years of age. People who came to college already flourished with backgrounds in ballet, jazz, tap, modern dance, and live theater.

I'm not sure I'd met anyone who'd done the type of dancing I had, primarily in what was still noncommercial Hip-Hop at the time and African styles. A ballet instructor (whom I really liked) couldn't contain her laughter one day when explaining to a class how I'd never be a principal ballerina or be featured in a ballet company, primarily due to my body composition and age. Still, as I'd experienced on the football field, no physical lesson could beat the lessons already moving me through mentally, energetically, and spiritually. As well, you can guess, that I kept showing up!

I also carried with me the inspiration of Sabra Johnson, third season winner of the popular Fox network show *So You Think You Can Dance*. She was a breathtakingly amazing, powerful, graceful, and captivating dancer. A vignette of her backstory revealed she hesitated to pursue dance because, according to industry standards, she'd started "too late." She decided to try it anyway, trained expressly hard, and emerged victorious on this national TV show four years later. She scored consistently high in the competition and, to me, looked better than many of the seasoned dancers who'd been studying for a lifetime. Her body, face, and outgoing energy also expressed a story and soul many others didn't or couldn't.

This example, among others, helped me through my dance education and challenging degree track. These inspirations and my desire to release the suppression and fighting of a lifetime certainly helped me as I walked into a wrestling ring for the first time.

Here I was, likewise, overriding the construct of "starting too late" to do something only a fraction of people on earth do professionally—*and* successfully. I was looking to put all I am and all I could give into something I'd loved since childhood. I would make right on my imagination, physical uniqueness, speaking ability, attraction to power, and desire for reverse anger management.

I'd lived a life between the lines of notebooks, in a boxing gym, on a football field, on theatrical stages, nestled in rap ciphers, swooning at poetry slams, grooving on dance floors, jungle-booking through New York City, and outwitting the weight of the world to my best ability. I was a spirit warrior, a warrior queen, an original woman, and a Black girl. Now, I would take it back to the ancients and play my cards in the grappling game. I would stand on business, "ten toes down," with the opportunity to express the fight I had in me. I would walk through the gates of the coliseum with a legend behind me and a new one to create. So, what would it be?

I had ideas but knew visions would also materialize naturally at the right time. I wanted training to tell me more about myself. The mental and physical demands were also enough to focus on just starting out. Still, I couldn't resist daydreaming and scribing away about all the scenarios I saw creatively in my head. I also couldn't resist thinking of the long line of Black and women wrestlers in similar but very different shoes years and decades ago.

Creativity and sports are freer but no different than academics to me, so I also had homework to do. Continually watching "tape," analyzing my inspirations, and questioning what's come before me continue to stimulate and fulfill me. I was already filling my notebooks with wrestling journals before I ever stepped foot into training. The following is an excerpt from an entry titled "On the Three Classes of Black Wrestlers."

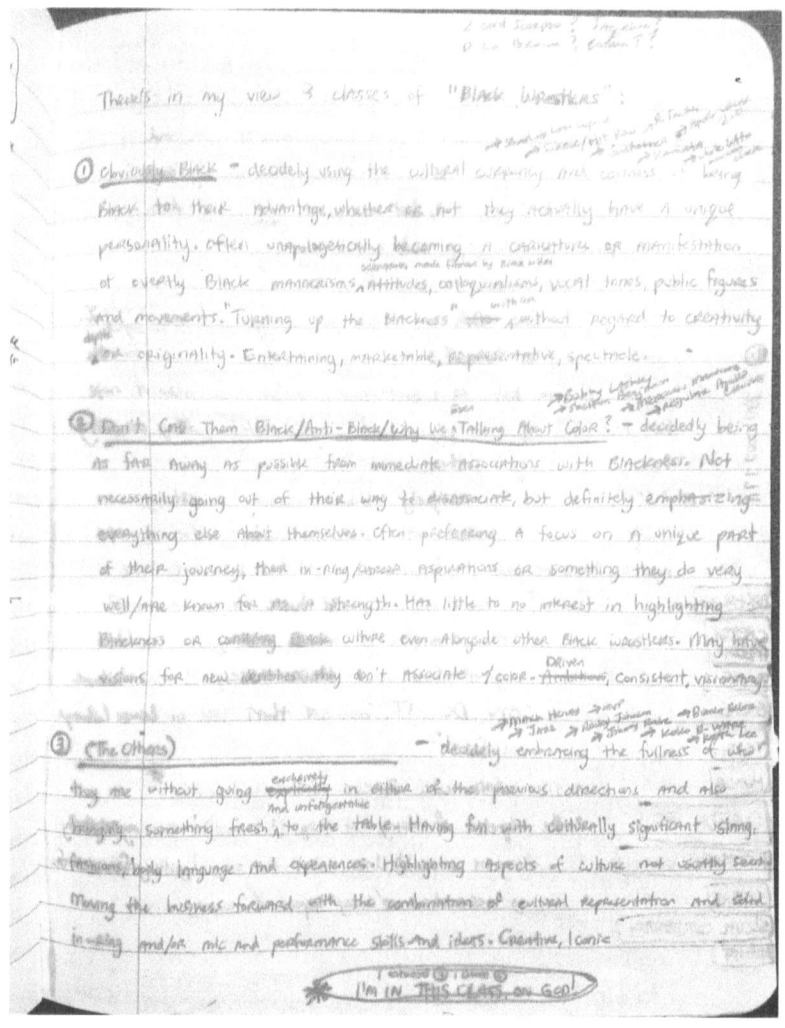

In my view, there are three classes of "Black wrestlers":

1. OBVIOUSLY BLACK—decidedly using the cultural currency and coolness of being Black to their advantage, regardless of whether they have a unique personality. Often unapologetically becoming a caricature or manifestation of overtly Black mannerisms, scenarios made famous by Black culture, attitudes, colloquialisms, vocal tones, public figures, and movements. "Turning up the Blackness" with or without regard to creativity, depth, or originality. Entertaining, marketable, representative, spectacle.
2. DON'T CALL THEM BLACK OR EVEN ANTIBLACK; MATTER FACT, WHY WE EVEN TALKING ABOUT COLOR?—decidedly being as far away as possible from immediate associations with Blackness. Not necessarily going out of their way to disassociate but definitely emphasizing everything else about themselves. Often preferring a focus on a unique part of their journey, their in-ring and career aspirations, or something they do very well and are known for as a strength. Has little to no interest in highlighting Blackness or centering Black culture, even alongside other Black wrestlers. May have visions for new identities they don't associate with color. Driven, consistent, visionary, and marketable, depending on strengths.
3. (THE OTHERS) CHECK BOX MARKED OTHER— decidedly embracing the fullness of who they are without going exclusively in the previous directions and bringing something fresh and unforgettable to the table. Having fun with culturally significant slang, fashions, body language, and experiences. Highlighting aspects of culture not usually seen. Moving the business forward with the combination of cultural representation and solid in-ring and/or mic

and performance skills and ideas. Creative, iconic, and marketable due primarily to differentiation.

I really enjoyed diving into the full scope of what being a professional wrestler is and the range of experiences one can have in a career. Putting my mind to success feels successful. Learning from the world-renowned legend Johnny Rodz and numerous club members was a perfect match for my goals, the mind-set required for them, and my intentions of authenticity. I had visions about every part of wrestling, and I wanted to do it in an authentic way.

Right before I started, I was fresh off moving back to New York after a painful breakup with a partner of three years who was a talented, creative, thriving entrepreneur, business partner, and my best friend. I'd also lost touch with my best girlfriend and most of my associates in the arts. I'd quietly hustled up the funds to successfully buy a one-way ticket back, miraculously land myself a new job, and, right at the threat of homelessness, a new apartment (amen!). I was working hard on creating my first album release, by then, over a year in the making with thousands of dollars invested and experiencing all types of independent artist hiccups. There were unknowns in every area of my life, and nothing was guaranteed except my bills.

When I was at my lowest in the relationship, dependent, and unsure how to change my life, I vowed to get out, reset, and truly live. I promised myself I'd return to New York and do something different, something I always wanted to do, and make a habit of it. I emptied the last of my savings to begin wrestling training and took months to pay the rest of my club fees. If I was investing in anything, it was because of the value it brought me or truly seeing a future with it. Everything about pro wrestling made sense to me and my life, and I love it when things make sense. Above all, I felt terrific doing it, and I *needed* this feeling.

I dove in admirably and intensely but soon found I had to learn to balance the intensity for myself. Other than rapid analysis of the experience as it was happening, much came to be realized in the first month and a half of my training because a major injury occurred in the ring while working out with an alternate trainer and relatively new trainees. As a result, a subtle line of "before and after" was created in my life. With the help of Johnny and several gracious veteran club members, I was revived after crashing to the mat, getting up, collapsing into unconsciousness, and eventually helped to emergency medical attention.

The diagnosis was a severe concussion and bleeding in my skull. It forced a halt in training for another eight weeks and forced me to contend with the seriousness of what I was doing with the sport and my body outside of it. It shined a brighter light on what I'd need to give myself amidst all this external giving for wrestling to work and to last. Most importantly, it emphasized what I'd need to understand, give up, and give myself for my life and any new chapters to work and last.

CHAPTER 20
THE REAL WORLD IS FAKER THAN WRESTLING, PT. 2

> *This is a way of life. I am a way of life. [Clutching championship belt] this is mine. Bought, paid for, with blood, sweat, and a ton of guts! The clothes, cars, women, money, all of them, are secondary to this! This is my life . . . brother, what you've done to me, has really sent me north of where I should be. I've lost it. I've lost reality!*
>
> —Ric Flair, World Championship Wrestling, Jim Crockett Promotions

---

I EXPERIENCED many things while healing through the severe concussion and skull injury diagnosis that no one prepared me for. I primarily relied on my own perceptions of pain tolerance, previous trauma survival, mental toughness, the controversial "Strong Black Woman" archetype, and spiritual beliefs to regain functionality. According to mental health research by the Concussion Alliance nonprofit organization, a concussion can have a more significant mental and emotional burden than its physical tax, especially for athletes and active individuals. Reevaluating identity, perceptions of weakness, and urgency to return to regular activity often cause people to engage in avoidance or rush the healing process. Lack of common knowledge and absence of visible indicators of post-concussion symptoms often leads to isolation, misunderstanding, and disconnection. Anxiety and stress can increase due to financial and social pressures, the inability to carry out daily activities, and barriers to the help one really needs.

Unfortunately, dealing with the complications following a concussion can result in increased stress levels. Uncertainty about how to resolve symptoms or find treatment can create a cycle of frustration and worry, which may be compounded by legal or insurance issues surrounding the event. Feeling overwhelmed or incapable of dealing with medical, social, or financial complications has the potential to worsen mental health symptoms following a concussion.

Most of my healing process was done in isolation while living alone. Other than insomnia, numbness, and privately intense emotional releases, cognitive and behavioral symptoms went mostly undetected in my self-awareness. By the time I was able to see a doctor and told of symptom possibilities such as "bad decision-making," I was so distrustful of the medical system and doctors and so faithful in my ability to heal myself that I decided not to internalize symptoms and only focus on my success in functionality. I was aware of numerous examples of athletes who incurred brain injuries and went on to violent and destructive behaviors. However, I decided I was still in enough self-control and self-determination for this not to be my reality. My suicide survival played a significant role in this thinking. I was willing to wager if my decision was a gamble at best. While mentally risky, I knew my wellness and greater healing powers were up to me. Being "uninsured" without material coverage, I was especially willing to nurture and carefully gaslight myself into better health.

The following are excerpts of journal entries written within the first three weeks of my recovery.

JOURNAL (A)

Lucky and deserving am I, indeed. God read these words.

On the healing path of my concussion diagnosis, I've sent my last "touch base, stay connected, follow-up" text to . . . well, everyone left standing in my life, other than the network-appropriate updates and inquiries. People indeed do what they want to do, as much as they may limit themselves, complain, or buck against circumstances. As the psychiatrist asked ex-husband Stan on "The Monkey Show, Part 1," season seven, episode of The Golden Girls, "Why would you want to be with someone who so obviously doesn't want to be with you?" Hmm. And even in that case was a lingering mother issue. But digressing . . .

There's no one to chase, beg, impress, or prove my worth to in this life. "The material speaks for itself," as they say, respectfully. Evidence clarifies beyond that. I'm ready to experience good people in my life who are independently healthy, in order, of harmony, good and kind to me, consistent, and securely take me personally. Not because I'm paying them, related to them, or forced to, situationally—just those who apply initiative to our connection.

With this concussion, I found myself, thankfully, lucky and deserving to be with people at the wrestling club and gym who cared about my health, safety, and whereabouts. I'm immensely grateful for this because I wasn't even coherent for much of it. The grace and favor were just happening for me, amen, aṣẹ. Pardon me, as my head is hurting. I may have to stop writing . . . sidebar: my tailbone has been so sore.

Now, Lord, you lined up all these people to help me while I was mostly unconscious, including someone who made the decision to drop everything, drive me to the hospital, and see to it I was cared for no matter what I insisted. Now this man was also fine. Fine or fine asf! Damn near . . . '90s R&B, Queen Latifah's Living Single fine. As my auntie says, in Uganda we don't say "eye candy." We say, "optical nutrition." Ha! You brought a fine man into my experience so closely and had him stick around, notably. And offer himself to me from the heart. And be upstanding and have integrity. And be financially empowered, upwardly mobile, and generous to me with these. You had him look me in the eyes. And for this, I'm certainly lucky and deserving! Yes, thank you! What a treat. I graciously understood he had to leave my side and continue the life he was living. Yet, since here, I've been facing this concussion alone. Facing mixed signals from people in my life again. Healing by myself. Why? After supporting so many others, and doing this by myself so many times now, I think I've used up all my rage about it. So, just . . . why?

Perhaps healing by oneself is the only accurate way to? An abundance of examples would prove that wrong. But this, like success in all things, is the pattern of my life. Why? And why not consistent warmth and kindness from good people who make room for me in their reality?

My mantra today: A LITTLE BETTER THAN YESTERDAY.

By the way, what is the perfect life?

All of what you want and none of what you don't want (?)

Peace, health, love, happiness, money, and success *Reverend Ike voice* (?)

Self-actualization and the support of it (?)

Let's clean some things out and reinforce some things in . . .

JOURNAL (B)

It's day nine. I had the sweetest dream last night, sweeter than I've had in a while. What's more, I finally closed all the windows firmly, blocked the sounds of outside (it's been torture all week. Why was I allowing this???), and let the air unit move some calm, cool, nonabrasive air into the house. Worrying about the bill was a waste of peace twice over—my healing is most important. Lastly, what's more, I did some research on sleeping positions for tailbone pain and corrected my pillow lineup and side postures. This has given me two solid options for lying down for the first time in days! So thankful, OMG. It's really the little things.

So, this dream . . .

JOURNAL (C)

You thought about reaching out to you know who for a brief, confidential vent, and sworn-to-secrecy hug-it-out. But you also heard the echo of Impact days and Jamal's infamous "Use it all!" You know the one. From that day you broke out crying in the middle of that big a** important rehearsal? Don't tell me you forgot about that embarrassing s***. Of course, you didn't. But you pulled it out! Brave, very brave. And you did use it all and put together one of your best performances. You've been "using it all" ever since! Now, we have this happening and a call of angel numbers through repeated sixes and fours. You read what the call said. So, before I reach out to anyone or any "material world resource," just try talking to me. What would you say, what do you have to vent about right now?

Exhale OK.

People think positive thinking is bull****, but it's my life. I get asked about it sometimes, and I think it's bull**** that it's a concept that needs to be grasped. That it's something to think about, like we must reprogram and reconsider it instead of it being our natural or normalized mindset. It's my number one job every day. It's been my life since I lost my life and tried to take it years ago. Ironically, I think the only thing I've ever legit failed at is killing myself. Sure, I've stumbled, fumbled, been embarrassed, and made tons of mistakes. Been at the wrong place at the wrong time or had the wrong words at the wrong time. Witnessed something I thought I'd have forever run its course or know it was time to pivot and put my energy somewhere better, but still held on. I've had "wins and learns" in damn near all those things, even still. Suicide is the one thing that was a "did-not-succeed" and "did-not-go-forward," which, to me, says a lot about bigger and deeper things at hand.

Look, the first week of this concussion was hell. It was a living hell. It was me, God, and the demons. An exorcism had to be happening. I don't know how to describe how this felt in my head and body . . . unable to be still, unable to move, then not wanting to because the pain was profoundly having its way. It was making arrogant announcements to every bloodstream, every joint, every organ, and every cell. Having to decide to surrender to this pain just for the chance it would stop or ease just a little bit. Or because there was no resistance left. Battling internally, completely alone, shuddering at every assault to the healing. Laughter at the will to heal. Light absolutely crushed by darkness without reprieve. A wired, haunting, trauma dusting, break you from the inside pain. If that damn medical staff knew the half, they sure didn't tell me.

Allow me to subtopic.

I've had a lot of intense physical experiences outside of sports and the performing arts, sure. Ones that had my entire being engaged for better or captured for worse. I remember once I was laid out on the floor of my first apartment. (It meant a lot to me because I was eighteen or nineteen when I got it and had been planning for it since I was fourteen.) I was writhing in emotional pain on the floor, addicted to cocaine after a crazy, unpredictable, three-week binge in which I had no business being involved. I was just laid out, facedown, crying hard. I was yelling, "What did you do to me?!" to the drug, about the drug. To myself, about myself.

I cried so hard from the emotional arrest of the experience, and when I got up that day, I knew it was over. It had to be over. You know why? Because I have something inside me that simply will not be conquered. Yes, I'm a very soft and submissive person in my overtly warm, very sensitive way, but this part is an undying leader and just will not be dominated. I mean, I've been off sugar for three years now, meat for over seven, and Black & Milds took awhile, but I nixed that too! I also quit that intense three-month bout with Newport menthol cigarettes "cold turkey." Now, in that moment, I was about to "cold turkey" cocaine. I've successfully detached from all my physical burdens and addictions, mainly because this part of me refused to be enslaved.

Highkey honorable mention goes to the fact this was also after I'd just returned from visiting my boyfriend at the time, who was in prison out of state. My addiction was so intense that I got high in a

Porta Potty outside the facility before the visit. I believe it was also the look in his eyes when he asked me if I was high, and I said yes, which forever rang a bell. I was taken aback as he said the words with rare tears in his eyes, "This is not you." I responded tearfully, "I know." And then, the usual sweetness of seeing him because of our emotional closeness, intellectual stimulation, genuine good times, and openness was overcast by the bitterness of knowing it was the cocaine visiting, not me. Additionally, I had the whole Greyhound bus ride back home to think about his tears, not being in his arms, and only going back to this supposed master. It may have been the first thing I did when I walked back into the apartment, to just drop down on the floor and cry. I prayed and cried myself into a power nap. Then got up to shower and never touched a drug like this again.

I thought I'd never feel that low again. Well . . . the first week of the concussion drew a parallel to this, just off the injury itself, which is crazy! I felt like I was on that floor again, excruciatingly. It was this amount of pain but concentrated physically and doing its best to mess with my mind psychologically. And this made me sad and angry at a lot of things.

On top of the excruciating pain, which not one doctor or nurse had prepared me for, was a subconscious pounding throughout my system of "this thing." An invader, intruder, imposter. "This thing" trying to arrest me, this expressly negative energy weaving a very grand illusion of harming me. I knew I couldn't give it power, but I was so angry for my inner child. "This thing" had gone behind me while I was doing something I loved, something which gave me life and which I put life into, and tried to get inside my mind! It got inside my skull and drew blood! Me! Little Em! Queen Em! Wild Lady Em! Goddess Em! HOW F****** DARE YOU! This is God's body; how f****** dare you.

So not only did this demon need to get the f*** out, but I didn't deserve to lose my ability to taste, smell, and hear frequencies. And not only be barred from in-ring training, running, weightlifting, or being able to touch my mf toes, but not be able to edit my videos, or create content, or read or write for long periods, or work on my voice, or rehearse, or listen to music, or dance, or approve my projects, or do the work which fulfills me and attracts money to me! All I could do was breathe and feel pain. I couldn't change my sheets. At first, I couldn't feed myself, I couldn't even bathe! If I tried to sleep, I would wake up with the pain every hour or two! It was sheer will to not go out like that! All I did was battle and pray. I didn't like seeing myself like that, which made me sad and angry at many things. Knowing I couldn't be sad and angry because I had to heal myself... made me sad and angry!

The other night, I did a SWOT report on myself (strengths, weaknesses, opportunities, threats). In the "weaknesses" section was my first admittance that the impact of the concussion and skull injury had me feeling highly emotional, with periodic anxiety and depression, which I didn't even realize until late week two. Everything up to this was straight survival, straight pain management, straight me against the demons—all day, every day.

After about day six, when I finally started getting a handle on this mysteriously shooting tailbone pain which made it almost impossible to sleep lying down, I finally felt coherent to life again. I was affirmatively back on my number one job of staying positive. It had gotten me through "hell week," and now, I could start to face the world with it in a bigger dose. So, I worked on the basics like it was Kill f****** Bill, and I could finally "wiggle my toe." I was working on lifting my foot off the floor. I practiced getting out of bed for a few days, then got my mind together for phone calls. I started making calls to schedule my concussion follow up as week-three approached, and, man... these mfs here. Now, I know there are plenty of places in the world, my home country included, where I wouldn't have gotten a fraction of the care and quality I got through this experience, so I'm very grateful. Very, very grateful. With that said, this mf system is so hit-or-miss, man!

I was crying between phone calls because I was so angry all over again. They had me "north of where I should be." I was losing it! Like bffr, tf y'all want me to do? I was relieved to get one or two people with the decency to say simple things like, "I hope you feel better" and "I'm sorry you're going through this." Like, yes, remind me we're humans again, please and thank you very much! There's no reason why a person who's dealing with an assault on their basic stability, excruciating pain, and following up on the help they need should have to go through such nonsense with a medical system rife with inconsistency, impersonal (mis)management, and frankly, extortion. Institutional extortion is all around. One of the biggest rackets. RACKETS, racketeering, Health & Racket Club chile, Venus and Serena! Whether medically insured or not! But ohhhh, the energy I've been given as someone with-not!

The hospital concussion clinic gave me an "after visit summary" document. It says on the paper, don't do s*** for two weeks, take pills (which had I listened to them, I'd be in worse shape and would've needed to return to the emergency room), then call back the concussion clinic. So that's what I do, and these mfs gon' tell me that they do not specialize in concussions and can't pull a doctor who does for at least another four to six weeks! The f***?! Then a monologue about paying to see a doctor again, then paying for the follow up test, which has to be ordered by said doctor, then paying again for the doctor to talk to me about the results from said test. The f***?! I'm like, well, are the results in English? Cause we can save a payment, and I'll talk to myself!

I'm on a scavenger hunt now because that's how they've made me feel, like a f****** scavenger. Anybody need anything while I'm out hunting-gathering?! I'm hunting for the help I was told would be there. I'm hunting for health; I'm hunting for the facilities which have the necessary machines I need. I'm hunting for the simplest resolution to a simple f****** thing which they've made layers of complicated. Outsourced this and private offices that and emergency this and affiliates that and this is on record, this isn't, and uninsured, self-pay, and the f***?!

I made a vow. In addition to everything I want to do to better this earth, be it art, kids, orcas, large cats, bees, butterflies, ancestral land, my people—whatever—I'm absolutely going to do something to help athletes going through medical emergencies. This includes dancers and stage performers, mental health, and wellness because I didn't deserve this, and no one going through an injury does. But I'm so thankful for these eyes, this mind, and those closest who helped me through this, especially at the gym. I know as a world-class artist, forthright, and influential individual, this is something God would have me succeed in because people of right, good, and influence are connected, have felt, and can see. This s*** has been virally ridiculous! "F****** ridiculous!" *RZA voice* Cue all seven minutes of "So Appalled" and turn that b**** tf up! Thank God I got a doctor to at least tell me something, though . . . finally.

A final note on my follow up with the medical system experience . . . They have my number and can text me from numerous parts of their affiliated institutions. The first day I hadn't even left the emergency room, I was already getting a text about a bill for $200-something. I could see it was for the brain scan, so I thought, "Oh, okay, that's understandable," and I paid it. Then I started getting texts and emails about a $400-something charge. Then a $14,000-something bill in my name. I'm like, the f******k?! The 14K just can't be real. In fact, at first, I flagged it as spam and said to myself, "Nah, somebody scamming my s***." Then I find out I'm within the salary range for this "Charity Care Support" thing (thank God!), so I apply, and they say they're sending me applications in the mail. I'm like, "Bet." Physical bills come first, though, for those two amounts again and another, and I'm like, again, what in the f***is going on?! The $400 one, I see and recognize the name of the doctor, the one who spoke to me the most. I see it shows the additional brain scans, so it seems legit, though I'm also thinking, Ain't that a b****? I was never told I'd be charged for the pop-up test they decided to redo at the last minute!

Subtopic on that: after Christian left me in the emergency room (I begged him to; he'd gone out of his way to drive me there and stayed supporting me all night) came a four in the morning repeat of brain scans. They came to roll me to the radiation room, leaving me alone in the f****** hallway. All types of s*** going on and going by. Sometimes even traffic jams of those left alone, taking up space. Then they pulled me in to take the second test. They rolled me back out, and I was waiting alone again. Then suddenly, the guy pops back out and says, "Ms. Ottoo, we actually need you back. The doctor ordered another test." I thought they made a mistake because of the way they rechecked my bracelet and spoke on my case number. But we went ahead and did another round. They rolled me back out, I waited alone again, and then they rolled me back to the base to wait some more. No one even told me why the third test was ordered suddenly, let alone that it was separate and I'd be charged for it. These mfs, man!

I'm full on staying positive about this, tho!!! I got me a follow up doctor, and I'm finna get my follow up test to confirm what's happening. But I'm not trusting these mfs farther than I can throw them! This type of s*** was precisely why I wasn't going to take myself into the emergency room in the first place, though I'm thankful Christian did because I was still losing consciousness in his passenger seat and was clearly not okay. Who knows what would've happened if I had gone home and stumbled about alone? So, I accept some things need to be known and happen this way. I also spoke with Johnny after his surgery, and he was even telling me to peep game and stay ahead of these doctors, my records, and my results. No one deserves this on top of what they're already going throughhhhh!!!

An aside: while living alone and dealing with something like this has its downsides, it's been a blessing to have my home clean and in order and, for the most part, be able to maneuver it through "hell week" and beyond. You know you get to a point where even though you want to train, create, work on your things, and enjoy life again, you just want your best opportunity at rest, peace, and quiet. This was its own challenge living in a New York City apartment, but better in my own home. Also, my father has been traveling again and is halfway across the world, which isn't new. But what is new is he also has a new wife and a new baby. I have a baby brother now!

So, I'd been babysitting and trying to get to know new wifey. But now, I'm also healing from a concussion. I'm very, very grateful for her, please understand. In this short time, she's exemplified a lot of grace, brightness, wisdom, and love in my life which many haven't shown in a lifetime. And she's an excellent mother to my first sibling, my first baby brother. But I also felt like I was on duty for his life decisions, which made me a little angry and sad. Like, why can't you just be home? What's wrong with home? This is exactly why I made a home for me, right for me. I'm doing home right for me, even with being in all these other places with all these goals, visions, and dreams. But concussion or not, I'll be damned if my little brother is going to grow up like I did, with nobody home physically or emotionally. Mfs checking in and out, not holding on to the master plan and s***. Wondering if I'm even part of it and s***. That ends with me! I saw brother Scotty at the baptism, and he told me to "stay in this baby's life." Word . . . Yet, something else also set in.

They're plainly a different family than we were. There's much more love in that house now. With the pandemic, my father's been home and "fathering" a lot more. Prior to this, he'd already really changed as a man for this new life, which I admired. My brother has two available parents ready to love him. The old issues aren't even factors anymore. They already ended, and maybe it's just what I had to experience within the circumstances of my parents. Neither of them seems to need me to be a family. But still . . . I've always been thoughtful about the duty of having children and felt responsible for any children around me. So, pops, baby bro, new wifey, new mom . . . Please give me a minute, and I'm going to be there for you in the doses I can manage. Absolutely. Sometimes, I just want to heal in peace, though.

It's also been nice to hear from my birth mother via text. Not gonna lie. During "hell week," I had a day where I just wanted to be held by my mommy. On my mama I just wanted my mama on some very basic s***, like my newborn baby brother. I haven't felt this in a while. I haven't desired it in even longer. Her caring made me feel that motherly thing again (positively), a feeling I'd forgotten. It came and went quickly, but the psychology of that energy is wild. I've also noticed while watching new wifey lovingly mother by herself. The womb bond is wild. With everything we've gone through, I wish my birth mother was here to soothe me quietly.

It's been about a month and ten days since formally entering wrestling training, and so much has happened. So many things have deliberately or unintentionally tried to energetically insert themselves into what God and I know can't be stopped or misdirected—not just in wrestling but in all I love. Of the few people I selectively chose to tell the diagnosis, one tried to tell me I have COVID and repeatedly referred to me as basically "down and out," which I vehemently rebuked in full and total whole! Word also got out at my job, and this girl kept wishing me well by affirming the negative I didn't even call attention to! People don't realize how much power they give away with words. I'm not "down and out." I'm up and in! I'm letting this contrast serve me. This will all work out in my favor even still. It's still all so sweet; y'all have no idea. Still, the sweetest life, sweetest pops for me and everyone I know! It's y'all that's lost it! I'm in my reality where I'm GOOD, and I'ma be aight! So, anywaysss . . . !

While in the wrestling club, I just want to train, learn, enjoy, mind my business, be positive, meet cool people, get better at coexisting with members' energies, and swerve guys in the gym trying to get at me for sexual conquest or control. Someone on the boxing side of the gym professed their love for me—no exaggeration—and how they're usually watching me in the gym, and not the only one doing so. I appreciated it, and . . . type cringe! Especially because I greet several people when I walk in. They also thought this honesty entitled them to me. They tried to get me to quit training with Johnny and pitched all they would do for me with a career in boxing. That's audacity. I'm not sure, but I think that's an illegal solicitation or questionable gym protocol, or maybe just in bad taste. I'd never do it like that even if this were my interest, but the point is, respect my s***! I'm already here, investing in my investment, so let me vest! S***! Then these doctors told me to be a vegetable for two weeks—no, actually—four to six weeks. Then my allergies flared up, and right when I thought "an orgasm would be fire right now," I got my mf period. Like, ahhhhhhh, f***$%@!!!!

All this, and then "this thing" drawing blood in my skull and shifting my systems around. Trying to get me to think outside my right mind. Trying to stop what can't be stopped, misdirect what can't be corrupted. All these things doing their best to stand in the way of the simple truth of me coming to do what I've decided to do. What I love. What I'm good at. What I'm good for, and what's good for me. I refuse, rebuke, and reject all the negative words and energies from people. It's just not cool. That's not what it is 'cause how f****** dare you?! This is God!

Y'ALL (NOT) GON' MAKE ME LOSE MY MIND

Exhale so, I'll take some breaths in silence now. When you're ready, I'll take my five-minute hug. Then I never want to hear about this again. I mean it. Everything I just said, the hug, the hug-request, none of it ever happened. Poof-dust-particles . . . and if you ever use this hug against me, I got something for that a**. I'ma breathe now. Thank you for listening.

I thank my rage for carrying me through my deepest brokenness. May this lull her back to sleep, until the next time she is truly needed.
—Ciran McDermott, "417 Hz | Clears Away of All Negative Energy & Blockages," Meditative Mind
#
Only the strong go crazy. The weak just go along.
—Assata Shakur

I soon returned to work. In realizing my sensitivity to computer screens, not just my eyes but how the device seemed to drain my entire body now, I knew I would have to make big changes and really listen to my body. So, I donned some anti-blue light glasses, resolved to take routine screen breaks, pull back on social media, hydrate more, and handle my business.

I was archiving digital media for *The Only*, a Paramount Streaming original documentary about famed athlete Briana Scurry. It profiles her as the highly talented US goalkeeper, two-time Olympic Gold Medalist, and World Cup Champion who made one of the most incredible saves in soccer (football) history. Great emphasis is placed on her highs, darks, and lows while breaking several barriers and doing her part to move the sport forward. I was intrigued by the featured images and the uniqueness of the situation while taken aback not to know her or her story. A Black woman sports hero I'd never seen before, holding up the American flag, glowing golden with sweat and a big smile under stadium lights, kneeling in the middle of a field with confetti falling all around her. The documentary was inherently justified to exist because a Black woman was a pioneer in the evolution of women's soccer (football), and I'd had no idea!

I couldn't watch the film or read too much as pushing screen-time would strain my eyes and induce concussion headaches, but something told me to run a search on her, and I'm glad I did. I found an NPR piece detailing her life and a severe concussion injury she incurred during a game in 2010. Though things were more advanced then, "concussion protocol" and follow up in professional sports were still developing. In many ways, it's still developing as there's a lot we don't know, totally, for sure, about the human brain and its communication with the body. Lasting traumas have still happened all over the world. The piece by Terry Gross was titled "A brain injury cut short Briana Scurry's soccer career. It didn't end her story."

The collision left Scurry with a traumatic brain injury, resulting in constant, excruciating headaches, blurred vision, cognitive problems, and depression. She was unable to work, and the league soon collapsed, leaving her without a medical team or training facility to help her. To make matters worse, Scurry's insurance company refused to cover the surgery she needed to repair the nerve that was the source of her pain and was reduced to pawning her gold medals.

"It was the most difficult thing I'd ever done in my life," Scurry says of selling her Olympic medals for $18,000. "But it was the patch and the temporary fix that I needed to get some stability in order to continue to press forward and get the help I needed."

"For the longest time, I was mad at [the player who crashed into me.] I realized over time that my anger towards her wasn't helping me and . . . for a long time, wished I could undo that hit. And when you're in an emotional state like a concussion, you are essentially disconnected from yourself. And I prayed so many days. Because I was a different person now. I changed emotionally, I was different. My confidence, my focus, all these different things. And I was so lost in the wilderness."

I feel seen, sis! My mind was opened by her description of the experience which rocked her athletic career but certainly hadn't ended her story. It was continuing to make a difference, now, for me. I hadn't talked to anyone about the more profound effects of the injury I experienced. Reading her article was the first time I realized how normal the darkness I was going through was. It was also the first time I heard depression, emotional twilight, and nonphysical effects linked to it. The standout parallel was even as an insured Olympic champion, she found herself in a position where the help she needed wasn't available to her, so quality of life may not always address the vulnerability one can experience systemically at any level. I greatly appreciated her candor on the subject, and this affirmed my wanting to improve it for myself and others.

At the time of this writing, it's been about six months since my initial concussion incident while wrestling. (With the time off for injury and attending in-ring sessions only three days a week, I've completed less than one hundred days of training in that time.) I've also been successfully cross-training, working full time, creating, taking care of myself, managing my home, and seeing family when possible. I stepped up my education and application of balance, rest, and recovery in a *big* way. I happily intend to continue pro wrestling training.

By the two-month mark postconcussion, I'd unexpectedly done my first show with the wrestling club, dubbed by Johnny as "Wild Lady Emilia," in a special rules, blindfolded, four-way match. Around the four-month mark, I was able to independently help fellow rookies with basics and get further in important rote work with veterans. Then by the five-month mark, I spontaneously asked if someone would be a body for me to spar a move named the "side Russian leg sweep." It entails hooking several body parts, folding forward, swinging up, and sending you and your opponent crashing back into the mat from a standing position.

I went through it several times off instinct of how I'd seen it done and explained and took sideline corrections from Johnny, who was watching. It went incredibly smoothly and left me so satisfied. It was also the first move I attempted to do, which wasn't taught or shown by the well-respected or highly skilled veterans. This was my first "I wanna try something" move. It was brought to my attention that affirmatively volunteering to do this move was also me blowing past any subconscious fears about the injury since crashing backward to the mat was how the concussion climaxed in the first place. It was evidence of my goal-driven attitude and fearlessly trusting myself again. Self-trust is a big deal for many athletes (and nonathletes) post-injury or post-trauma.

I appreciated this as I hadn't thought about this profoundly true perspective. My state of mind was focused on curiosity, creativity, the vision of seeing myself doing the move well, knowing I could, and wanting to feel my body do other things. Wanting to feel how my body could move with a bit more education. I was so focused on desire I had no time to even consider a fear could exist! Trusting myself and going for it felt great; this state of mind was priceless. I've come full circle to slaying the normal and abnormal fears and have slightly raised the level in which I'm doing it. Now *that's* the "cream rising to the top." **Randy Savage voice** Oohhhhh yeaaaa!

New challenges will arise with new levels, and I'll remember the sayings, "Feel the fear and do it anyway" or "If you're scared, then do it scared." But ultimately, the benefit of any challenge or healing process we desire is facing fears to make them obsolete.

If you're experiencing mental, emotional, or psychological symptoms from a physical injury or lacking support in your healing process, please consider talking about it, connecting to a healing community, or getting the help you need. Resources, support organizations, and help can also be found in the back of this book.

We are not robots. We don't just play the sport. We're people playing the sport and have things that happen to us that we feel with our platform we can shed light on.
   —*Briana Scurry*

PROSPERITY, BUSINESS & SOCIAL ENTREPRENEURSHIP

CHAPTER 21
DEAD PREZ, POLITICS & THE MODEL UNITED NATIONS

In the real world, these just people with ideas
  They just like me and you when the smoke and camera disappears .
. .

—Dead Prez, "It's Bigger Than Hip-Hop"

The personal is political.
  —Carol Hanisch

FORMAL EDUCATION CAN BE a cross between underfunded compliance training and an overpriced networking business. It can get more impersonal and political as one goes on. I've realized it's on me to make the knowledge I receive and am exposed to work for and personal to me. This is often through discernment, the art of framing questions, and trusting the strengths of what I already know.

Intellectual fearlessness is one of the best intangible returns on investment education can give, and though it can come from a classroom, it doesn't have to. For example, being a political science major (in addition to business and marketing courses within my arts management minor), constantly analyzing history, international relations, social systems, and law stripped me of being intimidated by contracts and agreements in home management, daily business, and entertainment. Understanding how contract law runs the world was an education in itself, especially in light of the social conditioning around it. Paperwork, fine print, terms, and conditions dictate many areas of our lives, especially for artists, entrepreneurs, and home managers. Yet, many undervalue them, shy away, or are afraid of what they don't understand. It's essential to unlearn fears which affect our well-being by facing them or replacing them with new thoughts. Consider the inspirations which enthuse you most about controlling your own destiny.

Being unafraid of what you don't know—not because the unknown isn't scary or uncomfortable, but because you trust what you *do* know about your strengths, what works, what makes sense to you, and your ability to feel when something's not right—is my view of intellectual fearlessness. It's one way to look at the infamous Jay-Z line, *"Show 'em how to move in a room full of vultures."* You may swim with sharks who seem to maneuver in intense, bold rhythms, hinting at your alleged inferiority. But perhaps you're the killer with the smile on its face, the orca (who's lowkey the superior predator) swimming majestically and peacefully to the sounds of Erykah Badu's "The Healer." From a spiritual perspective, fearlessness as inner security and groundedness often radiates as creation, attraction, and commanding energy. Interest in a particular decision, set of knowledge, or position brings an experience to you, meeting you where you are, and unfolding for you. What you may not know or feel less than about yourself may be inconsequential to the gains making themselves available to you.

Trying new and scary things is also important because many experiences are lucky to have you. Sometimes your value isn't tangible or in rote information. Rote information has its place, but there's a reason why we often learn more from a single activity or conversation than a class or entire semester, which also begins to escape our memory. Your value is in your entire presence. You bring all your qualities, strengths, unique experiences, and ability to grow with you. This layered understanding reflects how women doing "bad b**** rap," culture nerd rap, intellectually conscious Boom Bap, and all subgenres in between are important contributors to Hip-Hop. There's high value in the reminders of what we bring to every experience, to routinely edit what's undeserving of our attention or our desire for attention itself. Subject matter aside, feminine energy and the perspective of women and girls often impart much needed awareness, balance, receptivity, and emotional intelligence to our usually hard-nosed, transactional, two-dimensional masculine perspective mirrored by the bustling world. I can relate to the realizations of imbalance by Nichole Ann Guillory in her 2005 dissertation, "Schoolin' women: hip hop pedagogies of black women rappers."

Before beginning the writing of my understandings of black women rappers' lyrics, I could not connect with the stories they created about black women's lives because I only had a limited awareness of who I was. Unable to respond to the womanist call in many black women rappers' texts, I could not appreciate many of their songs. For a very long time, rap, for me, was coded male. All of my favorite rappers were black men . . . until I engaged in the process of uncovering the multiple, sometimes contradictory, layers of my own identity, I was unable to respond to and appreciate women rappers' cultural productions.

Much like Guillory and rap icon Lady of Rage (as told by Tom Maxwell's "Shelved: The Lady of Rage's Eargasm" on the online nonfiction platform *Longreads*), I was for a time moved and driven exclusively by the examples of male icons like Rakim and Chuck D of Public Enemy, in part because I was only resonating with parts of myself. While quite the soft-skilled creative, I've been very in touch with myself as a huntress with an analytical brain and clarity seeking, masculine, alpha energy. I'd also grown up around my father more than my mother and, thus, was more likely to pattern his mental approaches. Psychologists often analyze the patterns of adults who had to think for themselves through childhood traumas. As a general go-getter, largely independent child, and trauma survivor, I'd also done many things on my own, which necessitated mentally covering all my bases. This led to often being an aggressor in thought, bringing me out of myself where I may have been better served in supporting, reassuring, and protecting thoughts already serving and retaining my good. The latter is a balance of feminine energy, even in the alpha state.

I often benefit from the balance of my sensitive superpower, observation skills, ease, and creativity—and vice versa. To utilize masculine energy is to pursue our goals and desires with drive and clarity, which is important. To utilize feminine energy is to understand what we're bringing to these goals and desires, to nurture this value, and raise it in whatever we're doing without force or chasing, and this is important. You as you are a valuable source of energy and wealth. This is why advertisers are always after your attention, and companies want your labor. Don't be so easily moved from your sovereignty or whole self despite all urges, offers, and distractions.

> *The power of one who has claimed stewardship over his own life is in one's ability to screen and interpret the meaning of the information before it is ALLOWED inside oneself. Too many people are too suggestible, allowing anyone to just pour into their minds freely. Never. I have the first and final say when it comes to my life.*
> —@phantamzero100, "You're the Alpha of Your World," Rom Wills

---

As I've ventured into the world and weighed out being "in it but not of it," I've also observed how perception can and does change. Your own assessment of value and how you feel about yourself needs to remain as clear and robust as possible. If you don't like something about yourself physically or emotionally and you can't change it, or it would take a lot to adjust it, also consider whether you're taking vital energy and attention away from what you like about yourself or maybe a strength. Gold may exist there.

Dance legend Bob Fosse made a historically successful career out of choreography which embraced his physical flaws. Talk show pioneer and media mogul billionaire Oprah Winfrey was fired from her first job as a news anchor for being "too emotionally invested" in the stories she reported on. Switch something up when you feel it's right but also remember the public can be finicky, tastes can change, and a shift in your perspective, strategy, or approach may be for the best.

Our physical self-concept is one of our greatest ideas, and like everything, is mental first. In the fourth grade, I was teased for having a proportionally, naturally large butt, which I previously didn't think much about at all. Popular 1980s and '90s sitcoms routinely spun jokes and commentary about this being undesirable or cartoonish in women's bodies, even among Black women. When my attention was brought to it, I let myself be under the impression this was undesirable and cartoonish about me. My style of dress was usually modest and tomboyish. However, I still actively tried to cover it up and *exercise-it-away* ***Solange voice*** because I grew ashamed or uncomfortable about it. Imagine then . . . seeing the state of society's a** obsession which would come. Though strong opinions surrounded me, considering this opinion about myself was a misuse and misdirection of my valuable energy and attention. Sometimes, I feel I was happier not thinking about it at all. But really, I'm best with as clear and robust a self-image as possible.

Self-image and valuation also matter regarding opinions and offers in business and by businesses. At the time of this writing, I've been on Pinterest and YouTube more than any other digital social platforms ("It's the media without the social for me").

Because Pinterest has become much more popular, paid ads and targeted posts are more frequent (message!). Among them, lip-plumping products seem to be promoted a lot. Influencers of all types, including Black girls, are frequently shown demonstrating them on camera. Despite how anyone feels, they're popular because fuller and bolder lips are the latest rage. Fuller lips are a trait found naturally in my lineage, so it's been eye-opening to see them as "the rage" with a full-on commercial swing.

This raging swing of capitalism caught me off guard once. I braved a doctor's appointment and thought I'd treat myself by visiting a nearby Ulta Beauty store. I was very happy to buy some body butter and Black skincare products. A lovely lady put "free gifts" in my bag at the register. I usually give these back because many products are not for me nor made with me in mind, but I was in a receiving mood, so I took them. One was a lip moisturizing product, and being a notorious label reader, I found the ingredients okay. I put it on that night, but my lips immediately started burning—whoa! Wide-eyed, I picked the product back up like "hol' up, what are you?!" and indeed, I hadn't read the label closely enough. It was a lip-*plumping* moisturizer (slipped that in, didn't they!), and no, I wasn't interested. Because fuller lips are the rage, especially among those whom this trait isn't found naturally, and while bolder and more decorative lips are the rage among those whom it is, big business and the science which backs it have oriented to this. Not to people, to the rage. Not to bodies, to psychology.

It's assumed the average consumer wants fuller or bolder lips than they already have, so much so companies are willing to give their lip products out *freely* to attract undecided or open-minded lip product consumers. They're willing to bet this is everyone who buys anything related to their body. They're willing to bet anyone who invests in an idea of beauty, i.e., from a "beauty store," is willing to be swayed about theirs. Because a rage is always happening, and it's usually about a sway of psychology or self-image, they're looking to be in the mastery and moneymaking of it. I'm not that consumer, respectfully, but we all are to something. Had I not been on Pinterest or ventured into Ulta, I also wouldn't have known my natural trait's been out here setting off a chain reaction of billion-dollar business! Sometimes, it's not your factual input, rote information, physical presence, or tangible assets needed to bring value to the world, situations, or conversations. Often, your representation *is* the value. Be the first to understand this and be willing to understand it more because someone's always willing to gain from it.

While chopping away at my political science major, I took an opportunity to merge my skills and interests in intellectual fearlessness, performance, goal-based collaboration, and how to "work a room" through something called Model United Nations. Students would come together and learn ways and methods of how different bodies of the United Nations (UN) operate. They'd be assigned a specific committee focus and learn its inner workings. They'd be assigned a country to represent and research its characteristics. They'd drill in how to conduct official activities to UN standards and the strategies of being effective representatives. Then they'd leave their regular school, attend a mass conference, and be ambassadors with political objectives to see through for five straight days of conference sessions.

We'd be thrown in with thousands of students from prestigious schools worldwide. Since the event was being held in New York and we were English-speaking native New Yorkers from a high-ranking New York university, our group was expected to represent with high caliber. While technically, there'd be no sole winner, there were clear ways of determining who did well and excelled in their performance. Official observers would watch everyone in every committee activity, and in our case, veteran participants from our school would also covertly monitor us throughout the conference. Formal awards in each committee would be announced at the end.

This was the intellectual equivalent of *"Showtime!"* for knowledge nerds.

I was one of two new students to the Pace University Model UN team that year. The other was my partner, Kieran, an intelligent, ultracool, functioning weedhead from Queens who also worked at a luxury car dealership and wore a suit regularly. He was a marijuana connoisseur who had his life mapped around his wraps. He seemed to care little about much and, like me, saw through the façades of higher education. He could read people and rooms excellently and was always calm. We had instant respect and intellectual chemistry. He was also one of the few people I knew who focused better when they were high.

Though not a smoker at this time, I'd come out of a long "functioning weedhead" period myself, so I understood and respected his methods, and this understanding proved an asset to our partnership. We remained centered, positive, and supportive of each other throughout the experience. Much of the student-run team was more highly strung about the situation and not interested in us personally. They'd also done it before and were in each other's classes, so they seemed to have more of a rapport with one another. They relished the break in regular scheduling, which Model UN afforded them. As juniors and seniors, they were looking forward to other conferences, internships, and job opportunities related to the field.

Understandably, there wasn't a lot of time to prepare for the week of sessions, so they were short on "getting to know you" and strict on drilling us on the points of the simulation. Once we got our host country (Sierra Leone) and committee (World Intellectual Property), they ran us through how to represent the country accurately, put official documents together, strategically position ourselves, make impromptu speeches, and evaluate other teams to our advantage. While stimulating in my imagination, it was also methodical, dry, dense, and intense in real time.

I began dreading this decision as we continually drilled, but there was no turning back now. While the high level of preparation by the senior team turned out exactly right and invaluable to our independent execution, I'm also thankful to Kieran (and his weed) for the perspective, esteem, and appreciation of this unusual experience.

Preparation was now over; it was game time.

On orientation day, we arrived at a posh midtown Sheraton Hotel and met our entire senior team for the last time. Decked out in business attire, holding faux leather binders under our arms, and with our chins held at "We Run New York" level parallel to the glossy marble floors, we strutted through, checked in, and got our laminates. The other teams swarmed in with a mix of confident, superior, insecure, confused, and just-excited-to-be-here energy. Our senior leader snapped us to attention and explained we'd be on our own from here. Interestingly, he noted that many teams, especially from overseas, didn't care about doing well in the actual conference. They were simply there for a free trip to New York. I couldn't blame them, but Kieran and I would remember this.

While taking it all in, I was also low-key fighting insecurity because I didn't have pricey, coordinated business attire nor could I afford new clothes at the time. The best I could do was what I'd done . . . assembled a couple of dollar ties and a button-down shirt from a thrift store, pulled off some slack-ish pants, and through a vest, sweaters, and assortment of accessories, created a homemade line of "business attire." I was also on a natural hair transitioning journey which created a daily challenge. I'd dived into training and hadn't made time to organize my mane into a maintainable or protective style for the week.

So here I was, tired and not feeling my best next to students named "Maximillian" from countries I couldn't pronounce, dressed in three-piece Prada suits and matching leather binders. Still, something in me knew none of this mattered because of what I had in my mind. Not only did I belong, but I was also called to this opportunity, well trained, intellectually fearless, and by spiritual definition, qualified. I had the perfect eyes to see exactly what I needed to see in everyone and everything. I also had the perfect partner to exchange with, learn from, and ride this out. So, I adjusted the seams on my homemade high-fashion outfit and pressed on.

Day one introduced us to the rooms we'd work out of, the protocols of each day, and most importantly, the other teams. We mingled, and for a moment, we were simply meeting each other just as young students with different accents, handshakes, customs, and body language. It was clear who was genuinely goodhearted and who couldn't care less who you were. It was also clear or profoundly hinted at who were the sharks, orcas, seals, and little fish.

I enjoyed this time of graciousness as I realized we were all probably living slightly different versions of the same life. I looked into people's eyes and could tell they hadn't gotten a lot of sleep like me, may have been stressed like me, or were under various pressures from their school or home country like us. Nevertheless, I embraced the moment because where else would I be in a room with educated youth from over 100 countries?

We soon learned being English-speaking native New Yorkers was more than just swag; it was a clear advantage. Speaking other languages wouldn't be allowed during the simulation, thus, gutting at least half the teams' ability to communicate. Things were in our favor already. Of course, this made those focused on outmaneuvering us more disdained and motivated. A few three-piece Prada suits took it upon themselves to look at us like we were nothing. The gamesmanship had begun. I smiled and looked at Kieran as he smiled and looked at me. Without saying anything, we knew what it was from then on. In unison and without hesitation, we shifted gears mentally. This was *our* territory, this was *our* home court, and to quote legendary boxer-turned-rapper Roy Jones Jr., "Y'all Must've Forgot!"

Kieran and I fully understood the assignment, not just from

our senior team but with each other. This would be one of the best platonic partnership experiences I ever had. We moved as *one*, readily listening to each other, playing to our strengths, and maneuvering with clear mental unity even when separated. Our ability to divide and conquer the tasks at hand was seamless. Often, we could just look at each other across the space and register our messages. We'd huddle together to share information, update a course of action, then split the room and network with nearly every team in the committee. We soon were among the top teams and countries in operation.

Politically speaking, respectfully, for Sierra Leone to lead the room and committee documents alongside the "superpowers" of the United States, Russia, China, United Kingdom, and France was startling and said a lot about how we were playing the game. We didn't care about the advantage and perceived superiority of the superpowers. It didn't matter to us that we represented a country with less geographical significance, not the greatest gross domestic product, many developmental issues, and a continent whose autonomy was so negatively impacted by internal corruption, colonialism, and the world powers themselves. *Mmm!*

While I was proud to represent Africa and to source the strengths and uniqueness of Sierra Leone, you could've given us the continent of Antarctica to represent, and we would've had the same attitude. We were in the act of doing more than anyone thought we could with the power we had. We had bigger visions and a greater sense of independence. We were full-time employees and full-time students in a capital city of global industry. We were a kid from Harlem and a kid from Queens. We had instincts and seasoning nobody else had. We weren't in college for a college experience or at this conference to participate in a simulation. We were here to best a social construct. We were here to play the game. We were here to win at life.

For the next four days, every morning while riding the subway to the conference, my ritual became listening to "It's

Bigger Than Hip-Hop" by Dead Prez *strictly* on repeat. I wasn't sure why; it just fit my mood and aspiration exactly. I *felt* like Hip-Hop walking into the conference every day. Undervalued, overlooked, and pressured upon unfairly, yet possessing unthinkably pervasive creative power and unstoppable dominance.

This was top tier "show 'em how to move in a room full of vultures" energy with every step. Our cannot-be-dominated ease was matter-of-factly giving off "The Healer" energy, creating what some couldn't organize, listening to what many weren't hearing, looking for what most couldn't see, and speaking how many couldn't articulate. The point was, who we were was already bigger, and we made ourselves bigger than who we walked in as.

The bassline, cadence, rhythm, and energy of Dead Prez on "It's Bigger than Hip-Hop" seemed to seal the moment sonically and put me exactly where I desired to be. As author and inspirational speaker Abraham Hicks would say, "tuned in, tapped in, turned on." Centered, locked, and loaded. I'd zone out to it on the train ride, and no matter what happened before that morning, it was like an ordinance, prayer, or putting on face paint. I was completed as a warrior.

Every morning I'd then exit the subway, meet Kieran, and walk to a side street so he could smoke. We'd talk about our mental health, music, culture, what he was learning at the dealership, what I was learning doing shows, the "real life" college was supposedly painting, and the real life we designed in our minds. Finally, we'd solidify our game plan for the day, speak our final affirmations like *The Boondock Saints*, and proceed to check in quietly, without a doubt in our minds that we were the best. The work was demanding and involved, but we stayed on top of it. Several times we noticed veteran team members who'd come to monitor how we were doing. Every time they saw us, we were "working the room."

I got on the podium twice, which was twice as much as most

teams, and gave highly resonant speeches that drew us more positive attention. Being in the World Intellectual Property Committee, we noticed most were speaking about the political facts surrounding patent issues but largely ignoring how much of this was affecting the availability and distribution of medication, machinery, and infrastructure in places that needed it most.

I was sure to note this and appeal to empathic things like how people were dying and suffering as we stood around debating percentages of patent law which were already exploitative. But honestly, there was a lot I didn't understand. Still, I remembered my political science perspective as artful chess and drew imagination on the spot by getting "deeper into character." Access, relationships, power, control—this is what political science meant to me. Even when you don't have it, it's what you do with what you have and the influence you can create which makes it science.

I concluded my final speech à la Suge Knight on the 1995 Source Awards, saying something like, "If any of you other countries are interested in making *real* change and not just politicking, come meet us at such-and-such corner of the room where things that make sense are happening." To my surprise, many came to us before we even got to said corner. They expressed having no political power to sign our documents but how they'd back us in a vote, or how they loved our speeches, or admired our leadership even though we weren't one of the superpowers.

Ultimately, we were given the coveted "Outstanding Delegate" award in our committee and were one of few teams in our school to pull that overall. Unfortunately, due to a scheduling and capacity issue at the UN building, I couldn't get inside for the ceremony to receive the award officially; however, our committee was recognized, and we got a certificate. Kieran and I did what we knew we could do, and between us, victory was sweet. No odds, insecurities, or designer suits were greater than us. With the lasting effect of ritually listening to Dead Prez every morning, I credit them with one-third of this triumph. We'd raised our consciousness, strategized, put on for the people, and excelled in the politics of high stakes business. A kid from Harlem and a kid from Queens proved outstanding global UN delegates. Hip-Hop had bested *all* the nations.

CHAPTER 22
WALL STREET, NIPSEY HUSSLE & HIP-HOP BUSINESS HISTORY

MY CORE CURRICULUM at the public High School for Economics and Finance included classes like personal finance, accounting, and my favorite, "Welcome to Wall Street." Taught by Scott Schaffner, a cool, traditionally masculine, well respected American-White man who doubled as our successful basketball coach, I was always early and on time for this class. The zenith of the course was being enrolled in the Network for Teaching Entrepreneurship (NFTE) small business program. We'd review case studies, standard best practices, and basic understandings of marketing, inventory, and business management to eventually be given $25 and a partner with whom to start an actual business.

We'd have to keep records, make pitches, and presentations, problem-solve hypothetical issues thrown at our business, and do our best to make it to each milestone of existence. Once they explained we could keep all profits made after paying back the $25, I was "100 Miles and Runnin'." *NWA voice* My partner (who wasn't as enthused about the program) seemed to be going through the motions and quit halfway through. I was very happy because they felt like a dead weight to drag, and I knew I could do more without them. So, I gladly paid them half of the program's investment and profits to that point and became the sole proprietor without breaking a sweat.

The business was selling military-style belts of various colors and patterns retail, which I'd buy from the Wholesale Fashion District in Manhattan. Well—the *product* was the belts. The *business* was selling the ability to put yourself together in any situation. I was selling ease, style, and order. I quickly noticed the mechanics of the military-style belts made them easier to install, wear, and adjust. Their width and materials created a cleaner line in most outfits and looked newer for longer. The variety of colors and patterns allowed people to "dress for success" or make various personal statements. I set my mind to understanding the "belt needs" of every type of consumer and was happy to meet them where they were.

I became fixated on buying, selling, managing, making a profit, keeping, and creating customers. I began spending more time in the Wholesale District, keeping my inventory fresh and carrying belts everywhere I went. I sold them everywhere, every day of the week, even at rehearsals and after shows. Soon, people knew I had them and would come to me. By the end of the program, I walked away with an additional $136 and was floored. After paying back my half of the program's investment, I'd still made a five hundred percent increase in profits . . . with belts?! Suffice it to say, my eyes were wide open.

I continued selling without the program. When the belts seemed to get a bit saturated, I segued into shoelaces and then plain T-shirts. The shirts sold very well as I knew many athletes and street people who wore them like uniforms. I'd roll up to the likes of gym classes, sports practices, or pickup basketball games on the hunch people might need fresh tees. Guys would inquire about their girlfriends, and girls started asking me to accommodate them too, so I started carrying a few cuts in shapelier sizes. I'd also diversify into colored shirts, especially for major holidays and annual celebrations, which really got my creativity going!

For instance, I made sure to carry sets of red and pink shirts around Valentine's Day, kept a bouquet of fresh roses with me, and offered single florals with double purchases. Wholesalers began to know me and would throw in free or discounted items they had around if I wanted, which were never the same thing twice. I'd space out when I carried them, price them high, and flip them as exclusives. I made loyal customers out of guys who needed sizes they couldn't find, to which I made special trips to source shirts and deliver them in hallways or by their classrooms (which was an additional service and cost extra!). I shut down operations once the physical load of carrying things became too much, and more was happening in my life. I also wanted to sell something I had more of a personal connection to. But nothing could shake the feeling of this rhythm and affirmed self-determination.

I found a comfort zone I never quite shook the feeling of about business and the essence of money itself. Money as thought or energy in action. This feeling had everything to do with creativity, vision, self-determination, self-esteem, risk management, purpose, observing people, connecting with them in a real way, and becoming one with the energetic flow of success in the world. These were all things I found as a live performer, athlete, writer, and artist. I had started several businesses as a child but didn't stick with any idea longer than a season. Still, I always had a hunch I was onto something good about the energetic flow of success. "Welcome to Wall Street" and the NFTE program gave me constructive room to focus on my existing skills, stick to something, make money from knowledge, create my own opportunities, and leverage my natural feelings for success in anything. Now *that's* my idea of education!

I wasn't aware of most of my family's entrepreneurial history until I was an adult, so most of it didn't factor into my esteem, nor was it being applied consciously. However, I grew up surrounded by my father's indecipherable economics and finance books, filling every room's tall shelves. They towered over me, almost intimidatingly, and in my mind, represented the reason he was always away. He has since become a PhD Finance, certified Financial Risk Manager, and Chartered Financial Analyst—the latter of which is a high-level certification only a few people attain globally. I see him as the true rockstar between us, as he's traveled the world through business trips, conferences, and giving presentations for most of my life.

Knowing his intelligence was taking him somewhere, seeing those books, travel photos, and gifts from his international students allowed me to learn from exposure. Still, I was learning more about choices than the knowledge itself. We never sat and talked about money or business, and I never knew what he was teaching. My idea of business was bigger because of his example, yet when I told people I wanted to be "a businesswoman" when I grew up (I also had an answer for every day of the week), I had no idea what it meant. I just knew I would be living through the power of my mind, and the thought of this felt like freedom.

As a child, my father made bricks and sold them to construction sites (read *that* again!), as well as cut and sold sugarcane, bananas, and cabbage to earn money to go to school. When I met my maternal grandmother, she was handmaking gorgeous bags of intricate styles, shapes, and colors. I've continued to stumble on eye-opening evidence of my mother's education, activities, and career, which we never spoke about. Though while supplementing her development through professional growth events, groups, and conferences, she always kept a side hustle. While a single mom, she was an Amway lady, and by taking me with her to sales meetings, I caught whiffs of the intensity and possibility of entrepreneurship.

In 2016, my birth country of Uganda was ranked the "top entrepreneurial country in the world" from research done by the Global Entrepreneurship Monitor and covered by the UK publication, *The Guardian*. Also, local loaning, domestic trading, and door-to-door selling of fresh produce and products are still normal among people there. Yet, even before I knew all this, I always felt an orientation of business in my blood and believed this is ancestrally endowed in us all, regardless of whether we use it. It's why I'm never shocked to see the success of teen or child-run businesses and why "The Fundraiser" is in my top three favorite episodes of Aaron McGruder's legendary animated sitcom, *The Boondocks*.

While I don't agree with all the elements of capitalism, I've always firmly believed in self-determination, commerce, and the ability to create prosperous businesses. Trade, marketplace, entrepreneurship—these were major pillars in societies and human history long before colonialism and corporations reshaped the world. Historical accounts like *The Journal of African History* have detailed complex, preexisting systems and "subsistence economies" of precolonial trade established by aboriginal people for centuries.

History, as we've been taught (especially in the West), is in more cases than not, a strategic "capitalization" of what's already existed. This means, for instance, the old stereotype of the African "savage" or slave to be civilized also covered up an arguably superior history of skilled businessmen, women, and artisans who created well-developed networks and mastery of local resources. Some modern societies still utilize trade economies, such as the Trobriand Islanders of Papua New Guinea in the Oceania region (they use yams and banana leaves as a form of currency). If we're "social and political animals," as Greek philosopher Aristotle allegedly once stated, and economics is defined by most textbooks as "the distribution of goods and services," then conducting prosperous business is more natural than most of us have been conditioned to believe.

As a billion-dollar global industry, omnipresent, and invaluable culture, Hip-Hop is one of the most remarkable case studies of business in the modern world. Decades after its formal inception in the 1970s, it's shifted, adapted, or evolved multiple times through changes in business practice, copyright law, contracts, social trends, politics, transparency, public taste, global exposure, and technological evolution. The advanced marketplace it found itself in from 1998–2006 saw groundbreaking mergers at the corporate levels of the music industry amidst shakeups of the world economy.

Simultaneously, the Hip-Hop underground, mixtape marketplace, and independent artist landscape was also experiencing drastic changes into the decade and beyond the 2010s. The shifts in record label activity, internet usage, niche audiences, digital production, new sounds, digital consumption, and social media engagement allowed professional artists to break new ground in conducting themselves as creative businesses. The Crenshaw, Los Angeles-raised, Eritrean-Black multitalent known widely as Nipsey Hussle is one of Hip-Hop's most outstanding individual case studies in this area.

I remember Nipsey Hussle on his come-up as a Hip-Hop artist, already segueing into strategic business by the time he'd made quite the name for himself as a rapper. Not only did he have an intriguingly diverse following, unique story, and strong cultural connection with his community, but he was also routinely noted among movers and shakers of rap's elite. An air of quality, order, and professionalism surrounding his brand also made him stand out from the sea of artists clamoring for attention at every level. His "value over vanity" ethos was not only good for business and a generational teaching tool but also made having integrity look cool. Dorian of the *82 Points of View* podcast briefly discusses this in the episode titled "I Asked Nipsey Hussle for a Feature. This was his price." Regarding contacting Nipsey's management company, he states, "The level of professionalism that the Marathon Agency showed was indicative of what Nipsey stood for." His growing empire was covered by renowned publications such as *Forbes*, the *LA Times*, *Inc.*, magazine, *Entrepreneur* magazine, and more.

As dope as he was musically, it was always the mindset for me. Since his transition from the physical, numerous book clubs have sprung up to read the books he read, multiple think pieces have been created about the methods to his success, and many students and families have prospered utilizing the investments he made. So, when I learned from the *Wall Street Journal* of his community and development interests (including real estate, entrepreneurship, job creation, STEM programs, and various social services) totaling a value of over $200 million in his short time on earth, I was floored! *Wayment, hol up now, let's take a time out.* "Blow the Whistle!" *Too Short voice* We usually hear about rappers' earnings, houses, cars, jewelry, etc., being in the millions, but . . . community investments? I had no idea it was this much and wondered why it wasn't spoken of more. Due to his spirit in action and speech in interviews, I can only imagine this number would've grown.

This immediately reminded me of several things surrounding individual success, wealth, giving, and the common good. Nipsey's community-business portfolio was in the hundreds of millions because he built it that way, directly with the communities he looked to uplift in mind, and diversification of investments which meant something to him. "Giving," as we know it, being the general call to action and result of donations and charitable contributions, is often manipulated and taken for granted at every level. Whether in times of crises or underserved people swamped in political poverty, too many times, the money never reaches or truly uplifts the communities who could use it. There's also a big difference between investing in people, solutions, and the health of a community—and throwing money at a problem (which never goes away).

As discussed in "What Is Behind Foreign Aid Ineffectiveness?" by Mohamed Mounir Sraieb, the billions of dollars annually distributed as "giving" to countries and regions in need hasn't created meaningful change in decades, primarily due to "corruption, limited absorption capacity, and lack of good governance in recipient countries." Let's briefly take the focus off the flawed recipient and look at the errors of the unintentionally or willfully flawed giver. When it comes to "giving" or investing, if the thought really does count, *what is the thought* behind all the money which hasn't worked in decades, which either never reaches, never goes, or never grows? In Nipsey's case, one man in an unexpectedly shortened lifespan has done more for more people economically than multiple governments. Regardless of one's wealth, the principles of this can and should be replicated.

"The Giving Pledge" sprang up some years ago amidst growing economic attention to "wealth hoarding" (its myth or reality, depending on what you're looking at) and a charge for billionaires to give half of their net worths away. It states on its website:

The Giving Pledge is a movement of philanthropists who commit to giving most of their wealth to charitable causes during their lifetimes or in their wills. As of 2022, the pledge has 236 signatories from twenty-eight countries.

Ironically, I found out about this soon after getting my hands on the 2010 edition of *Forbes* magazine, which featured another top tier case study in Hip-Hop business history, Jay-Z, joined by Warren Buffet on its cover. Alongside pieces like "Jay-Z, Buffet, and Forbes on Success and Giving Back," the issue featured America's top fifty billionaires and several honorable mentions. From 2010–2020, the top ten of this list, which the public now knows quite well, increased anywhere from ten to $99 billion richer. My point here has nothing to do with an emotion about people who "possess" this "type of money."

Reading the magazine copy on these fifty or so billionaires revealed enormously scaled family businesses, private equity, opportune advances in communications and technology, strategic acquisitions, cash-cows-turned-enterprises, and strongholds in natural resources. Seeing how much money is floating around this earth at any given time was eye-opening. Also, being a multibillionaire is not as rare a human achievement as I thought. I thought there were only a few in the world, but many hundreds exist! How much long-money energy is moving behind closed doors and in complete silence? "A lot." *21 Savage voice*

A complementing contrast is how loud-money energy is so visible to us, and while not being long, is what seems to be celebrated most. Pieces like "Black Wealth Hardly Exists, Even When You Include NBA, NFL And Rap Stars" by Antonio Moore make many eye-opening points about comparative amounts of communal wealth and political power. Still, money-energy of every type is all around us, and being made choices about every day, at every level. This makes my limited financial thinking of the past seem almost silly.

Nipsey Hussle's $200 million community investment portfolio also reminded me of the *trillion*-dollar nonprofit industry, which, while being in the trillions, could always use more dollars. His example prompts the question, is it a double standard to expect celebrities in the public eye to be more giving of their wealth when there are numerous abundantly moneyed whom we'll never know about and may have no interest in "The Giving Pledge" or similar attitudes? (There's also an ongoing debate about whether wealthy Black celebrities should be expected to be more socially responsible than wealthy celebrities of other races.)

From a broader perspective, are the measurements of wealth fixed or always shifting according to the narrative? *Who is rich?* I think of myself as a rich person. *What is rich?* Are the communities who make people monetarily rich, rich themselves? Are the celebrities we know even wealthy? Do you have to be wealthy to create wealth that gives back? Or is a desire and strategy to create it and distribute it enough, since even some millionaires won't, and some billionaires don't? Nipsey creating such a level of effective community investment in his lifetime made me think

. . . If he could do that, can't anyone with similar values, principles, or capital? If so, then what's *everyone* really doing? "What's Going On?" *Marvin Gaye voice*

In 2012, I studied the impact of individuals and nonprofit organizations doing the work which governments and institutions don't. These studies climaxed in a semester-long project for a writing-enhanced "Political Economy and Globalization" class where I used my former arts program, Impact Repertory Theatre, as a case study. I also produced a mini-documentary to accompany the 47-page, peer-reviewed, scholarly thesis. Its meaning was raised by powerful quotes from anonymous interviews with ten significant people who graciously gave their valuable insights. Spotlighting the politics of the common good and why some nonprofits have or have not, it was titled, "What We Do Now Matters Forever: The Politics of the Nonprofit Industry." I presented it to the honors program of the Dyson College of Arts and Sciences at Pace University and was inducted into the Society of Fellows for that year.

I've always known money is not the only thing making the world go round. It's also people with thinking minds. Everything we can see results from someone's belief and dedication to an idea. As described in the book "Dollars Want Me: The New Road to Opulence" by Henry Harrison Brown, initially published in 1903 (read that year again!)—the dollar itself is lifeless until we give it life and powerless until we give it power. In many ways, *we* are the money. I believe money is an energy and a frequency beginning in the mind. I'm also a believer that business school is everywhere.

If Nipsey could make a multimillion-dollar portfolio because he wanted to and learned how to, I believe a like-mind can meet or exceed him today. To me, he always represented someone who just "got it," and this encouraged me to stay in the energy of "getting it." To keep my business mind open and remain a person who's about something.

Several other individual examples in Hip-Hop culture have

taught me this, from the more visibly mastery of names like Sylvia Robinson, Cindy Campbell, Queen Latifah, MC Lyte, Yo-Yo, Sister Souljah, Kimora Lee Simmons, Missy Elliott, Karrine Steffans, Remy Ma, Nicki Minaj, Issa Rae, Keyshia Ka'oir, and Cardi B, to behind-the-scenes visionaries like Martha Diaz, Toni Blackman, Abhita Austin, Sylvia Rhone, Rayna Bass, Karen Civil, Heather Lowery, dream hampton, and many more. Their energy of creative control, scalable business, iconic artistry, and broader horizons because-we-said-so continue to clear pathways beyond music, movies, and media.

The groundbreaking contributions of Hip-Hop's other affluent or influential business leaders—the likes of Master P, Sean "Diddy" Combs, Jay-Z, Dr. Dre, Kanye West, J. Prince, Dapper Dan, Daymond John, Pharrell Williams, Andre Harrell, Timbaland, and Swizz Beatz to name a few—are often overshadowed by perceptions of two-dimensional financial motivations and public controversy. It's not uncommon for blame to be aimed at them for the commercialization or gentrification of Hip-Hop culture. This perspective is as unfair as it is reasonable since almost every generation after Hip-Hop's inception gained sustainable success by merging tactics of urban life with the business opportunism of the traditional American Dream. In the 1980s, America's zeal for corporate and political domination revved up and paralleled the bloom of Hip-Hop culture in almost synchronized timing.

Successful mainstream movies in the US bookending the first Golden Era of Hip-Hop include *Risky Business*, *Wall Street*, *Scarface*, *Trading Places*, and *The Secret of My Success*. Greed as a virtue, shrewd deal making, zero-sum thinking, mergers, acquisitions, hostile takeovers, gamesmanship, mob politics, ruthless franchising, social manipulation, and usurps of power are debatably as American as apple pie. As stated in "Selling the ghetto, rap music and entrepreneurialism," by Stuart Lucas Tully in 2009, "Though rap music claims to be counter-cultural, the economic designs of the genre assert a much more conservative ethos. While making money through business is not necessarily conservative, the manner in which these moguls acted harks more to old entrepreneurs than African-American culture."

However, the uniqueness of the numerous faces of the Hip-Hop business Mount Rushmore is in their shaping of new norms and things to come, more than their visibility or sheer desires for wealth. As they pushed forward, so did old lines of limitation. Some artists influence how music looks and sounds in the eras following them. Without them, things would be very different. Likewise, there are managers, executives, and entrepreneurs in Hip-Hop who've influenced how business has been conducted at every level.

It's more than valid to say not everything has changed for the better. There's progress to be made in ownership, professional politics, equal pay, equity, underutilized markets, access, safety in the workplace, institutional building, and communal independence. Hip-Hop has done as much looking in the mirror as outward social commentary at several points in its history of rapid growth. Yet, it hasn't always carried this to solutions of groundbreaking change for itself. Tully continues about contentiously historic business decisions which forecasted decades of rappers grabbing valuable market share while navigating being the new "pop."

. . . because of this infusion of traditional American economic values with the emerging sounds of hip-hop, [early moguls were] able to achieve a level of wealth previously unseen in black music [and] provide a blueprint for future hip-hop artists to follow. Indeed, because of Run-DMC's success with Adidas, future rappers followed their example by actively seeking endorsement deals with various levels of success. Furthermore, because of the saturation of upstart artists seeking endorsement deals, companies no longer felt obligated to financially compensate those who mention their brands. The practice had become so common that companies began to try and distance themselves from the hip-hop market by publicly distancing themselves from the rapper lifestyle. No longer is any advertising or publicity good

publicity. However, not all rappers have the management of [an early mogul] type entrepreneur backing them and actively bringing elements together. In short, these subsequent rappers are listening to the persona of Run-DMC's success rather than the actual occurrence.

[Nasir] Jones released "Hip-Hop is Dead" and the ensuing controversy about the statement's factual nature . . . [it] included "Black Republican," a collaboration with [Shawn] Carter, demonstrating of their reconciliation from their earlier feud. While Jones might decry the results of their commercial influence, he still recognized their importance within the advancement of the genre.

As evidenced by these moguls, rap music is not a rebuke of capitalism, but rather a reaffirmation of its potency. Rappers were not attempting to change the system, but rather utilize the current status quo for their own means. While [one mogul] might claim, "I have never targeted any of my products to African Americans . . . What I do is for cool Americans," there is the understanding that those who follow the trends will be more than willing to pay. Likewise, the subsequent rappers inspired to not only rap, but become moguls of their own, also pay homage to this initial concept. In addition, the sustainment of this mainstream audience was paramount, as evidenced by [Sean] Combs' deliberate rebranding of his name. Were it not for the economic drive of [these] individuals . . . in addition to the lines of national distribution provided by linking with larger record labels, there is no way rap music could have reached as large of an audience, let alone developed into a cultural movement for both black and white.

Even when mainstream markets haven't aligned with Hip-Hop culture, there's been enough of a cultural infrastructure for artists and entrepreneurs to build foundations, followings, networks, and portfolios until the right scaling opportunities occur. This has made it more possible for those who do seek to change the status quo to also engage in mass promotion and prosperous business. Rappers as resources in the modern knowledge-economy and as self-contained businesses in non-rap fields (Chuck D of Public Enemy, Chamillionaire, Soulja Boy, Stic of Dead Prez, T-Pain, Pharoahe Monch, Mia X, A$AP Rocky,

Bahamadia . . .) are possible because of our entrepreneurial ancestry.

While business management, promotion, and marketing existed in the earliest eras of Hip-Hop through party planning and event management, certain mindsets about money and markets didn't exist until the culture's trailblazers evolved. As they continue to, many validly argue whether such evolution has been natural, good, or genuinely constructive for the Hip-Hop community. Motivations and controversies aside, trailblazers made important marks because, creatively and prosperously, history was never the same after them. As Ralph Waldo Emerson said, "The mind, once stretched by a new idea, never returns to its original dimensions." Neither can the business of Hip-Hop.

CHAPTER 23
THE KRS-ONE GUIDE TO BEING IRREPLACEABLE

BY AUGUST 2020, the COVID-19 pandemic was in startling swing worldwide. Unemployment was up, the word "essential" was redefined, venues began closing for good, most stimulus checks were depleted, and "quarantine life" started to set in for many. As we mourned heartbreak, loss, and questioned the future, this period also provided an intense time of reflection for many who sheltered in place. Social media simultaneously provided spaces for much needed humor, candor, connection, knowledge exchange, and positive support. Releasing "Dear Corona," my Emzkey One-produced song, self-made art, and codirected music video months earlier had connected me to thousands of well-receiving people in numerous countries. Its modest success turned my depression into direction and reinvigorated my desire to truly live. In this spirit, I tried something new and created my first Twitter thread. The topic surrounded one of the most contentious interactions I ever had on a "regular job."

While not necessarily the most entertaining thread, it helped me lay out a breakthrough I previously undervalued and pushed past my anxieties about sharing details of my life on social media. (The irony of a lyricist at a loss for tweets!) With the help of Hip-Hop and the pioneering efforts of Bronx legend KRS-One, also known as "The Teacha," for groundbreaking records with Boogie Down Productions and numerous iconic solo efforts, it helped me see myself better and creatively make some healthy points. These points were dually shaped by the objectives of well-known business analysis approaches like SWOT, NOISE, TOWS, PESTEL, and Porter's Five Forces. Building it out with visual media also exposed me to meaningful memes and quotes I hadn't known.

My intended moral was—special, rare, and unique exist for a reason—everyone and everything *aren't* replaceable. So, while the earth *is* truly abundant, and order and humility are great virtues to uphold in it, uniquely valuable people, places, and things shouldn't be taken for granted.

The artistry of KRS-One "begat this" in near perfect parallel as his contributions to Hip-Hop in voice, sound, attitude, and intellect created a uniquely consistent impact on the culture. His roaring energy, bold style, and fearlessness have given me courage, resilience, and much needed excitement in some of my lowest moods. He's also been a vital representation and balance to the landscape by embodying intelligence as cool and powerful. He's been an inspiration to stay present, "unf***witable," and in good spirit, rightfully take up space.

When you're ongoingly unappreciated, or your environment is determined to remain unhealthy, sometimes it's best to let people learn the lesson of losing you. There's as much an art to removing yourself from a circumstance as there's an art to existing and growing from it. Be convinced of the truth of your value, and never allow anyone to diminish it in your mind, even when you're humbly moving toward a bigger gain. The following are these lessons and cross-cultural connections illustrated through my first original Twitter thread.

EMMA LEE M.C.
@emiliaisemma

i do SWOT reports (strengths, weaknesses, opportunities, threats) on myself & my niche(s). i like to know where i stand & what work really matters. in all my business studies i really got this mentality from KRS-ONE, who always kept a verse for everybody in the game.

A THREAD:

EMMA LEE M.C.
@emiliaisemma

i was once highkey triggered being called "replaceable" in a group chat by an owner of a startup which highkey mistreated & underpaid my team. i understand the perspective of utility & in capitalist clarity we all are. but i understand value & vision where they clearly did not.

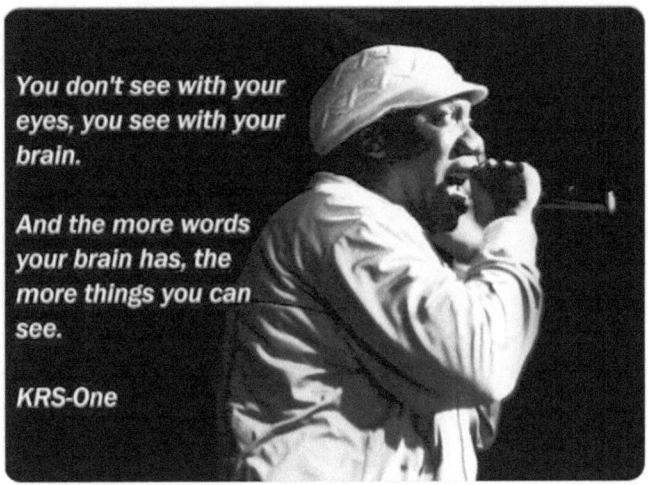

You don't see with your eyes, you see with your brain.

And the more words your brain has, the more things you can see.

KRS-One

EMMA LEE M.C.
@emiliaisemma

i was the only black person & for awhile only woman...but i digress. i stood my ground in our groupchat (as most of my team who i huddled with prior were suddenly quiet or wanted me to chill) fell back, prepared a detailed SWOT report of the company & followed w. my resignation.

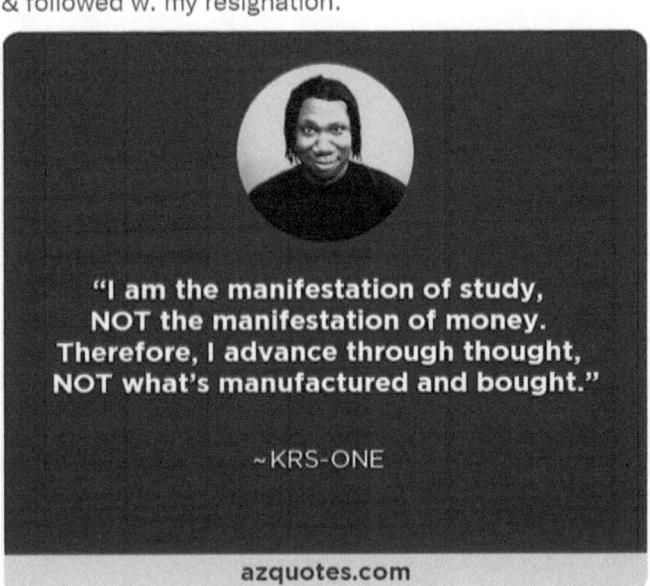

EMMA LEE M.C.
@emiliaisemma

the owner who called me replaceable was crickets, the team was shocked (the "chill" nigga was crickets) & the other owners called themselves trying to reel him in. "he don't know what he be saying" type vibe. when i say i professionally gave them the ether, the rapture...ayye.

#KRSOne #StepIntoAWorld
KRS-One - Step Into A World (Rapture's Delight)

EMMA LEE M.C.
@emiliaisemma

the smart owner (whom said little if ever to me before) said he'd been to harvard business school & my report was among the top best he's ever seen. pleaded that i stay. i told him why that "replaceable" shit was honest but inaccurate & not OK. that i appreciated him but nahhh...

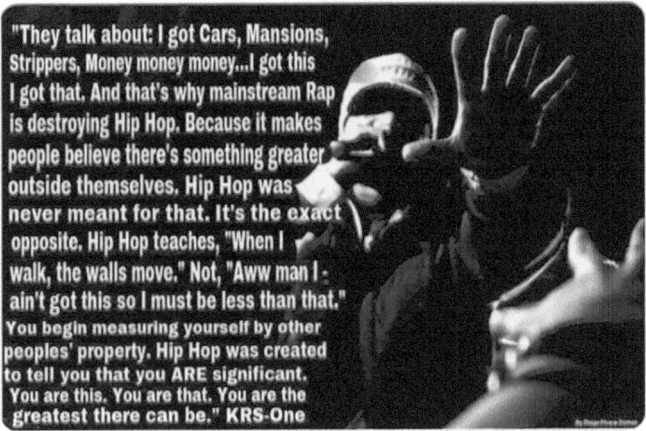

"They talk about: I got Cars, Mansions, Strippers, Money money money...I got this I got that. And that's why mainstream Rap is destroying Hip Hop. Because it makes people believe there's something greater outside themselves. Hip Hop was never meant for that. It's the exact opposite. Hip Hop teaches, "When I walk, the walls move." Not, "Aww man I ain't got this so I must be less than that." You begin measuring yourself by other peoples' property. Hip Hop was created to tell you that you ARE significant. You are this. You are that. You are the greatest there can be." KRS-One

EMMA LEE M.C. 🏳️‍🌈 👽 ✊🏽
@emiliaisemma

i realized even more in that convo that i was of the worth, intellect, insight, leadership & compassion to be a managing partner (ownership level) of this company & could've build out our NY team to do damage. they had successfully expanded but NY was proving a different animal.

EMMA LEE M.C.
@emiliaisemma

decided tho, never would i work for or with someone who was this willfully deaf, dumb & blind to my value and contribution. or with spineless people willing to abuse & silence me or sideline themselves in battle for their convenience (as i also fought for them.)

EMMA LEE M.C.
@emiliaisemma

KRS-ONE not only cut his teeth in battles & ciphers, his tenacity & understanding of his ability moved him from homelessness to sustainable independent icon of rap & global legend of hip hop. he stands behind a strong catalog that's also a critical curriculum of edu-tainment.

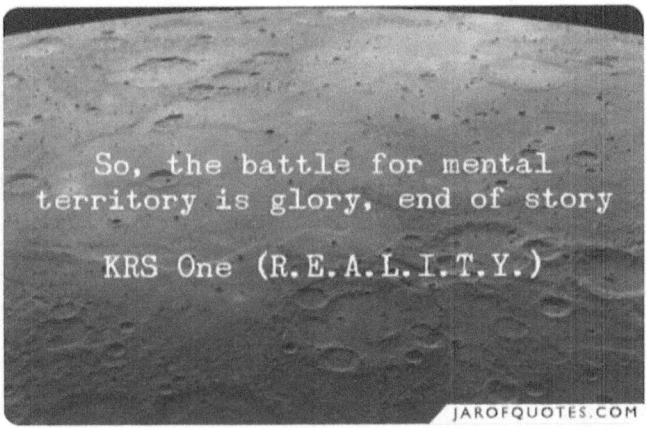

EMMA LEE M.C.
@emiliaisemma

he said in an interview he periodically looks at the top 10 charting hip hop artists & keeps a battle verse for them at all times. in every era. some may think this is unnecessary but this is elite emcee behavior (and practiced by top corporations.)

KRS-One vs MC Shan from the BEEF DVD

EMMA LEE M.C.
@emiliaisemma

he's also made a point to prepare detailed rhymes/songs about things like disaster preparation & correcting revisionist history..so to see him have the same energy for creative & spiritual competition is telling.

KRS-One Disaster Kit (Official Video) Prod. By MAD LION

EMMA LEE M.C.
@emiliaisemma

it's really about self-respect, owning your own voice & agency and accurately diagnosing power. with the expressed understanding that forces are in motion around you at all times. where do you begin reclaim?

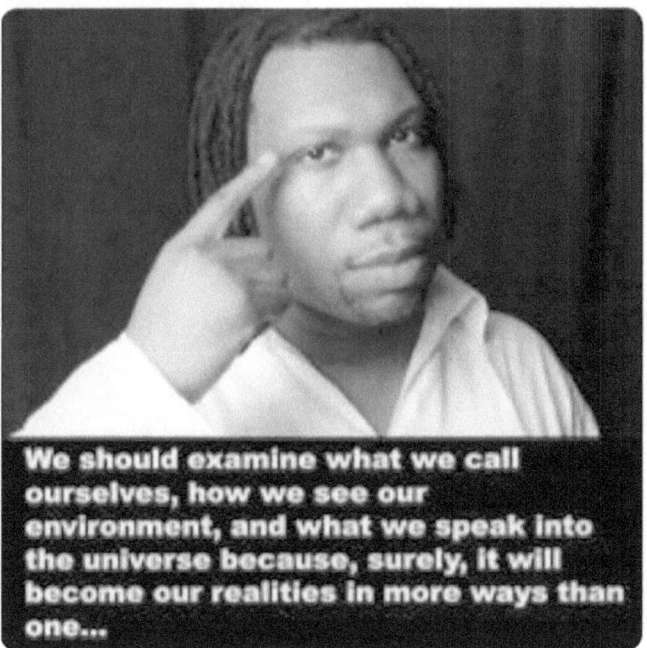

We should examine what we call ourselves, how we see our environment, and what we speak into the universe because, surely, it will become our realities in more ways than one...

EMMA LEE M.C. 🏳️‍🌈☮️⚖️
@emiliaisemma

with all problematic issues recognized i can't separate the value of this energy and consistent example of KRS-ONE. another example of why HIP HOP is so powerful it's weaponized against us.

EMMA LEE M.C.
@emiliaisemma

so in conclusion: making some minutes to do a SWOT report on your niche(s) & yourself will serve you in a number of ways no matter what you're into! especially if you feel overwhelmed by your goals. train your mind's eye.

remember knowledge reigns supreme over nearly everyone.

#BoogieDownProductions #MyPhilosophy
Boogie Down Productions - My Philosophy

PLEASE TAKE CARE. I LOVE YOU. THANKS FOR READING.

In Memory Of

Stephen "tWitch" Boss
Robin Williams
Capital Steez
Dave Mirra
Daphne Dorman
Freddy E
KayO Redd
Riky Rick
Edot Baby
R5 Homixide
Disco D
Chris Cornell
Kurt Cobain
Chester Bennington
Michael Hutchence
Bradley Delp
Elliott Smith
Bob Welch
Tim "Avicii" Bergling
Karyn Washington
Cheslie Kryst
Simone Battle

Hana Kimura
Shannon "Daffney Unger" Spruill
Crash Holly
Chris Kanyon
Mike Von Erich
Chris Von Erich
Kerry Von Erich
Junior Seau
Kenny McKinley
Terry Long
Dave Duerson
Adrian Robinson
Chris Lighty
Shakir Stewart
Johnny "J" Jackson
Weldon Irvine
Phyllis Hyman
Donny Hathaway
Don Cornelius
Vincent van Gogh

. . . and many more who are not forgotten.

RESOURCES, ORGANIZATIONS & SUPPORT

Mental Health Promotion & "What Survivors of Suicide Want You to Know" Fact Sheet

---

Maryland Department of Health Suicide Prevention Program
https://health.maryland.gov/bha/suicideprevention/Pages/Healing-After-a-Suicide-Loss.aspx

---

National Suicide Prevention Lifeline
1-800-273-8255

American Foundation for Suicide Prevention (AFSP)
988 Suicide & Crisis Lifeline
http://www.afsp.org
https://988lifeline.org
Dial 988 or text TALK to 741741

RESOURCES, ORGANIZATIONS & SUPPORT

National Sexual Assault Hotline
RAINN (Rape, Abuse & Incest National Network)
https://www.rainn.org
1-800-656-HOPE (4673)

Substance Abuse and Mental Health Services Administration Hotline (SAMHSA)
http://www.samhsa.gov
1-800-662-4357

National Human Trafficking Hotline
1-888-373-7888 or TEXT 233733

Self-Harm Hotline
1-800-DONT CUT (1-800-366-8288)

IMAlive
1-800-784-2433

Veterans Crisis Line
http://www.veteranscrisisline.net
1-800-273-8255 and press 1

RESOURCES, ORGANIZATIONS & SUPPORT

Silence the Shame
https://silencetheshame.com/

Sad Girls Club
https://sadgirlsclub.org/

Suicide Awareness Voices of Education (SAVE)
http://www.save.org

Athletes Against Anxiety and Depression (AAAD)
https://aaadfoundation.org/

Mental Health in Athletes: 45 Resources to Help You Cope
https://www.onlinemswprograms.com/resources/mental-health-resources-for-athletes/

Concussion Alliance
https://www.concussionalliance.org/find-providers

Association for Applied Sports Psychology
https://appliedsportpsych.org/

RESOURCES, ORGANIZATIONS & SUPPORT

The Defensive Line
https://thedefensiveline.org/

The Changing Tides
https://thechangingtides.org

A Safe Space to Be
https://www.asafespacetobe.com/

Your Life Counts
https://yourlifecounts.org/find-help/

Inclusive Therapists
https://www.inclusivetherapists.com/

Melanin & Mental Health
https://www.melaninandmentalhealth.com/

Black Girls Smile
https://www.blackgirlssmile.org/

RESOURCES, ORGANIZATIONS & SUPPORT

Brother, You're on My Mind
https://oppf.org/byomm/

Therapy for Black Girls
https://therapyforblackgirls.com/

Therapy for Black Men
https://therapyforblackmen.org/

Blackline (BIPOC)
1-800-604-5841

Black Emotional and Mental Health Collective
https://beam.community/

AAKOMA Project
https://aakomaproject.org/

Therapy for Latinx
https://www.therapyforlatinx.com/

RESOURCES, ORGANIZATIONS & SUPPORT

Life is Precious/La Vida es Preciosa
https://www.comunilifelip.org/
917-304-3645

SanaMente/Each Mind Matters
https://www.sanamente.org/

The National Asian American Pacific Islander Mental Health Association
https://www.naapimha.org/aanhpi-service-providers

Asians Do Therapy
https://asiansdotherapy.com/

South Asian Mental Health Initiative & Network (SAMHIN)
https://samhin.org/

Indian Health Service (IHS)
http://www.ihs.gov/suicideprevention/

We R Native
https://www.wernative.org/

Zero Suicide in Indian Country (Toolkit)
https://zerosuicide.edc.org/toolkit/toolkit-adaptations/indian-country

---

The Trevor Project
https://www.thetrevorproject.org/
1-866-488-7386 (Trevor Lifeline)
Text the word START to 678678

THRIVE Lifeline (18+)
https://thrivelifeline.org/index.html
Text THRIVE or oSTEM to 1-313-662-8209

SAGE (LGBTQ Elder)
https://www.sageusa.org/
1-877-360-LGBT (5428)

GLBT National Help Center
https://www.lgbthotline.org/
1-888-843-4564 (National Hotline)
1-800-246-7743 (Youth Hotline)

RESOURCES, ORGANIZATIONS & SUPPORT

Trans Lifeline
https://translifeline.org/
1-877-565-8860 (U.S.)
1-877-330-6366 (Canada)

ABOUT THE AUTHOR

- EMMA LEE M.C. (Emilia A. Ottoo) is an award-winning Hip-Hop creative, performer, athlete, digital producer, and ARTivist born in Uganda and raised in Harlem, New York City. She has performed at the American Museum of Natural History, Green Haven Correctional Facility, Apollo Theater, and the Academy Awards. Her works have appeared in the BronxArtSpace, Brooklyn University, Black Panther Film Festival, and World Health Organization. She is passionate about cultural exchange, creative intelligence, and positive social impact.

        facebook.com/emiliaisemmalee
        instagram.com/emiliaisemmalee

www.ingramcontent.com/pod-product-compliance
Lightning Source LLC
Chambersburg PA
CBHW022026050526
44107CB00096B/7